PRE-RAPHAELITE AND OTHER POETS

PRE-RAPHAELITE
AND OTHER POETS

lectures by

LAFCADIO HEARN

Selected and Edited with an Introduction

by

JOHN ERSKINE
Professor of English
Columbia University

Essay Index Reprint Series

Originally published by:

DODD, MEAD AND COMPANY

BOOKS FOR LIBRARIES PRESS, INC.
FREEPORT, NEW YORK

First Published 1922
Reprinted 1968

Reprinted from a copy in the collections of
The New York Public Library
Astor, Lenox and Tilden Foundations

LIBRARY OF CONGRESS CATALOG CARD NUMBER:
68-22096

PRINTED IN THE UNITED STATES OF AMERICA

INTRODUCTION

THIS volume is issued in response to a demand from students of literature for the best lectures of Lafcadio Hearn in a more accessible form than the library editions in which they first appeared. It seemed advisable to bring together these chapters from "Interpretations of Literature," 1915, "Appreciations of Poetry," 1916, and "Life and Literature," 1917, in order to provide under one cover—and let us hope, in spite of the cost of printing, at a lower price—a fair example of Hearn's critical felicity in the field of modern poetry, where perhaps he was at his best. The choice of lectures has been governed largely by the manuscripts available; the studies of Rossetti, Swinburne, Browning, Morris, and Meredith are among the longest and clearest of the texts; the lecture on Robert Bridges is one of those kindling analyses which Hearn gave only when he was most happy, and only of the writers he loved; the brief notes on Rossetti's prose and on the "Shaving of Shagpat" were added as naturally complementing the verse-writings of their respective authors; and the account of Buchanan's ballad not only helps to round out a portrait of the modern muse, but it also illustrates Hearn's keen recognition of a great note in minor poets, and his ability to make us feel the greatness.

Those who have not read the prefaces to the library editions of Hearn's lectures should be reminded that

[v]

Introduction

he gave them before Japanese students at the University of Tokyo, in the years between 1896 and 1902. He lectured without manuscript, and since he died before he had the opportunity of formulating in writing for Western readers his judgments of European literature, it is entirely to the devotion of his students that we owe the present chapters. Out of consideration for his audience, whose English was but recently acquired, Hearn lectured slowly. Some dozen of his pupils were able, therefore, to write down practically every word he said. After his death they presented the manuscripts to Mrs. Hearn, who put them in the hands of her husband's friend and literary executor, Mitchell McDonald, Pay Director U. S. N., who in turn brought them to the present publishers.

In editing these lectures for the volumes in which they first appeared, I tried to make as few alterations as possible. Only those manuscripts have been published which were fairly clear; all passages which were so mangled as to call for a reconstruction of the text, I omitted, and if the omission seemed to affect in any essential way what remained, I rejected the whole lecture. No additions whatever were made to the text; only the punctuation was made uniform, and the numerous quotations verified. Undaunted by many misprints and many oversights of my own in the citations of the four thick volumes, I have once more verified the quotations in this present book, and dare hope that few errors now survive.

Allowing, therefore, for such mistakes as are incident to proofreading, the reader will find here a close record of Hearn's daily instruction to his Japanese

[vi]

Introduction

class in English literature. The record is unique. I
never read these chapters without marvelling at their
simplicity, at the volume, if I may say so, of Hearn's
critical faculty, and at the integrity of his character.
The simplicity of the lectures is deceptive. The jaded
book reviewer, coming, for example, on these transparent summaries or paraphrases of verse just quoted,
feels that such repetitions may have aided the Japanese
boys, but are only encumbrances for the reader born to
the command of the English language. Against a judgment so shallow or so blind, I am somewhat put on
my guard by my own experience with Hearn's lectures;
for having been a student of the English language and
a devoted lover of English poetry all my life, I am glad
to acknowledge that Hearn's simple paraphrases of
well-known poems have taught me truths about the
poems which I never learned from the poems themselves,
nor from critics of poetry to whom simplicity seems a
fault. In editing these lectures of Hearn's, in this and
the other volumes, I have had occasion to read every
chapter many times, and I have read at least once the
manuscripts which have not been printed. Simple as
each lecture seems, the mass effect of them all, delivered day in and day out, on all the great themes of
Western literature, is nothing short of titanic. In criticism as well as in creation, volume counts. To have a
sound reasoned opinion of one book is beyond the
power of the average reader. To be expert in all the
writings of one author is to be a more than average
critic. To know all the writers in one period is to be
an authority. But to have so mature a knowledge of
life and of art, so wide an outlook on experience and

Introduction

so philosophic a control of it, as to find consistently the
meaning of any book, classic or modern, is to be among
the few great critics, the few in whom criticism is a
function and not an event. Hearn is, I believe, among
the greatest of critics. It should be remembered also
that his many lectures, all illustrating this high dis-
crimination, were delivered in a foreign land, before a
group of young men who could understand only the
general drift of them, and with no likelihood, as it
seemed, that they would ever come under the review of
Western readers. Yet day in and day out Hearn lectured at Tokyo before his boys with the same care and
with the same elevation of spirit as though he had been
addressing an audience at the Sorbonne or at Oxford
—or better, as though he had been the official instead
of the accidental spokesman for Western letters, and
as though the whole East, and not only his limited
classroom, were hanging on his words. This consecra-
tion to work done in obscurity is as rare in teaching as
in other human activities. Observing it on every page
of Hearn's lectures, I marvel at the integrity of his
character.

One is tempted to speak in detail of all the lectures
in this book—of the special merit of each, and of the
relation of one to the other. It will be sufficient, however, to say a word of the chapter on Rossetti, which
exhibits Hearn's method and his success. Rossetti
usually seems, even to his admirers, a poet of temperament and color, diffuse temperament and exotic color;
in so much sensuousness it has not been easy for the
casual critic to trace the intellectual fibre. But Hearn
observes that the plots of Rossetti's ballads, stripped

Introduction

somewhat of their Rossetti decorations, are stirring plots, contrived by an energetic mind. With this clue he undertakes to show us that Rossetti's work is all of an intellectual architecture, however emotional the surface of it may be. To read what Hearn says of the "Staff and Scrip," and then to read the ballad, is to discover a new poem, with the conviction besides that the poem is what Hearn discovered it to be. If the reader of Rossetti thinks this praise of Hearn's chapter is excessive, let him run over at his leisure all the other criticism of Rossetti he can find. He will agree at last that here is criticism of the first order—the criticism which opens our eyes to things in books, and thereby to the things in life of which books are only the mirror.

JOHN ERSKINE.

CONTENTS

PRE-RAPHAELITE AND OTHER POETS

CHAPTER I

STUDIES IN ROSSETTI

I

WE must rank Dante Gabriel Rossetti as not inferior
to Tennyson in workmanship—therefore as occupying
the very first rank in nineteenth century poetry. He
was not inferior to Tennyson either as a thinker, but
his thinking was in totally different directions. He
had no sympathy with the ideas of his own century; he
lived and thought in the Middle Ages; and while one of
our very greatest English poets, he takes a place apart,
for he does not reflect the century at all. He had the
dramatic gift, but it was a gift in his case much more
limited than that of Browning. Altogether we can
safely give him a place in the first rank as a maker
of poetry, but in all other respects we cannot classify
him in any way. He remains a unique figure in the
Victorian age, a figure such as may not reappear for
hundreds of years to come. It was as if a man of the
thirteenth century had been reborn into the nineteenth
century, and, in spite of modern culture, had continued

to think and to feel very much as men felt and thought in the time of the great Italian poete Dante.

One reason for this extraordinary difference between himself and his contemporaries was that Rossetti was not an Englishman but an Italian by blood, religion, and feeling. In his verse we might expect to find something that we cannot find in any other English poet; and I think that we shall find it. The facts of his life— strange and pathetic—need not occupy us now. You need only remember for the present that he was a great painter before becoming a great poet, and that his painting, like his poetry, was the painting of another century than his own. Also it will be well to bear in mind that he detested modern science and modern philosophy—which fact makes it all the more remarkable that he uttered some great thoughts quite in harmony with the most profound philosophy of the Orient.

In studying the best of his poetry, it will be well for us to consider it by groups, taking a few specimens from each group as examples of the rest; since we shall not have time to read even a quarter of all his production. Taking the very simplest of his work to begin with, I shall make a selection from what I might call the symbolic group, for want of a better name. I mean those poems which are parables, or symbolic illustrations of deep truths—poems which seem childishly simple, but are nevertheless very deep indeed. We may begin with a little piece called "The Mirror."

> She knew it not,—most perfect pain
> To learn: this too she knew not. Strife
> For me, calm hers, as from the first.

Studies in Rossetti

'Twas but another bubble burst
Upon the curdling draught of life,—
My silent patience mine again.

As who, of forms that crowd unknown
Within a distant mirror's shade,
Deems such an one himself, and makes
Some sign; but when the image shakes
No whit, he finds his thought betray'd,
And must seek elsewhere for his own.

So far as the English goes, this verse is plain enough;
but unless you have met with the same idea in some other
English writer, you will find the meaning very obscure.
The poet is speaking of a universal, or almost universal, experience of misplaced love. A man becomes passionately attached to a woman, who treats him with
cold indifference. Finally the lover finds out his mistake; the woman that he loved proves not to be what
he imagined; she is not worthy of his love. Then what
was he in love with? With a shadow out of his brain,
with an imagination or ideal very pure and noble, but
only an imagination. Supposing that he was worshipping good qualities in a noble woman, he deceived himself; the woman had no such qualities; they existed only
in his fancy. Thus he calls her his mirror, the human
being that seemed to be a reflection of all that was good
in his own heart. She never knows the truth as to why
the man loved her and then ceased to love her; he could
not tell her, because it would have been to her "most
perfect pain to learn."

A less obscure but equally beautiful symbolism, in another metre, is "The Honeysuckle."

[3]

Pre-Raphaelite and Other Poets

I plucked a honeysuckle where
  The hedge on high is quick with thorn,
  And climbing for the prize, was torn,
And fouled my feet in quag-water;
  And by the thorns and by the wind
  The blossom that I took was thinn'd,
And yet I found it sweet and fair.

Thence to a richer growth I came,
  Where, nursed in mellow intercourse,
  The honeysuckles sprang by scores,
Not harried like my single stem,
  All virgin lamps of scent and dew.
  So from my hand that first I threw,
Yet plucked not any more of them.

It often happens that a young man during his first struggle in life, when all the world seems to be against him, meets with some poor girl who loves him. She is not educated as he has been; she is ignorant of many things, and she has suffered herself a great deal of hardship, so that although beautiful naturally and good-hearted, both her beauty and her temper have been a little spoiled by the troubles of life. The young man whom she loves is obliged to mix with a very poor and vulgar class of people in order to become intimate with her. There are plenty of rough common men who would like to get that girl; and the young man has a good deal of trouble in winning her away from them. With all her small faults she seems for the time very beautiful to her lover, because he cannot get any finer woman while he remains poor. But presently success comes to him, and he is able to enter a much higher

[4]

class of society, where he finds scores of beautiful girls, much more accomplished than his poor sweetheart; and he becomes ashamed of her and cruelly abandons her. But he does not marry any of the rich and beautiful women. Perhaps he is tired of women; perhaps his heart has been spoiled. The poet does not tell us why. He simply tells a story of human ingratitude which is as old as the world.

One more simple poem before we take up the larger and more complicated pieces of the group.

THE WOODSPURGE

The wind flapped loose, the wind was still,
Shaken out dead from tree and hill:
I had walked on at the wind's will,—
I sat now, for the wind was still.

Between my knees my forehead was,—
My lips, drawn in, said not Alas!
My hair was over in the grass,
My naked ears heard the day pass.

My eyes, wide open, had the run
Of some ten weeds to fix upon;
Among those few, out of the sun,
The woodspurge flowered, three cups in one.

From perfect grief there need not be
Wisdom or even memory:
One thing then learnt remains to me,—
The woodspurge has a cup of three!

The phenomenon here described by the poet is unconsciously familiar to most of us. Any person who has suffered some very great pain, moral pain, is apt to observe during that instant of suffering things which he never observed before, or to notice details never noticed before in common things. One reason is that at such a time sense-impressions are stimulated to a strange degree by the increase of circulation, while the eyes and ears remain automatically active only. Whoever among you can remember the pain of losing a parent or beloved friend, will probably remember with extraordinary vividness all kinds of little things seen or heard at the time, such as the cry of a bird or a cricket, the sound of the dripping of water, the form of a sunbeam upon a wall, the shapes of shadows in a garden. The personage of this poem often before saw the woodspurge, without noticing anything particular about it; but in a moment of great sorrow observing the plant, he learns for the first time the peculiar form of its flower. In a wonderful novel by Henry Kingsley, called "Ravenshoe," there is a very striking example of the same thing. A cavalry-soldier, waiting in the saddle for the order to charge the enemy, observes on the back of the soldier before him a grease-spot which looks exactly like the map of Sweden, and begins to think that if the outline of Norway were beside it, the upper part of the map would go over the shoulder of the man. This fancy comes to him in a moment when he believes himself going to certain death.

Now we will take a longer poem, very celebrated, entitled "The Cloud Confines."

> The day is dark and the night
> To him that would search their heart;
> No lips of cloud that will part
> Nor morning song in the light:

Studies in Rossetti

Only, gazing alone,
To him wild shadows are shown,
Deep under deep unknown,
And height above unknown height.
Still we say as we go,—
"Strange to think by the way,
Whatever there is to know,
That shall we know one day."

The Past is over and fled;
Named new, we name it the old;
Thereof some tale hath been told,
But no word comes from the dead;
Whether at all they be,
Or whether as bond or free,
Or whether they too were we,
Or by what spell they have sped.
Still we say as we go,—
"Strange to think by the way,
Whatever there is to know,
That shall we know one day."

What of the heart of hate
That beats in thy breast, O Time?—
Red strife from the furthest prime,
And anguish of fierce debate;
War that shatters her slain,
And peace that grinds them as grain,
And eyes fixed ever in vain
On the pitiless eyes of Fate.
Still we say as we go,—
"Strange to think by the way,
Whatever there is to know,
That shall we know one day."

[7]

What of the heart of love
  That bleeds in thy breast, O Man?—
  Thy kisses snatched 'neath the ban
Of fangs that mock them above;
  Thy bells prolonged unto knells,
  Thy hope that a breath dispels,
  Thy bitter forlorn farewells
And the empty echoes thereof?
  Still we say as we go,—
    "Strange to think by the way,
    Whatever there is to know,
    That shall we know one day."

The sky leans dumb on the sea,
  Aweary with all its wings;
  And oh! the song the sea sings
Is dark everlastingly.
  Our past is clean forgot,
  Our present is and is not,
  Our future's a sealed seedplot,
And what betwixt them are we?
  We who say as we go,—
    "Strange to think by the way,
    Whatever there is to know,
    That shall we know one day."

This dark poetry is very different from the optimism
of Tennyson; and we uncomfortably feel it to be much
more true. In spite of all its wonderful tenderness and
caressing hopefulness, we feel that Tennyson's poetry
does not illuminate the sombre problems of life. But
Rossetti will not be found to be a pessimist. I shall
presently show, by examples, the difference between
poetical pessimism and Rossetti's thoughtful melancholy. He is simply communing with us about the

mystery of the universe—sadly enough, but always truthfully. We may even suspect a slight mockery in the burthen of his poem:

> Whatever there is to know,
> That shall we know one day.

Suppose there is nothing to know? "Very well," the poet would answer, "then we shall know nothing." Although by education and by ancestry a Roman Catholic, Rossetti seems to have had just as little faith as any of his great contemporaries; the artistic and emotional side of Catholicism made strong appeal to his nature as an artist, but so far as personal belief is concerned we may judge him by his own lines:

> Would God I knew there were a God to thank
> When thanks rise in me!

Nevertheless we have here no preacher of negation, but a sincere doubter. We know nothing of the secret of the universe, the meaning of its joy and pain and impermanency; we do not know anything of the dead; we do not know the meaning of time or space or life. But just for that reason there may be marvellous things to know. The dead do not come back, but we do not know whether they could come back, nor even the real meaning of death. Do we even know, he asks, whether the dead were not ourselves? This thought, like the thought in the poem "Sudden Light," is peculiar to Rossetti. You will find nothing of this thought in any other Victorian poet of great rank—except, indeed, in some of the work of O'Shaughnessy, who is now coming

into a place of eminence only second to that of the
four great masters.

Besides this remarkable line, which I have asked you
to put in italics, you should remember those two very
splendid lines in the third stanza:

> War that shatters her slain,
> And peace that grinds them as grain.

These have become famous. The suggestion is that
peace is more cruel than war. In battle a man is dashed
to pieces, and his pain is immediately over. In the competition of civil life, the weak and the stupid, no matter
how good or moral they may be, are practically crushed
by the machinery of Western civilisation, as grain
might be crushed in a mill.

In the last stanza of the composition you will doubtless have observed the pathetic reference to the meaning of the song of the sea, mysterious and awful beyond
all other sounds of nature. Rossetti has not failed
to consider this sound, philosophically and emotionally,
in one of his most beautiful poems. And now I want
to show you, by illustration, the difference between a
really pessimistic treatment of a subject and Rossetti's
treatment of it. Perhaps the very finest example of
pessimism in Victorian poetry is a sonnet by Lee-Hamilton, on the subject of a sea-shell. You know that if
you take a large sea-shell of a particular form, and
hold it close to your ear, you will hear a sound like the
sound of the surf, as if the ghost of the sea were in the
shell. Nearly all English children have the experience
of listening to the sound of the sea in a shell; it startles
them at first; but nobody tells them what the sound

really is, for that would spoil their surprise and delight. You must not tell a child that there are no ghosts or fairies. Well, Rossetti and Lee-Hamilton wrote about this sound of the sea in a shell—but how differently! Here is Lee-Hamilton's composition:

> The hollow sea-shell, which for years hath stood
> On dusty shelves, when held against the ear
> Proclaims its stormy parent; and we hear
> The faint far murmur of the breaking flood.
> We hear the sea. The sea? It is the blood
> In our own veins, impetuous and near,
> And pulses keeping pace with hope and fear,
> And with our feelings' ever-shifting mood.
>
> Lo! in my heart I hear, as in a shell,
> The murmur of a world beyond the grave,
> Distinct, distinct, though faint and far it be.
> Thou fool; this echo is a cheat as well,—
> The hum of earthly instincts; and we crave
> A world unreal as the shell-heard sea.

Of course this is a very fine poem, so far as the poetry is concerned. But it is pessimism absolute. Its author, a brilliant graduate of Oxford University, entered the English diplomatic service as a young man, and in the middle of a promising career was attacked by a disease of the spine which left him a hopeless invalid. We might say that he had some reason to look at the world in a dark light. But such poetry is not healthy. It is morbid. It means retrogression. It brings a sharp truth to the mind with a painful shock, and leaves an after-impression of gloom unspeakable. As I said before, we must not spoil the happiness of children by

[11]

telling them that there are no ghosts or fairies. So we must not tell the humanity which believes in happiness after death that there is no heaven. All progress is through faith and hope in something. The measure of a poet is in the largeness of the thought which he can apply to any subject, however trifling. Bearing this in mind, let us now see how the same subject of the sea-shell appeals to the thought of Rossetti. You will then perceive the difference between pessimism and philosophical humanitarianism.

THE SEA-LIMITS

Consider the sea's listless chime:
 Time's self it is, made audible,—
 The murmur of the earth's own shell.
Secret continuance sublime
 Is the sea's end: our sight may pass
 No furlong further. Since time was,
This sound hath told the lapse of time.

No quiet, which is death's,—it hath
 The mournfulness of ancient life,
 Enduring always at dull strife.
As the world's heart of rest and wrath,
 Its painful pulse is in the sands.
 Last utterly, the whole sky stands,
Grey and not known, along its path.

Listen alone beside the sea,
 Listen alone among the woods;
 Those voices of twin solitudes
Shall have one sound alike to thee:
 Hark where the murmurs of thronged men
 Surge and sink back and surge again,—
Still the one voice of wave and tree.

Studies in Rossetti

Gather a shell from the strown beach
And listen at its lips: they sigh
The same desire and mystery,
The echo of the whole sea's speech.
And all mankind is thus at heart
Not anything but what thou art:
And Earth, Sea, Man, are all in each.

In the last beautiful stanza we have a comparison as
sublime as any ever made by any poet—of the human
heart, the human life, re-echoing the murmur of the
infinite Sea of Life. As the same sound of the sea is
heard in every shell, so in every human heart is the
same ghostly murmur of Universal Being. The sound
of the sea, the sound of the forest, the sound of men
in cities, not only are the same to the ear, but they
tell the same story of pain. The sound of the sea is
a sound of perpetual strife, the sound of the woods
in the wind is a sound of ceaseless struggle, the tumult
of a great city is also a tumult of effort. In this sense
all the three sounds are but one, and that one is the
sound of life everywhere. Life is pain, and therefore
sadness. The world itself is like a great shell full of
this sound. But it is a shell on the verge of the Infinite. The millions of suns, the millions of planets and
moons, are all of them but shells on the shore of the
everlasting sea of death and birth, and each would,
if we could hear it, convey to our ears and hearts the
one same murmur of pain. This is, to my thinking,
a much vaster conception than anything to be found
in Tennyson; and such a poem as that of Lee-Hamilton dwindles into nothingness beside it, for we have here
all that man can know of our relation to the universe,

and the mystery of that universe brought before us by a simile of incomparable sublimity.

Before leaving this important class of poems, let me cite another instance of the comparative nearness of Rossetti at times to Oriental thought. It is the fifteenth of that wonderful set of sonnets entitled the "House of Life."

THE BIRTH-BOND

Have you not noted, in some family
  Where two were born of a first marriage-bed,
  How still they own their gracious bond, though fed
And nursed on the forgotten breast and knee?—
How to their father's children they shall be
  In act and thought of one goodwill; but each
  Shall for the other have, in silence speech,
And in a word complete community?

Even so, when first I saw you, seemed it, love,
  That among souls allied to mine was yet
One nearer kindred than life hinted of.
  O born with me somewhere that men forget,
  And though in years of sight and sound unmet,
Known for my soul's birth-partner well enough!

This beautiful little thought of love is almost exactly the same as that suggested in a well-known Japanese proverb about the relations of a previous existence. We have here, in an English poet, who very probably never read anything about Buddhism, the very idea of the Buddhist *en*. The whole tendency of the poet's mind was toward larger things than his early training had prepared him for.

[14]

Studies in Rossetti

Yet it would be a mistake to suppose Rossetti a pure mystic; he was too much of an artist for that. No one felt the sensuous charm of life more keenly, nor the attraction of plastic beauty and grace. By way of an interlude, we may turn for a time to his more sensuous poetry. It is by this that he is best known; for you need not suppose that the general English public understands such poems as those which we have been examining. Keep in mind that there is a good deal of difference between the adjectives "sensuous" and "sensual." The former has no evil meaning; it refers only to sense-impression—to sensations visual, auditory, tactile. The other adjective is more commonly used in a bad sense. At one time an attempt was made to injure Rossetti by applying it to his work; but all good critics have severely condemned that attempt, and Rossetti must not be regarded as in any sense an immoral poet.

II

To the cultivated the very highest quality of emotional poetry is that given by blending the artistically sensuous with the mystic. This very rare quality colours the greater part of Rossetti's work. Perhaps one may even say that it is never entirely absent. Only, the proportions of the blending vary, like those mixtures of red and blue, crimson and azure, which may give us either purple or violet of different shades according to the wish of the dyer. The quality of mysticism dominates in the symbolic poems; we might call those deep purple. The sensuous element dominates in most of the ballads and narrative poems; we might say

[15]

that these have rather the tone of bright violet. **But**
even in the ballads there is a very great difference in
the proportions of the two qualities. The highest tone
is in the "Blessed Damozel," and in the beautiful narrative poem of the "Staff and Scrip"; while the lowest
tone is perhaps that of the ballad of "Eden Bower,"
which describes the two passions of lust and hate at
their greatest intensity. But everything is beautifully
finished as work, and unapproachably exquisite in feeling. I think the best example of what I have called the
violet style is the ballad of "Troy Town."

> Heavenborn Helen, Sparta's Queen,
> *(O Troy Town!)*
> Had two breasts of heavenly sheen,
> The sun and moon of the heart's desire:
> All Love's lordship lay between.
> *(O Troy's down!*
> *Tall Troy's on fire!)*
>
> Helen knelt at Venus' shrine,
> *(O Troy Town!)*
> Saying, "A little gift is mine,
> A little gift for a heart's desire.
> Hear me speak and make me a sign!
> *(O Troy's down!*
> *Tall Troy's on fire!)*
>
> "Look! I bring thee a carven cup;
> *(O Troy Town!)*
> See it here as I hold it up,—
> Shaped it is to the heart's desire,
> Fit to fill when the gods would sup.
> *(O Troy's down!*
> *Tall Troy's on fire!)*

[16]

Studies in Rossetti

"It was moulded like my breast;
   (*O Troy Town!*)
He that sees it may not rest,
Rest at all for his heart's desire.
O give ear to my heart's behest!
   (*O Troy's down!*
   Tall Troy's on fire!)

"See my breast, how like it is;
   (*O Troy Town!*)
See it bare for the air to kiss!
Is the cup to thy heart's desire?
O for the breast, O make it his!
   (*O Troy's down!*
   Tall Troy's on fire!)

"Yea, for my bosom here I sue;
   (*O Troy Town!*)
Thou must give it where 'tis due,
Give it there to the heart's desire.
Whom do I give my bosom to?
   (*O Troy's down!*
   Tall Troy's on fire!)

"Each twin breast is an apple sweet!
   (*O Troy Town!*)
Once an apple stirred the beat
Of thy heart with the heart's desire:—
Say, who brought it then to thy feet?
   (*O Troy's down!*
   Tall Troy's on fire!)

"They that claimed it then were three:
   (*O Troy Town!*)
For thy sake two hearts did he
Make forlorn of the heart's desire.

[17]

Do for him as he did for thee!
  (*O Troy's down!*
  Tall Troy's on fire!)

"Mine are apples grown to the south,
  (*O Troy Town!*)
Grown to taste in the days of drouth,
Taste and waste to the heart's desire:
Mine are apples meet for his mouth!"
  (*O Troy's down!*
  Tall Troy's on fire!)

Venus looked on Helen's gift,
  (*O Troy Town!*)
Looked and smiled with subtle drift,
Saw the work of her heart's desire:—
"There thou kneel'st for Love to lift!"
  (*O Troy's down!*
  Tall Troy's on fire!)

Venus looked in Helen's face,
  (*O Troy Town!*)
Knew far off an hour and place,
And fire lit from the heart's desire;
Laughed and said, "Thy gift hath grace!"
  (*O Troy's down!*
  Tall Troy's on fire!)

Cupid looked on Helen's breast,
  (*O Troy Town!*)
Saw the heart within its nest,
Saw the flame of the heart's desire,—
Marked his arrow's burning crest.
  (*O Troy's down!*
  Tall Troy's on fire!)

[18]

Studies in Rossetti

Cupid took another dart,
   (*O Troy Town!*)
Fledged it for another heart,
Winged the shaft with the heart's desire,
Drew the string, and said "Depart!"
   (*O Troy's down!*
   Tall Troy's on fire!)

Paris turned upon his bed,
   (*O Troy Town!*)
Turned upon his bed, and said,
Dead at heart with the heart's desire,—
"O to clasp her golden head!"
   (*O Troy's down!*
   Tall Troy's on fire!)

This wonderful ballad, with its single and its double refrains, represents Rossetti's nearest approach to earth, except the ballad of "Eden Bower." Usually he seldom touches the ground, but moves at some distance above it, just as one flies in dreams. But you will observe that the mysticism here has almost vanished. There is just a little ghostliness to remind you that the writer is no common singer, but a poet able to give a thrill. The ghostliness is chiefly in the fact of the supernatural elements involved; Helen with her warm breast we feel to be a real woman, but Venus and love are phantoms, who speak and act as figures in sleep. This is true art under the circumstances. We feel nothing more human until we come to the last stanza; then we hear it in the cry of Paris. But why do I say that this is high art to make the gods as they are made here? The Greeks would have made Venus and Cupid purely human. But Rossetti is not taking the Greek view of the subject at all. He is taking the mediæval one. He is writing of Greek gods and Greek legends as such subjects were felt by Chaucer and by the French poets of the thirteenth and fourteenth centuries. It would not be easy to explain the mediæval tone of the poem to you; that would require a comparison with the work of very much older poets. I only want now to call your attention to the fact that even in a Greek subject of the sensuous kind Rossetti always keeps the tone of the Middle Ages; and that tone was mystical.

Having given this beautiful example of the least mystical class of Rossetti's light poems, let us pass at once to the most mystical. These are in all respects, I am not afraid to say, far superior. The poem by which Rossetti became first widely known and admired was "The Blessed Damozel." This and a lovely narrative poem entitled "Staff and Scrip" form the most exquisite examples of the poet's treatment of mystical love. You should know both of them; but we shall first take "The Blessed Damozel."

This is the story of a woman in heaven, speaking of the man she loved on earth. She is waiting for him. She watches every new soul that comes to heaven, hoping that it may be the soul of her lover. While waiting thus, she talks to herself about what she will do to make her lover happy when he comes, how she will show him all the beautiful things in heaven, and will introduce him to the holy saints and angels. That is all. But it is very wonderful in its sweetness of simple pathos, and in a peculiar, indescribable quaintness which is not of the nineteenth century at all. It is of the Middle

Studies in Rossetti

Ages, the Italian Middle Ages before the time of Raphael. The heaven painted here is not the heaven of modern Christianity—if modern Christianity can be said to have a heaven; it is the heaven of Dante, a heaven almost as sharply defined as if it were on earth.

THE BLESSED DAMOZEL

> The blessed damozel leaned out
> From the gold bar of Heaven;
> Her eyes were deeper than the depth
> Of waters stilled at even;
> She had three lilies in her hand,
> And the stars in her hair were seven.

Damozel. This is only a quaint form of the same word which in modern French signifies a young lady—demoiselle. The suggestion is not simply that it is a maiden that speaks, but a maiden of noble blood. The idea of the poet is exactly that of Dante in speaking of Beatrice. Seven is the mystical number of Christianity.

> Her robe, ungirt from clasp to hem,
> No wrought flowers did adorn,
> But a white rose of Mary's gift,
> For service meetly worn;
> Her hair that lay along her back
> Was yellow like ripe corn.

Clasp. The ornamental fastening of the dress at the neck. "From clasp to hem" thus signifies simply "from neck to feet," for the hem of a garment means especially its lower edge. *Wrought flowers* here means embroidered flowers. The dress has no ornament and no girdle; it is a dress of the thirteenth century as to form; but it may interest you to know that usually in religious pictures of angels and heavenly souls (the French religious prints are incomparably the best) there is no girdle, and the robe falls straight from neck to feet. *Service.* The maiden in heaven becomes a servant of the Mother of God. But the mediæval idea was that the daughter of a very noble house, entering heaven, might be honoured by being taken into the service of Mary, just as in this world one might be honoured by being taken into the personal service of a queen or emperor. A white rose is worn as the badge or mark of this distinction, because white is the symbol of chastity, and Mary is especially the patron of chastity. In heaven also—the heaven of Dante—the white rose has many symbolic significations. *Yellow.* Compare "Elle est *blonde comme le blé.*" (De Musset.)

> Herseemed she scarce had been a day
> One of God's choristers;
> The wonder was not yet quite gone
> From that still look of hers;
> Albeit, to them she left, her day
> Had counted as ten years.

Herseemed. This word is very unusual, even obsolete. Formerly instead of saying "it seems to me," "it seems to him," English people used to say meseems, himseems, herseems. The word "meseems" is still used, but only in the present, with rare exceptions. It is becoming obsolete also. *Choristers.* Choir-singers. The daily duty of angels and souls in heaven was supposed to be to sing the praises of God, just as on earth hymns

[22]

are sung in church. *Albeit.* An ancient form of "although."

> (To one, it is ten years of years,
> . . . Yet now, and in this place,
> Surely she leaned o'er me—her hair
> Fell all about my face. . . . ,
> Nothing: the autumn-fall of leaves.
> The whole year sets apace.)

Ten years of years. That is, years composed not of three hundred and. sixty-five days, but of three hundred and sixty-five years. To the lover on earth, deprived of his beloved by death, the time passes slowly so that a day seems as long as a year. Sometimes he imagines that he feels the dead bending over him—that he feels her hair falling over his face. When he looks, he finds that it is only the leaves of the trees that have been falling upon him; and he knows that the autumn has come, and that the year is slowly dying.

> It was the rampart of God's house
> That she was standing on;
> By God built over the sheer depth
> The which is Space begun;
> So high, that looking downward thence
> She scarce could see the sun.

Rampart, you know, means part of a fortification; all the nobility of the Middle Ages lived in castles or fortresses, and their idea of heaven was necessarily the idea of a splendid castle. In the "Song of Roland" we find the angels and the saints spoken of as knights and ladies, and the language they use is the language of chivalry. *Sheer depth,* straight down, perpendicularly, absolute. God's castle overlooks, not a landscape, but space; the sun and the stars lie far below.

> It lies in Heaven, across the flood
>   Of ether, as a bridge.
> Beneath, the tides of day and night
>   With flame and darkness ridge
> The void, as low as where this earth
>   Spins like a fretful midge.
>
> Around her, lovers, newly met
>   'Mid deathless love's acclaims,
> Spoke ever more among themselves
>   Their heart-remembered names;
> And the souls mounting up to God
>   Went by her like thin flames.

Ether. This is not the modern word, the scientific ether, but the Greek and also mediæval ether, the most spiritual form of matter. The house of God, or heaven, rests upon nothing, but stretches out like a bridge over the ether itself. Far below something like enormous waves seem to be soundlessly passing, light and dark. Even in heaven, and throughout the universe, it was supposed in the Middle Ages that there were successions of day and night independent of the sun. These are the "tides" described. *Ridge the void* means, make ridges or wave-like lines in the ether of space. *Midge* is used in English just as the word *kobai* is used in Japanese. Fretful midge, a midge that moves very quickly as if fretted or frightened.

> And still she bowed herself and stooped
>   Out of the circling charm;
> Until her bosom must have made

[24]

Studies in Rossetti

The bar she leaned on warm,
And the lilies lay as if asleep
Along her bended arm.

Charm. The circling charm is not merely the gold
railing upon which she leans, but the magical limits of
heaven itself which holds the souls back. She cannot
pass beyond them. Otherwise her wish would take
her back to this world to watch by her living lover.
But only the angels, who are the messengers of heaven,
can go beyond the boundaries.

From the fixed place of Heaven she saw
    Time like a pulse shake fierce
Through all the worlds. Her gaze still strove
    Within the gulf to pierce
Its path; and now she spoke as when
    The stars sang in their spheres.

Shake. Here in the sense of to beat like a heart or
pulse. Heaven about her is motionless, fixed; but looking down upon the universe she sees a luminous motion,
regular like a heart-beat; that is Time. *Its path.*
Her eyes tried to pierce a way or path for themselves
through space; that is, she made a desperate effort to
see farther than she could see. She is looking in vain
for the coming of her lover. *Their spheres.* This is
an allusion to a Biblical verse, "when the morning stars
sang together." It was said that when the world was
created the stars sang for joy.

The sun was gone now; the curled moon
    Was like a little feather
Fluttering far down the gulf; and now
    She spoke through the still weather.

[25]

Pre-Raphaelite and Other Poets

Her voice was like the voice the stars
    Had when they sang together.

(Ah sweet!   Even now, in that bird's song,
    Strove not her accents there,
Fain to be hearkened?   When those bells
    Possessed the mid-day air,
Strove not her steps to reach my side
    Down all the echoing stair?)

Stair.   We must suppose the lover to be in or near
a church with a steeple, or lofty bell tower.   Outside he
hears a bird singing; and in the sweetness of its song
he thinks that he hears the voice of the dead girl speaking to him.   Then, as the church bells send down to
him great sweet waves of sound from the tower, he imagines that he can hear, in the volume of the sound, something like a whispering of robes and faint steps as of
a spirit trying to descend to his side.

"I wish that he were come to me,
    For he will come," she sa'd.
"Have I not prayed in Heaven?—on earth,
    Lord, Lord, has he not prayed?
Are not two prayers a perfect strength?
    And shall I fell afraid?

An allusion to a verse in the New Testament—"if
two of you shall agree on earth as touching anything
that they shall ask, it shall be done for them."   She is
a little afraid that her lover may not get to heaven after
all, but she suddenly remembers this verse, and it gives
her encouragement.   *Perfect strength* means strength
of prayer, the power of the prayer to obtain what is

[26]

prayed for. As she and he have both been praying for reunion in heaven, and as Christ has promised that whatever two people pray for, shall be granted, she feels consoled.

> "When round his head the aureole clings,
> And he is clothed in white,
> I'll take his hand and go with him
> To the deep wells of light;
> As unto a stream we will step down,
> And bathe there in God's sight.

The *aureole* is the circle or disk of golden light round the head of a saint. Sometimes it is called a "glory." In some respects the aureole of Christian art much resembles that of Buddhist art, with this exception, that some of the Oriental forms are much richer and more elaborate. Three forms in Christian art are especially common—the plain circle; the disk, like a moon or sun, usually made in art by a solid plate of gilded material behind the head; the full "glory," enshrining the whole figure. There is only one curious fact to which I need further refer here; it is that the Holy Ghost in Christian art has a glory of a special kind—the triangle. *White.* This is a reference to the description of heaven in the paradise of St. John's vision, where all the saints are represented in white garments. *Deep wells of light.* Another reference to St. John's vision, Rev. xxii, 1— "And he showed me a pure river of water of life, clear as crystal, proceeding out of the throne of God." In the heaven of the Middle Ages, as in the Buddhist paradise, we find also lakes and fountains of light, or of liquid jewels.

[27]

Pre-Raphaelite and Other Poets

"We two will stand beside that shrine,
    Occult, withheld, untrod,
Whose lamps are stirred continually
    With prayer sent up to God;
And see our old prayers, granted, melt
    Each like a little cloud.

Shrine. The Holy of Holies, or innermost sanctuary of heaven, imagined by mediæval faith as a sort of reserved chapel. But the origin of the fancy will be explained in the next note. *Lamps.* See again St. John's vision, Rev. iv, 5—"And there were seven lamps of fire burning before the throne, which are the seven Spirits of God." These mystical flames, representing special virtues and powers, would be agitated according to the special virtues corresponding to them in the ascending prayers of men. But now we come to another and stranger thought. *A little cloud.* See again Rev. v, 8, in which reference is made to "golden vials, full of incense, which are the prayers of the saints." Here we see the evidence of a curious belief that prayers in heaven actually become transformed into the substance of incense. By the Talmudists it was said that they were turned into beautiful flowers. Again, in Rev. viii, 3, we have an allusion to this incense, made of prayer, being burned in heaven—"And there was given unto him much incense, that he should offer it with the prayers of all saints." Now the poem can be better understood. The Blessed Damozel thinks that her old prayers, that is to say, the prayers that she made on earth, together with those of her lover, are in heaven in the shape of incense. As long as prayer is not granted, it remains incense; when granted it becomes

[28]

perfume smoke and vanishes. Therefore she says, "We shall see our old prayers, granted, melt each like a little *cloud*"—that is, a cloud of smoke of incense.

> "We two will lie i' the shadow of
> That living mystic tree
> Within whose secret growth the Dove
> Is sometimes felt to be,
> While every leaf that His plumes touch
> Saith His Name audibly.

The heavenly tree of life is described in Rev. xxvii, 2, as bearing twelve different kinds of fruit, one for each of the twelve months of the year, while its leaves heal all diseases or troubles of any kind. The Dove is the Holy Ghost, who is commonly represented in Christian art by this bird, when he is not represented by a tongue or flame of fire. Every time that a leaf touches the body of the Dove, we are told that the leaf repeats the name of the Holy Ghost. In what language? Probably in Latin, and the sound of the Latin name would be like the sound of the motion of leaves, stirred by a wind: *Sanctus Spiritus*.

> "And I myself will teach to him,
> I myself, lying so,
> The songs I sing here; which his voice
> Shall pause in, hushed and slow,
> And find some knowledge at each pause,
> Or some new thing to know."

> (Alas! we two, we two, thou say'st!
> Yea, one wast thou with me
> That once of old. But shall God lift
> To endless unity

Pre-Raphaelite and Other Poets

The soul whose likeness with thy soul
Was but its love for thee?)

It is the lover who now speaks, commenting upon
the imagined words of the beloved in heaven. *Endless
unity* here has a double meaning, signifying at once
the mystical union of the soul with God, and the reunion forever of lovers separated by death. The lover
doubts whether he can be found worthy to enter heaven,
because his only likeness to the beloved was in his love
for her; that is to say, his merit was not so much in
being good as in loving good in another.

"We two," she said, "will seek the groves
    Where the lady Mary is,
With her fine handmaidens, whose names
    Are five sweet symphonies,
Cecily, Gertrude, Magdalen,
    Margaret, and Rosalys.

Notice the mediæval method of speaking of the
mother of God as "the lady Mary"; such would have
been the form of address for a princess or queen in
those times. So King Arthur's wife, in the old romance, is called the lady Guinevere. *Symphonies* here
has only the simplest meaning of a sweet sound, not of
a combination of sounds; but the use of the word nevertheless implies to a delicate ear that the five names make
harmony with each other. They are names of saints,
but also favourite names given to daughters of great
families as Christian names. The picture is simply
that of the lady of a great castle, surrounded by her
waiting women, engaged in weaving and sewing.

[30]

Studies in Rossetti

"Circlewise sit they, with bound locks
And foreheads garlanded;
Into the fine cloth white like flame
Weaving the golden thread,
To fashion the birth-robes for them
Who are just born, being dead.

With bound locks means only with the hair tied up,
not flowing loose, as was usual in figures of saints and
angels. They are weaving garments for new souls
received into heaven, just as mothers might weave cloth
for a child soon to be born. The description of the
luminous white cloth might be compared with descriptions in Revelation. *Being dead.* Christianity, like
the Oriental religions, calls death a rebirth; but the
doctrinal idea is entirely different. You will remember that the Greeks represented the soul under the form
of a butterfly. Christianity approaches the Greek
fancy by considering the human body as a sort of cater-
pillar, which enters the pupa-state at death; the soul
is like the butterfly leaving the chrysalis. So far
everything is easy to understand; but this rebirth of
the soul is only half a rebirth in the Christian sense.
The body is also to be born again at a later day. At
present there are only souls in heaven; but after the
judgment day the same bodies which they used to have
during life are to be given back to them. Therefore
Rossetti is not referring here to rebirth except in the
sense of spiritual rebirth, as Christ used it, in saying
"Ye must be born again"—that is, obtain new hearts,
new feelings. What in Oriental poetry would represent a fact of belief, here represents only the symbol of
a belief, a belief of a totally different kind.

[31]

Pre-Raphaelite and Other Poets

"He shall fear, haply, and be dumb:
    Then will I lay my cheek
To his, and tell about our love,
    Not once abashed or weak:
And the dear Mother will approve
    My pride, and let me speak.

"Herself shall bring us, hand in hand,
    To Him round whom all souls
Kneel, the clear-ranged unnumbered heads
    Bowed with their aureoles:
And angels meeting us shall sing
    To their citherns and citoles.

"There will I ask of Christ the Lord
    Thus much for him and me:—
Only to live as once on earth
    With Love, only to be,
As then awhile, forever now
    Together, I and he."

The Damozel's idea is that her lover will be ashamed and afraid to speak to the mother of God when he is introduced to her; but she will not be afraid to say how much she loves her lover, and she will cause the lady Mary to bring them both into the presence of God himself, identified here rather with the Son than with the Father. *Citherns and citoles.* Both words are derived from the Latin *cithara*, a harp, and both refer to long obsolete kinds of stringed instruments used during the twelfth, thirteenth, and fourteenth centuries.

She gazed and listened and then said,
    Less sad of speech than mild,—
"All this is when he comes." She ceased.

[32]

Studies in Rossetti

The light thrilled toward her, filled
With angels in strong level flight.
Her eyes prayed, and she smiled.

(I saw her smile.)   But soon their path
Was vague in distant spheres:
And then she cast her arms along
The golden barriers,
And laid her face between her hands,
And wept.   (I heard her tears.)

In these beautiful lines we are reminded of the special
duty of angels, from which they take their name, "messenger"—the duty of communicating between earth and
heaven and bringing the souls of the dead to paradise.
The Damozel, waiting and watching for her lover,
imagines, whenever she sees the angels coming from
the direction of the human world, that her lover may
be coming with them.   At last she sees a band of angels
flying straight toward her through the luminous ether,
which shivers and flashes before their coming.   "Her
eyes prayed," that is, expressed the prayerful desire
that it might be her beloved; and she feels almost sure
that it is.   Then comes her disappointment, for the
angels pass out of sight in another direction, and she
cries—even in heaven.   At least her lover imagines that
he saw and heard her weeping.

The use of the word Damozel needs a little more
explanation, that you may understand the great art
with which the poem was arranged.   The Old French
damoisel (later *damoiseau*) signified a young lad of
noble birth or knightly parentage, employed in a noble
house as page or squire.   Originally there was no

[33]

feminine form; but afterwards the form *damoselle* came into use, signifying a young lady in the corresponding capacity. Thus Rossetti in choosing the old English form *damozel* selected perhaps the only possible word which could exactly express the position of the Damozel in heaven, as well as the mediæval conception of that heaven. Our English word "damsel," so common in the Bible, is a much later form than damozel. There was, however, a Middle English form spelled almost like the form used by Rossetti, except that there was an "s" instead of a "z."

Now you will better see the meaning of Rossetti's mysticism. When you make religion love, without ceasing to be religious, and make love religion, without ceasing to be human and sensuous, in the good sense of the word, then you have made a form of mysticism. The blending in Rossetti is very remarkable, and has made this particular poem the most famous thing which he wrote. We have here a picture of heaven, with all its mysteries and splendours, suspended over an ocean of ether, through which souls are passing like an upward showering of fire; and all this is spiritual enough. But the Damozel, with her yellow hair, and her bosom making warm what she leans upon, is very human; and her thoughts are not of the immaterial kind. The suggestions about bathing together, about embracing, cheek against cheek, and about being able to love in heaven as on earth, have all the delightful innocence of the Middle Ages, when the soul was thought of only as another body of finer substance. Now it is altogether the human warmth of the poem that makes its intense attraction. Rarely to-day can any Western

[34]

poet write satisfactorily about heavenly things, because we have lost the artless feeling of the Middle Ages, and we cannot think of the old heaven as a reality. In order to write such things, we should have to get back the heart of our fathers; and Rossetti happened to be born with just such a heart. He had probably little or no real faith in religion; but he was able to understand exactly how religious people felt hundreds of years ago.

Let us now turn to a more earthly phase of the same tone of love which appears in "The Blessed Damozel." Now it is the lover himself on earth who is speaking, while contemplating the portrait of the dead woman whom he loved. We shall only make extracts, on account of the extremely elaborate and difficult structure of the poem.

THE PORTRAIT

This is her picture as she was:
  It seems a thing to wonder on,
As though mine image in the glass
  Should tarry when myself am gone.
I gaze until she seems to stir,—
Until mine eyes almost aver
  That now, even now, the sweet lips part
  To breathe the words of the sweet heart:—
And yet the earth is over her.

.   .   .   .

Even so, where Heaven holds breath and hears
  The beating heart of Love's own breast,—
Where round the secret of all spheres
  All angels lay their wings to rest,—

[35]

Pre-Raphaelite and Other Poets

> How shall my soul stand rapt and awed,
> When, by the new birth borne abroad
> Throughout the music of the suns,
> It enters in her soul at once
> And knows the silence there for God!

Here is the very highest form of mystical love; for love is identified with God, and the reunion in heaven is a blending, not with a mere fellow soul, but with the Supreme Being. By "silence" here you must understand rest, heavenly peace. The closing stanza of the poem contains one of the most beautiful images of comparison ever made in any language.

> Here with her face doth memory sit
>   Meanwhile, and wait the day's decline,
> Till other eyes shall look from it,
>   Eyes of the spirit's Palestine,
> Even than the old gaze tenderer:
> While hopes and aims long lost with her
>   Stand round her image side by side,
>   Like tombs of pilgrims that have died
> About the Holy Sepulchre.

What the poet means is this: "Now I sit, remembering the past, and look at her face in the picture, as long as the light of day remains. Presently, with twilight the stars will shine out like eyes in heaven—heaven which is my Holy Land, because she is there. Those stars will then seem to me even as her eyes, but more beautiful, more loving than the living eyes. The hopes and the projects which I used to entertain for her sake, and which died when she died—they come back to mind, but like the graves ranged around the grave of Christ

Studies in Rossetti

at Jerusalem." The reference is of course to the great pilgrimages of the Middle Ages made to Jerusalem.

More than the artist speaks here; and if there be not strong faith, there is at least beautiful hope. A more tender feeling could not be combined with a greater pathos; but Rossetti often reaches the very same supreme quality of sentiment, even in poems of a character closely allied to romance. We can take "The Staff and Scrip" as an example of mediæval story of the highest emotional quality.

"Who rules these lands?" the Pilgrim said.
"Stranger, Queen Blanchelys."
"And who has thus harried them?" he said.
"It was Duke Luke did this;
God's ban be his!"

The Pilgrim said, "Where is your house?
I'll rest there, with your will."
"You've but to climb these blackened boughs
And you'll see it over the hill,
For it burns still."

"Which road, to seek your Queen?" said he.
"Nay, nay, but with some wound
You'll fly back hither, it may be,
And by your blood i' the ground
My place be found."

"Friend, stay in peace. God keep your head,
And mine, where I will go;
For He is here and there," he said.
He passed the hillside, slow,
And stood below.

[37]

Pre-Raphaelite and Other Poets

So far the poem is so simple that no one could expect anything very beautiful in the sequence. We only have a conversation between a pilgrim from the Holy Land, returned to his native country (probably mediæval France), and a peasant or yeoman belonging to the estate of a certain Queen. We may suspect, however, from the conversation, that the pilgrim is a knight or noble, and probably has been a crusader. He sees that the country has been ravaged by some merciless enemy; and the peasant tells him that it was Duke Luke. The peasant's house is burning; he himself is hiding in terror of his life. But the pilgrim is not afraid, and goes to see the Queen in spite of all warning. One can imagine very well that the purpose of the Duke in thus making war upon a woman was to force a marriage as well as to acquire territory. Now it was the duty of a true knight to help any woman unjustly oppressed or attacked; therefore the pilgrim's wish to see the Queen is prompted by this sense of duty. Hereafter the poem has an entirely different tone.

> The Queen sat idle by her loom:
>   She heard the arras stir,
> And looked up sadly: through the room
>   The sweetness sickened her
>   Of musk and myrrh.
>
> Her women, standing two and two,
>   In silence combed the fleece.
> The Pilgrim said, "Peace be with you,
>   Lady"; and bent his knees.
>   She answered, "Peace."

Studies in Rossetti

Her eyes were like the wave within;
Like water-reeds the poise
Of her soft body, dainty-thin;
And like the water's noise
    Her plaintive voice.

The naked walls of rooms during the Middle Ages
were covered with drapery or tapestry, on which figures
were embroidered or woven. *Arras* was the name given
to a kind of tapestry made at the town of Arras in
France.

For him, the stream had never well'd
In desert tracts malign
So sweet; nor had he ever felt
So faint in the sunshine
    Of Palestine.

Right so, he knew that he saw weep
Each night through every dream
The Queen's own face, confused in sleep
With visages supreme
    Not known to him.

At this point the poem suddenly becomes mystical.
It is not chance nor will that has brought these two
together, but some divine destiny. As he sees the
Queen's face for the first time with his eyes, he remembers having seen the same face many times before in
his dreams. And when he saw it in dreams, it was also
the face of a woman weeping; and there were also other
faces in the dream, not human but "supreme"—probably angels or other heavenly beings.

"Lady," he said, "your lands lie burnt
And waste: to meet your foe
All fear: this I have seen and learnt.
Say that it shall be so,
And I will go."

She gazed at him. "Your cause is just,
For I have heard the same:"
He said: "God's strength shall be my trust.
Fall it to good or grame,
'Tis in His name."

"Sir, you are thanked. My cause is dead.
Why should you toil to break
A grave, and fall therein?" she said.
He did not pause but spake:
"For my vow's sake."

"Can such vows be, Sir—to God's ear,
Not to God's will?" "My vow
Remains: God heard me there as here,"
He said, with reverent brow,
"Both then and now."

They gazed together, he and she,
The minute while he spoke;
And when he ceased, she suddenly
Looked round upon her folk
As though she woke.

"Fight, Sir," she said; "my prayers in pain
Shall be your fellowship."
He whispered one among her train,—
"To-morrow bid her keep
This staff and scrip."

Studies in Rossetti

The scrip was a kind of wallet or bag carried by pilgrims. Now we have a few sensuous touches, of the kind in which Rossetti excels all other poets, because they always are kept within the extreme limits of artistic taste.

> She sent him a sharp sword, whose belt
> About his body there
> As sweet as her own arms he felt.
> He kissed its blade, all bare,
> Instead of her.
>
> She sent him a green banner wrought
> With one white lily stem,
> To bind his lance with when he fought.
> He writ upon the same
> And kissed her name.

"Wrought" here signifies embroidered with the design of the white lily. Remember that the Queen's name is white lily (Blanchelys), and the flower is her crest. It was the custom for every knight to have fastened to his lance a small flag or pennon—also called sometimes "pennant."

> She sent him a white shield, whereon
> She bade that he should trace
> His will. He blent fair hues that shone,
> And in a golden space
> He kissed her face.

Being appointed by the Queen her knight, it would have been more customary that she should tell him what design he should put upon his shield—heraldic privileges coming from the sovereign only. But she tells him generously that he may choose any design that he pleases. He returns the courtesy very beautifully by painting the Queen's face on the shield upon a background of gold, and kissing the image. By "space" here must be understood a quarter, or compartment, of the shield, according to the rules of heraldry.

> Born of the day that died, that eve
> Now dying sank to rest;
> As he, in likewise taking leave,
> Once with a heaving breast
> Looked to the west.
>
> And there the sunset skies unseal'd,
> Like lands he never knew,
> Beyond to-morrow's battle-field
> Lay open out of view
> To ride into.

Here we have the suggestion of emotions known to us all, when looking into a beautiful sunset sky in which there appeared to be landscapes of gold and purple and other wonderful colours, like some glimpse of a heavenly world. Notice the double suggestion of this verse. The knight, having bidden the Queen good-bye, is riding home, looking, as he rides, into the sunset and over the same plain where he must fight to-morrow. Looking, he sees such landscapes—strangely beautiful, more beautiful than anything in the real world. Then he thinks that heaven might be like that. At the same time he has a premonition that he is going to be killed the next day, and this thought comes to him: "Perhaps I shall ride into that heaven to-morrow."

[42]

Studies in Rossetti

Next day till dark the women pray'd;
　Nor any might know there
How the fight went; the Queen has bade
　That there do come to her
　　No messenger.

The Queen is pale, her maidens ail;
　And to the organ-tones
They sing but faintly, who sang well
　The matin-orisons,
　　The lauds and nones.

Orison means a prayer; *matin* has the same meaning
as the French word, spelled in the same way, for morning. Matin-orisons are morning prayers, but special
prayers belonging to the ancient church services are
intended; these prayers are still called matins. *Lauds*
is also the name of special prayers of the Roman morning service; the word properly means "praises." *Nones*
is the name of a third special kind of prayers, intended
to be repeated or sung at the ninth hour of the morning—hence nones.

Lo, Father, is thine ear inclin'd,
　And hath thine angel pass'd?
For these thy watchers now are blind
　With vigil, and at last
　　Dizzy with fast.

Weak now to them the voice o' the priest
　As any trance affords;
And when each anthem failed and ceas'd,
　It seemed that the last chords
　　Still sang the words.

[43]

Pre-Raphaelite and Other Poets

By *Father* is here meant God—probably in the person of Christ. To incline the ear means to listen. When this expression is used of God it always means listening to prayer. In the second line angel has the double signification of spirit and messenger, but especially the latter. Why is the expression "at last" used here? It was the custom when making special prayer both to remain without sleep, which was called "keeping vigil" or watch, and to remain without food, or "to fast." The evening has come and the women have not eaten anything all day. At first they were too anxious to feel hungry, but *at last* as the night advances, they become too weak.

"Oh, what is the light that shines so red?
'Tis long since the sun set";
Quoth the youngest to the eldest maid:
" 'Twas dim but now, and yet
The light is great."

Quoth the other: " 'Tis our sight is dazed
That we see flame i' the air."
But the Queen held her brows and gazed,
And said, "It is the glare
Of torches there."

Held her brows—that is, put her hand above her eyes so as to see better by keeping off the light in the room. There is a very nice suggestion here; the Queen hears and sees better than the young girls, not simply because she has finer senses, or because she has more to fear by the loss of her kingdom. It is the intensification of the senses caused by love that makes her see and hear so well.

[44]

Studies in Rossetti

"Oh what are the sounds that rise and spread?
All day it was so still;"
Quoth the youngest to the eldest maid:
"Unto the furthest hill
    The air they fill."

Quoth the other: " 'Tis our sense is blurr'd
With all the chants gone by."
But the Queen held her breath and heard,
And said, "It is the cry
    Of Victory."

The first of all the rout was sound,
The next were dust and flame,
And then the horses shook the ground;
And in the thick of them
    A still band came.

I think that no poet in the world ever performed a greater feat than this stanza, in which, and in three lines only, the whole effect of the spectacle and sound of an army returning at night has been given. We must suppose that the women have gone out to wait for the army. It comes; but the night is dark, and they hear at first only the sound of the coming, the tramp of black masses of men passing. Probably these would be the light troops, archers and footmen. The lights are still behind, with the cavalry. Then the first appearance is made in the light of torches—foot soldiers still, covered with dust and carrying lights with them. Then they feel the ground shake under the weight of the feudal cavalry—the knights come. But where is the chief? No chief is visible; but, surrounded by the mounted knights, there is a silent company of men on foot carrying something. The Queen wants to know what it is. It is covered with leaves and branches so that she cannot see it.

> "Oh what do ye bring out of the fight,
>   Thus hid beneath these boughs?"
> "Thy conquering guest returns to-night,
>   And yet shall not carouse,
>   Queen, in thy house."

After a victory there was always in those days a great feast of wine-drinking, or carousal. *To carouse* means to take part in such noisy festivity. When the Queen puts her question, she is kindly but grimly answered, so that she knows the dead body of her knight must be under the branches. But being a true woman and lover, her love conquers her fear and pain; she must see him again, no matter how horribly his body may have been wounded.

> "Uncover ye his face," she said.
>   "O changed in little space!"
> She cried, "O pale that was so red!
>   O God, O God of grace!
>   Cover his face!"

> His sword was broken in his hand
>   Where he had kissed the blade.
> "O soft steel that could not withstand!
>   O my hard heart unstayed,
>   That prayed and prayed!"

Why does she call her heart hard? Because she naturally reproaches herself with his death. *Unstayed* means uncomforted, unsupported. There is a sugges-

[46]

tion that she prayed and prayed in vain because her
heart had suffered her to send that man to battle.

> His bloodied banner crossed his mouth
> Where he had kissed her name.
> "O east, and west, and north, and south,
> Fair flew my web, for shame,
> To guide Death's aim!"

> The tints were shredded from his shield
> Where he had kissed her face.
> "Oh, of all gifts that I could yield,
> Death only keeps its place,
> My gift and grace!"

The expression "*my* web" implies that the Queen had
herself woven the material of the flag.   The word "web"
is not now often used in modern prose in this sense—
we say texture, stuff, material instead.   *A shred* especially means a small *torn* piece.   "To shred from"
would therefore mean to remove in small torn pieces—
or, more simply expressed, to scratch off, or rend away.
Of course the rich thick painting upon the shield is
referred to.   Repeated blows upon the surface would
remove the painting in small shreds.   This is very
pathetic when rightly studied.   She sees that all the
presents she made to him, banner, sword, shield, have
been destroyed in the battle; and with bitter irony, the
irony of grief, she exclaims, "The only present I made
him that could not be taken back or broken was death.
Death was my grace, my one kindness!"

> Then stepped a damsel to her side,
> And spoke, and needs must weep;

[47]

Pre-Raphaelite and Other Poets

"For his sake, lady, if he died,
He prayed of thee to keep
This staff and scrip."

That night they hung above her bed,
Till morning wet with tears.
Year after year above her head
Her bed his token wears,
Five years, ten years.

That night the passion of her grief
Shook them as there they hung
Each year the wind that shed the leaf
Shook them and in its tongue
A message flung.

We must suppose the Queen's bed to have been one of the great beds used in the Middle Ages and long afterwards, with four great pillars supporting a kind of little roof or ceiling above it, and also supporting curtains, which would be drawn around the bed at night. The staff and scrip and the token would have been hung to the ceiling, or as the French call it *ciel*, of the bed; and therefore they might be shaken by a passion of grief—because a woman sobbing in the bed would shake the bed, and therefore anything hung to the awning above it.

And once she woke with a clear mind
That letters writ to calm
Her soul lay in the scrip; to find
Only a torpid balm
And dust of palm.

Sometimes when we are very unhappy, we dream that

[48]

what we really wish for has happened, and that the sorrow is taken away. And in such dreams we are very sure that what we were dreaming is true. Then we wake up to find the misery come back again. The Queen has been greatly sorrowing for this man, and wishing she could have some news from his spirit, some message from him. One night she dreams that somebody tells her, "If you will open that scrip, you will find in it the message which you want." Then she wakes up and finds only some palm-dust, and some balm so old that it no longer has any perfume—but no letter.

> They shook far off with palace sport
>   When joust and dance were rife;
> And the hunt shook them from the court;
>   For hers, in peace or strife,
>   Was a Queen's life.
>
> A Queen's death now: as now they shake
>   To gusts in chapel dim,—
> Hung where she sleeps, not seen to wake
>   (Carved lovely white and slim),
>   With them by him.

It would be for her, as for any one in great sorrow, a consolation to be alone with her grief. But this she cannot be, nor can she show her grief to any one, because she is a Queen. Only when in her chamber, at certain moments, can she think of the dead knight, and see the staff and scrip shaking in their place, as the castle itself shakes to the sound of the tournaments, dances, and the gathering of the great hunting parties in the court below.

[49]

Pre-Raphaelite and Other Poets

In that age it was the custom when a knight died
to carve an image of him, lying asleep in his armour,
and this image was laid upon his long tomb. When
his wife died, or the lady to whom he had been pledged,
she was represented as lying beside him, with her hands
joined, as if in prayer. You will see plenty of these
figures upon old tombs in England. Usually a nobleman was not buried in the main body of a large church,
but in a chapel—which is a kind of little side-church,
opening into the great church. Such is the case in
many cathedrals; and some cathedrals, like Westmin-
ster, have many chapels used as places of burial and
places of worship. On the altar in these little chapels
special services are performed for the souls of the dead
buried in the chapel. It is not uncommon to see, in
such a chapel, some relics of the dead suspended to the
wall, such as a shield or a flag. In this poem, by the
Queen's own wish, the staff and scrip of the dead knight
are hung on the wall above her tomb, where they are
sometimes shaken by the wind.

> Stand up to-day, still armed, with her,
>   Good knight, before His brow
> Who then as now was here and there,
>   Who had in mind thy vow
>   Then even as now.

> The lists are set in Heaven to-day,
>   The bright pavilions shine;
> Fair hangs thy shield, and none gainsay;
>   The trumpets sound in sign
>   That she is thine.

[50]

Studies in Rossetti

Not tithed with days' and years' decease
He pays thy wage He owed,
But with imperishable peace
Here in His own abode,
    Thy jealous God.

Still armed refers to the representation of the dead knight in full armour. Mediæval faith imagined the warrior armed in the spiritual world as he was in this life; and the ghosts of dead knights used to appear in armour. The general meaning of these stanzas is, "God now gives you the reward which he owed to you; and unlike rewards given to men in this world, your heavenly reward is not diminished by the certainty that you cannot enjoy it except for a certain number of days or years. God does not keep anything back out of his servants' wages—no tithe or tenth. You will be with her forever." The adjective "jealous" applied to God is a Hebrew use of the term; but it has here a slightly different meaning. The idea is this, that Heaven is jealous of human love when human love alone is a motive of duty. Therefore the reward of duty need not be expected in this world but only in Heaven.

Outside of the sonnets, which we must consider separately, I do not know any more beautiful example of the mystical feeling of love in Rossetti than this. It will not be necessary to search any further for examples in this special direction; I think you will now perfectly understand one of the peculiar qualities distinguishing Rossetti from all the other Victorian poets—the mingling of religious with amatory emotion in the highest form of which the language is capable.

[51]

Pre-Raphaelite and Other Poets`

While we are discussing the ballads and shorter narrative poems, let us now consider Rossetti simply as a story-teller, and see how wonderful he is in some of those lighter productions in which he brought the art of the refrain to a perfection which nobody else, except perhaps Swinburne, has equalled. Among the ballads there is but one, "Stratton Water," conceived altogether after the old English fashion; and this has no refrain. I do not know that any higher praise can be given to it than the simple statement that it is a perfect imitation of the old ballad—at least so far as a perfect imitation is possible in the nineteenth century. Should there be any criticism allowable, it could be only this, that the tenderness and pathos are somewhat deeper, and somewhat less rough in utterance, than we expect in a ballad of the fourteenth or fifteenth century. Yet there is no stanza in it for which some parallel might not be found in ballads of the old time. It is nothing more than the story of a country girl seduced by a nobleman, who nevertheless has no intention of being cruel or unfaithful. Just as she is about to drown herself, or rather to let herself be drowned, he rescues her from the danger, marries her in haste to save appearances, and makes her his wife. There is nothing more of narrative, and no narrative could be more simple. But as the great pains and great joys of life are really in simple things, the simplest is capable of almost infinite expansion when handled by a true artist. Certainly in English poetry there is no ballad more beau-

[52]

tiful than this; nor can we imagine it possible to do anything more with so slight a theme. It contains nothing, however, calling for elaborate explanation or comment; I need only recommend you to read it and to feel it.

It is otherwise in the case of such ballads as "Sister Helen" and "The White Ship." "The White Ship" is a little too long for full reproduction in the lecture; but we can point out its special beauties. "Sister Helen," although rather long also, we must study the whole of, partly because it has become so very famous, and partly because it deals with emotions and facts of the Middle Ages requiring careful interpretation. Perhaps it is the best example of story telling in the shorter pieces of Rossetti—not because its pictures are more objectively vivid than the themes of the "White Ship," but because it is more subjectively vivid, dealing with the extremes of human passion, hate, love, revenge, and religious despair. All these are passions peculiarly coloured by the age in which the story is supposed to happen, the age of belief in magic, in ghosts, and in hell-fire.

I think that in nearly all civilised countries, East and West, from very old times there has been some belief in the kind of magic which this poem describes. I have seen references to similar magic in translations of Chinese books, and I imagine that it may have been known in Japan. In India it is still practised. At one time or other it was practised in every country of Europe. Indeed, it was only the development of exact science that rendered such beliefs impossible. During the Middle Ages they caused the misery of many thousands of lives, and the fear born of them weighed upon men's minds like a nightmare.

This superstition in its simplest form was that if you wished to kill a hated person, it was only necessary to make a small statue or image of that person in wax, or some other soft material, and to place the image before a fire, after having repeated certain formulas. As the wax began to melt before the fire, the person represented by the image would become sick and grow weaker and weaker, until with the complete melting of the image, he would die. Sometimes when the image was made of material other than wax, it was differently treated. Also it was a custom to stick needles into such images, for the purpose of injuring rather than of killing. By putting the needles into the place of the eyes, for example, the person would be made blind; or by putting them into the place of the ears, he might be rendered deaf. A needle stuck into the place of the heart would cause death, slow or quick according to the slowness with which the needle was forced in.

But there were many penalties attaching to the exercise of such magic. People convicted of having practised it were burned alive by law. However, burning alive was not the worst consequence of the practice, according to general belief; for the church taught that such a crime was unpardonable, and that all guilty of it must go to hell for all eternity. You might destroy your enemy by magic, but only at the cost of your own soul. A soul for a life. And you must know that the persons who did such things believed the magic was real, believed they were killing, and believed they were condemned to lose their souls in consequence. Can we conceive of hatred strong enough to satisfy itself at this price? Certainly, there have been many examples in the history of those courts in which trials for witchcraft were formerly held.

Now we have the general idea behind this awful ballad. The speakers in the story are only two, a young woman and her brother, a little boy. We may suppose the girl to be twenty and the boy about five years old or even younger. The girl is apparently of good family, for she appears to be living in a castle of her own—at least a fortified dwelling of some sort. We must also suppose her to be an orphan, for she avenges herself—as one having no male relative to fight for her. She has been seduced under promise of marriage; but before the marriage day, her faithless lover marries another woman. Then she determines to destroy his life by magic. While her man of wax is melting before the fire, the parents, relatives, and newly-wedded bride of her victim come on horseback to beg that she will forgive. But forgive she will not, and he dies, and at the last his ghost actually enters the room. This is the story.

You will observe that the whole conversation is only between the girl and this baby-brother. She talks to the child in child language, but with a terrible meaning behind each simple word. She herself will not answer the prayers of the relatives of the dying man; she makes the little brother act as messenger. So all that is said in the poem is said between the girl and the little boy. Even in the opening of the ballad there is a terrible pathos in the presence of this little baby brother. What does he know of horrible beliefs, hat-

[55]

red, lust, evil passion of any sort? He only sees that his sister has made a kind of wax-doll, and he thinks that it is a pretty doll, and would like to play with it. But his sister, instead of giving him the doll, begins to melt it before the fire, and he cannot understand why.

One more preliminary observation. What is the meaning of the refrain? This refrain, in italics, always represents the secret thought of the girl, what she cannot say to the little brother, but what she thinks and suffers. The references to Mary refer to the Virgin Mary of course, but with the special mediæval sense. God would not forgive certain sins; but, during the Middle Ages at least, the Virgin Mary, the mother of God, was a refuge even for the despairing magician or witch. We could not expect one practising witchcraft to call upon the name of Christ. But the same person, in moments of intense pain, might very naturally ejaculate the name of Mary. And now we can begin the poem.

SISTER HELEN

"Why did you melt your waxen man,
    Sister Helen?
To-day is the third since you began."
"The time was long, yet the time ran,
    Little brother."
    (*O Mother, Mary Mother,*
Three days to-day, between Hell and Heaven!)

"But if you have done your work aright,
    Sister Helen,
You'll let me play, for you said I might."

[56]

Studies in Rossetti

"Be very still in your play to-night,
    Little brother."
    (*O Mother, Mary Mother,*
Third night, to-night, between Hell and Heaven!)

"You said it must melt ere vesper-bell,
    Sister Helen;
If now it be molten, all is well."
"Even so,—nay, peace! you cannot tell,
    Little brother!"
    (*O Mother, Mary Mother,*
O what is this, between Hell and Heaven?)

"Oh, the waxen knave was plump to-day,
    Sister Helen;
How like dead folk he has dropped away!"
"Nay now, of the dead what can you say,
    Little brother?"
    (*O Mother, Mary Mother,*
What of the dead, between Hell and Heaven?)

"See, see, the sunken pile of wood,
    Sister Helen,
Shines through the thinned wax red as blood!"
"Nay now, when looked you yet on blood,
    Little brother?"
    (*O Mother, Mary Mother,*
How pale she is, between Hell and Heaven!)

"Now close your eyes, for they're sick and sore,
    Sister Helen,
And I'll play without the gallery door."
"Aye, let me rest,—I'll lie on the floor,
    Little brother."
    (*O Mother, Mary Mother,*
What rest to-night, between Hell and Heaven?)

[57]

Pre-Raphaelite and Other Poets

"Here high up in the balcony,
    Sister Helen,
The moon flies face to face with me."
"Aye, look and say whatever you see,
    Little brother."
    (*O Mother, Mary Mother,*
What sight to-night, between Hell and Heaven?)

"Outside, it's merry in the wind's wake,
    Sister Helen;
In the shaken trees the chill stars shake."
"Hush, heard you a horse-tread as you spake,
    Little brother?"
    (*O Mother, Mary Mother,*
What sound to-night, between Hell and Heaven?)

"I hear a horse-tread, and I see,
    Sister Helen,
Three horsemen that ride terribly."
"Little brother, whence come the three,
    Little brother?"
    (*O Mother, Mary Mother,*
Whence should they come, between Hell and Heaven?)

In this last stanza the repetition of the words "little brother" indicates intense eagerness. The girl has been expecting that the result of her enchantments would force the relatives of her victim to come and beg for mercy. The child's words therefore bring to her a shock of excitement.

"They come by the hill-verge from Boyne Bar,
    Sister Helen,
And one draws nigh, but two are afar."

[58]

Studies in Rossetti

"Look, look, do you know them who they are,
    Little brother?"
    (O Mother, Mary Mother,
Who should they be, between Hell and Heaven?)

"Oh, it's Keith of Eastholm rides so fast,
    Sister Helen,
For I know the white mane on the blast."
"The hour has come, has come at last,
    Little brother!"
    (O Mother, Mary Mother,
Her hour at last, between Hell and Heaven!)

Those who come are knights, and the child can know
them only by the crest or by the horses; as they are very
far he can distinguish only the horses, but he knows
the horse of Keith of Eastholm, because of its white
mane, floating in the wind. From this point the poem
becomes very terrible, because it shows us a play of
terrible passion—passion all the more terrible because
it is that of a woman.

"He has made a sign and called Halloo!
    Sister Helen,
And he says that he would speak with you."
"Oh, tell him I fear the frozen dew
    Little brother."
    (O Mother, Mary Mother,
Why laughs she thus, between Hell and Heaven?)

"The wind is loud, but I hear him cry,
    Sister Helen,
That Keith of Ewern's like to die."

Pre-Raphaelite and Other Poets

"And he and thou, and thou and I,
  Little brother."
  (*O Mother, Mary Mother,*
And they and we, between Hell and Heaven!)

"Three days ago, on his marriage-morn,
  Sister Helen,
He sickened, and lies since then forlorn."
"For bridegroom's side is the bride a thorn,
  Little brother?"
  (*O Mother, Mary Mother,*
Cold bridal cheer, between Hell and Heaven!)

We now can surmise the story from the girl's own lips. There are wrongs that a woman cannot forgive, unless she is of very weak character indeed. But this woman is no weakling; she can kill, and laugh while killing, because she is a daughter of warriors, and has been cruelly injured. Notice the bitter mockery of every word she utters, especially the exulting reference to the unhappy bride. We imagine that she might be sorry for killing a man whom she once loved; but we may be perfectly sure that she will feel no pity for the woman that he married.

"Three days and nights he has lain abed,
  Sister Helen,
And he prays in torment to be dead."
"The thing may chance, if he have prayed,
  Little brother!"
  (*O Mother, Mary Mother,*
If he have prayed, between Hell and Heaven!)

"But he has not ceased to cry to-day,
  Sister Helen,
That you should take your curse away."

[60]

Studies in Rossetti

"*My* prayer was heard,—he need but pray,
  Little brother!"
 (*O Mother, Mary Mother,*
Shall God not hear, between Hell and Heaven?)

"But he says till you take back your ban,
  Sister Helen,
His soul would pass, yet never can."
"Nay then, shall I slay a living man,
  Little brother?"
 (*O Mother, Mary Mother,*
A living soul, between Hell and Heaven!)

"But he calls for ever on your name,
  Sister Helen,
And says that he melts before a flame."
"My heart for his pleasure fared the same,
  Little brother."
 (*O Mother, Mary Mother,*
Fire at the heart, between Hell and Heaven!)

"Here's Keith of Westholm riding fast,
  Sister Helen,
For I know the white plume on the blast."
"The hour, the sweet hour I forecast,
  Little brother!"
 (*O Mother, Mary Mother,*
Is the hour sweet, between Hell and Heaven?)

"He stops to speak, and he stills his horse,
  Sister Helen,
But his words are drowned in the wind's course."
"Nay hear, nay hear, you must hear perforce,
  Little brother!"
 (*O Mother, Mary Mother,*
What word now heard, between Hell and Heaven?)

Pre-Raphaelite and Other Poets

"Oh, he says that Keith of Ewern's cry,
  Sister Helen,
Is ever to see you ere he die."
"In all that his soul sees, there am I,
  Little brother!"
  (*O Mother, Mary Mother,*
The soul's one sight, between Hell and Heaven!)

"He sends a ring and a broken coin,
  Sister Helen,
And bids you mind the banks of Boyne."
"What else he broke will he ever join,
  Little brother?"
  (*O Mother, Mary Mother,*
No, never joined, between Hell and Heaven!)

It was a custom, and in some parts of England still is a custom, for lovers not only to give each other rings, but also to divide something between them—such as a coin or a ring, for pledge and remembrance. Sometimes a ring would be cut in two, and each person would keep one-half. Sometimes a thin coin, gold or silver money, was broken into halves and each of the lovers would wear one-half round the neck fastened to a string. Such pledges would be always recognised, and were only to be sent back in time of terrible danger—in a matter of life and death. There are many references to this custom in the old ballads.

"He yields you these, and craves full fain,
  Sister Helen,
You pardon him in his mortal pain."
"What else he took will he give again,
  Little brother?"

Studies in Rossetti

(O Mother, Mary Mother,
Not twice to give, between Hell and Heaven!)

"He calls your name in an agony,
  Sister Helen,
That even dead Love must weep to see."
"Hate, born of Love, is blind as he,
  Little brother!"
(O Mother, Mary Mother,
Love turned to hate, between Hell and Heaven!)

"Oh it's Keith of Keith now that rides fast,
  Sister Helen,
For I know the white hair on the blast."
"The short, short hour will soon be past,
  Little brother!"
(O Mother, Mary Mother,
Will soon be past, between Hell and Heaven!)

"He looks at me and he tries to speak,
  Sister Helen,
But oh! his voice is sad and weak!"
"What here should the mighty Baron seek,
  Little brother?"
(O Mother, Mary Mother,
Is this the end, between Hell and Heaven?)

"Oh his son still cries, if you forgive,
  Sister Helen,
The body dies, but the soul shall live."
"Fire shall forgive me as I forgive,
  Little brother!"
(O Mother, Mary Mother,
As she forgives, between Hell and Heaven!)

This needs some explanation in reference to religious belief. The witch, you will observe, has the power to destroy the soul as well as the body, but on the condition of suffering the same loss herself. Yet how can this be? It could happen thus: if the dying man could make a confession before he dies, and sincerely repent of his sin before a priest, his soul might be saved; but while he remains in the agony of suffering caused by the enchantment, he cannot repent. Not to repent means to go to Hell for ever and ever. If the woman would forgive him, withdrawing the curse and pain for one instant, all might be well. But she answers, "Fire shall forgive me as I forgive"—she means, "The fire of Hell shall sooner forgive me when I go to Hell, than I shall forgive him in this world." There will be other references to this horrible belief later on. It was very common in the Middle Ages.

> "Oh he prays you, as his heart would rive,
>   Sister Helen,
> To save his dear son's soul alive."
> "Fire cannot slay it, it shall thrive,
>   Little brother!"
> (*O Mother, Mary Mother,*
> *Alas, alas, between Hell and Heaven!*)

Rive is seldom used now in prose, though we have "riven" very often. To rive is to tear. The last line of this stanza is savage, for it refers to the belief that the black fire of Hell preserves the body of the damned person instead of consuming it.

> "He cries to you, kneeling in the road,
>   Sister Helen,
> To go with him for the love of God!"

Studies in Rossetti

"The way is long to his son's abode,
    Little brother!"
(*O Mother, Mary Mother,*
The way is long, between Hell and Heaven!)

"A lady's here, by a dark steed brought,
    Sister Helen,
So darkly clad, I saw her not."
"See her now or never see aught,
    Little brother!"
(*O Mother, Mary Mother,*
What more to see, between Hell and Heaven?)

As the horse was black and the lady was all dressed in black, the child could not at first notice either in the shadows of the road. On announcing that he had seen her at last, the excitement of the sister reaches its highest and wickedest; she says to him, "Nay, you will never be able to see anything in this world, unless you can see that woman's face and tell me all about it." For it is the other woman, who has made forgiveness impossible; it is the other woman, the object of her deepest hate.

"Her hood falls back, and the moon shines fair,
    Sister Helen,
On the Lady of Ewern's golden hair."
"Blest hour of my power and her despair,
    Little brother!"
(*O Mother, Mary Mother,*
Hour blessed and bann'd, between Hell and Heaven!)

"Pale, pale her cheeks, that in pride did glow,
    Sister Helen,
'Neath the bridal-wreath three days ago."

[65]

Pre-Raphaelite and Other Poets

"One morn for pride, and three days for woe,
      Little brother!"
    (*O Mother, Mary Mother,*
Three days, three nights, between Hell and Heaven!)

"Her clasped hands stretch from her bending head,
      Sister Helen;
With the loud wind's wail her sobs are wed."
"What wedding-strains hath her bridal bed,
      Little brother?"
    (*O Mother, Mary Mother,*
What strain but death's, between Hell and Heaven?)

You must remember that the word "strains" is
nearly always used in the sense of musical tones, and
that "wedding-strains" means the joyful music played
at a wedding. Thus the ferocity of Helen's mockery
becomes apparent, for it was upon the bridal night
that the bridegroom was first bewitched; and from the
moment of his marriage, therefore, he has been screaming in agony.

The climax of hatred is in the next stanza. After
that the tone begins to reverse, and gradually passes
away in the melancholy of eternal despair.

"She may not speak, she sinks in a swoon,
      Sister Helen,—
She lifts her lips and gasps on the moon."
"Oh! might I but hear her soul's blithe tune,
      Little brother!"
    (*O Mother, Mary Mother,*
Her woe's dumb cry, between Hell and Heaven!)

To "gasp" means to open the mouth in the effort
to get breath, as one does in a fit of hysterics, or in

time of great agony. "Gasps on the moon" means that she gasps with her face turned up toward the moon. In the last line we have the words "blithe tune" used in the same tone of terrible irony as that with which the word "wedding-strain" was used in the preceding stanza. "Blithe" means "merry." Helen is angry because the other woman has fainted; having fainted, she has become for the moment physically incapable of suffering. But Helen thinks that her soul must be conscious and suffering as much as ever; therefore she wishes that she could hear the suffering of the soul, since she cannot longer hear the outcries of the body.

> "They've caught her to Westholm's saddle-bow,
>   Sister Helen,
> And her moonlit hair gleams white in its flow."
> "Let it turn whiter than winter-snow,
>   Little brother!"
>   (*O Mother, Mary Mother,*
> *Woe-withered gold, between Hell and Heaven!*)

The allusion is to the physiological fact that intense moral pain, or terrible fear, sometimes turns the hair of a young person suddenly white.

> "O Sister Helen, you heard the bell,
>   Sister Helen!
> More loud than the vesper-chime it fell."
> "No vesper-chime, but a dying knell,
>   Little brother!"
>   (*O Mother, Mary Mother,*
> *His dying knell, between Hell and Heaven!*)

[67]

Pre-Raphaelite and Other Poets

"Alas, but I fear the heavy sound,
    Sister Helen;
Is it in the sky or in the ground?"
"Say, have they turned their horses round,
    Little brother?"
    (*O Mother, Mary Mother,*
What would she more, between Hell and Heaven?)

"They have raised the old man from his knee,
    Sister Helen,
And they ride in silence hastily."
"More fast the naked soul doth flee,
    Little brother!"
    (*O Mother, Mary Mother,*
The naked soul, between Hell and Heaven!)

"Flank to flank are the three steeds gone,
    Sister Helen,
But the lady's dark steed goes alone."
"And lonely her bridegroom's soul hath flown,
    Little brother!"
    (*O Mother, Mary Mother,*
The lonely ghost, between Hell and Heaven!)

"Oh the wind is sad in the iron chill,
    Sister Helen,
And weary sad they look by the hill."
"But he and I are sadder still,
    Little brother!"
    (*O Mother, Mary Mother,*
Most sad of all, between Hell and Heaven!)

"See, see, the wax has dropped from its place,
    Sister Helen,
And the flames are winning up apace!"

[68]

Studies in Rossetti

"Yet here they burn but for a space,
  Little brother!"
(O Mother, Mary Mother,
Here for a space, between Hell and Heaven!)

"Ah! what white thing at the door has cross'd,
  Sister Helen?
Ah! what is this that sighs in the frost?"
"A soul that's lost as mine is lost,
  Little brother!"
(O Mother, Mary Mother,
Lost, lost, all lost, between Hell and Heaven!)

Notice how the action naturally dies off into despair. From the beginning until very nearly the close, we had an uninterrupted crescendo, as we should say in music —that is, a gradual intensification of the passion expressed. With the stroke of the death-bell the passion subsides. The revenge is satisfied, the irreparable wrong is done to avenge a wrong, and with the entrance of the ghost the whole consequence of the act begins to appear within the soul of the actor. I know of nothing more terrible in literature than this poem, as expressing certain phases of human feeling, and nothing more intensely true. The probability or improbability of the incidents is of no more consequence than is the unreality of the witch-belief. It is enough that such beliefs once existed to make us know that the rest is not only possible but certain. For a time we are really subjected to the spell of a mediæval nightmare.

As we have seen, the above poem is mainly a subjective study. As an objective study, "The White Ship" shows us an equal degree of power, appealing to the visual faculty. We cannot read it all, nor is this necessary. A few examples will be sufficient. This ballad is in distichs, and has a striking refrain. The story is founded upon historical fact. The son and heir of the English king Henry I, together with his sister and many knights and ladies, was drowned on a voyage from France to England, and it is said that the king was never again seen to smile after he had heard the news. Rossetti imagines the story told by a survivor—a butcher employed on the ship, the lowest menial on board. Such a man would naturally feel very differently toward the prince from others of the train, and would criticise him honestly from the standpoint of simple morality.

> Eighteen years till then he had seen,
> And the devil's dues in him were eighteen.

The peasant thus estimates the ruler who breaks the common laws of God and man. Nevertheless he is just in his own way, and can appreciate unselfishness even in a man whom he hates.

> He was a Prince of lust and pride;
> He showed no grace till the hour he died.
> .   .   .   .
> God only knows where his soul did wake,
> But I saw him die for his sister's sake.

It is a simple mind of this sort that can best tell a tragical story; and the butcher's story is about the most perfect thing imaginable of its kind. Here also we have one admirable bit of subjective work, the narration of the butcher's experience in the moment of drowning. I suppose you all know that when one is just about to die, or in danger of sudden death, the memory becomes extraordinarily vivid, and things long forgotten flash into the mind as if painted by lightning, together with voices of the past.

> I Berold was down in the sea;
> Passing strange though the thing may be,
> Of dreams then known I remember me.

Not dreams in the sense of visions of sleep, but images of memory.

> Blithe is the shout on Harfleur's strand
> When morning lights the sails to land:
>
> And blithe is Honfleur's echoing gloam
> When mothers call the children home:
>
> And high do the bells of Rouen beat
> When the Body of Christ goes down the street.
>
> These things and the like were heard and shown
> In a moment's trance 'neath the sea alone;
>
> And when I rose, 'twas the sea did seem,
> And not these things, to be all a dream.

In the moment after the sinking of the ship, under the water, the man remembers what he most loved at home— mornings in a fishing village, seeing the ships return; evenings in a like village, and the sound of his own mother's voice calling him home, as when he was a little child at play; then the old Norman city that he knew

well, and the church processions of Corpus Christi
(Body of Christ), the great event of the year for the
poorer classes. Why he remembered such things at
such a time he cannot say; it seemed to him a very
ghostly experience, but not more ghostly than the sight
of the sea and the moon when he rose again.

> The ship was gone and the crowd was gone,
> And the deep shuddered and the moon shone;
>
> And in a strait grasp my arms did span
> The mainyard rent from the mast where it ran;
> And on it with me was another man.
>
> Where lands were none 'neath the dim sea-sky,
> We told our names, that man and I.
>
> "O I am Godefroy de l'Aigle hight,
> And son I am to a belted knight."
>
> "And I am Berold the butcher's son,
> Who slays the beasts in Rouen town."

The touch here, fine as it is, is perfectly natural. The
common butcher finds himself not only for the moment
in company with a nobleman, but able to talk to him as
a friend. There is no rank or wealth between sky and
sea—or, as a Japanese proverb says, "There is no king
on the road of death." The refrain of the ballad utters
the same truth:

> *Lands are swayed by a King on a throne,*
> *The sea hath no King but God alone.*

Both in its realism and in its emotion this ballad is

a great masterpiece. It is much superior to "The King's Tragedy," also founded upon history. "The King's Tragedy" seems to us a little strained; perhaps the poet attempted too much. I shall not quote from it, but will only recommend a reading of it to students of English literature because of its relation to a very beautiful story—the story of the courtship of James I of Scotland, and of how he came to write his poem called "The King's Quhair."

Another ballad demands some attention and explanation, though it is not suitable for reading in the classroom. It is an expression of passion—but not passion merely human; rather superhuman and evil. For she who speaks in this poem is not a woman like "Sister Helen"; she is a demon.

> Not a drop of her blood was human,
> But she was made like a soft sweet woman.

Perhaps the poet desired to show us here the extremest imaginative force of hate and cruelty—not in a mortal being, because that would repel us, but in an immortal being, in whom such emotion can only inspire fear. Emotionally, the poet's conception is of the Middle Ages, but the tradition is incomparably older; we can trace it back to ancient Assyrian beliefs. Coming to us through Hebrew literature, this strange story has inspired numberless European poets and painters, besides the author of "Eden Bower." You should know the story, because you will find a great many references to it in the different literatures of Europe.

Briefly, Lilith is the name of an evil spirit believed by the ancient Jews and by other Oriental nations to cause nightmare. But she did other things much more evil, and there were curious legends about her. The Jews said that before the first woman, Eve, was created, Adam had a demon wife by whom he became the father of many evil spirits. When Eve was created and given to him in marriage, Lilith was necessarily jealous, and resolved to avenge herself upon the whole human race. It is even to-day the custom among Jews to make a charm against Lilith on their marriage night; for Lilith is especially the enemy of brides.

But the particular story about Lilith that mostly figures in poetry and painting is this: If any young man sees Lilith, he must at once fall in love with her, because she is much more beautiful than any human being; and if he falls in love with her, he dies. After his death, if his body is opened by the doctors, it will be found that a long golden hair, one strand of woman's hair, is fastened round his heart. The particular evil in which Lilith delights is the destruction of youth.

In Rossetti's poem Lilith is represented only as declaring to her demon lover, the Serpent, how she will avenge herself upon Adam and upon Eve. The ideas are in one way extremely interesting; they represent the most tragical and terrible form of jealousy—that jealousy written of in the Bible as being like the very fires of Hell. We might say that in Victorian verse this is the unique poem of jealousy, in a female personification. For the male personification we must go to Robert Browning.

But there is a masterly phase of jealousy described in one of Rossetti's modern poems, "A Last Confession." Here, however, the jealousy is of the kind with which

we can humanly sympathise; there is nothing monstrous
or distorted about it. The man has reason to suspect
unchastity, and he kills the woman on the instant. I
should, therefore, consider this poem rather as a simple
and natural tragedy than as a study of jealousy. It
is to be remarked here that Rossetti did not confine
himself to mediæval or supernatural subjects. Three
of his very best poems are purely modern, belonging to
the nineteenth century. This "Last Confession," ap-
propriately placed in Italy, is not the most remarkable of the three, but it is very fine. I do not know
anything in even French literature to be compared with
the pathos of the murder scene, unless it be the terrible
closing chapter of Prosper Merimée's "Carmen." The
story of "Carmen" is also a confession; but there is a
great difference in the history of the tragedies. Carmen's lover does not kill in a moment of passion. He
kills only after having done everything that a man
could do in order to avoid killing. He argues, prays,
goes on his knees in supplication—all in vain. And
then we know that he must kill, that any man in the
same terrible situation must kill. He stabs her; then
the two continue to look at each other—she keeping
her large black eyes fixed on the face of her murderer,
till suddenly they close, and she falls. No simpler fact
could occur in the history of an assassination; yet how
marvellous the power of that simple fact as the artist
tells it. We always see those eyes. In the case of
Rossetti's murderer, the incidents of the tragedy differ
somewhat, because he is blind with passion at the moment that he strikes, and does not see. When his
vision clears again, he sees the girl fall, and

Pre-Raphaelite and Other Poets

—her stiff bodice scooped the sand
Into her bosom.

As long as he lived, he always saw that—the low stiff
front of the girl's dress with the sand and blood. In
its way this description is quite as terrible as the last
chapter of "Carmen"; and it would be difficult to say
which victim of passion most excites our sympathies.
The other two poems of modern life to which I have
referred are "The Card-Dealer" and "Jenny." "The
Card-Dealer" represents a singular faculty on the poet's
part of seeing ordinary facts in their largest relations.
In many European gambling houses of celebrity, the
cards used are dealt—that is, given to the players—by
a beautiful woman, usually a woman not of the virtuous kind. The poet, entering such a place, watches
the game for a time in silence, and utters his artistic
admiration of the beauty of the card-dealer, merely as
he would admire a costly picture or a statue of gold.
Then suddenly comes to him the thought that this
woman, and the silent players, and the game, are but
symbols of eternal fact. The game is no longer to his
eyes a mere game of cards; it is the terrible game of
Life, the struggle for wealth and vain pleasures. The
woman is no longer a woman, but Fate; she plays the
game of Death against Life, and those who play with
her must lose. However, the allusions in this poem
would require for easy understanding considerable fa-
miliarity with the terms of card-play and the names of
the cards. If you know these, I think you will find
this poem a very solemn and beautiful composition.

Much more modern is "Jenny," a poem which

greatly startled the public when it was first published. People were inclined for the moment to be shocked; then they studied and admired; finally they praised unlimitedly, and the poem deserved all praise. But the subject was a very daring one to put before a public so prudish as the English. For Jenny is a prostitute. Nevertheless the prudish public gladly accepted this wonderful psychological study, which no other poet of the nineteenth century, except perhaps Browning, could have attempted.

The plan of the poem is as follows: A young man, perhaps the poet himself, finds at some public place of pleasure a woman of the town who pleases him, and he accompanies her to her residence. Although the young man is perhaps imprudent in seeking the company of such a person, he is only doing what tens of thousands of young men are apt to do without thinking. He represents, we might say, youth in general. But there is a difference between him and the average youth in one respect—he thinks. On reaching the girl's room, he is already in a thoughtful mood; and when she falls asleep upon his knees, tired with the dancing and banqueting of the evening, he does not think of awakening her. He begins to meditate. He looks about the room and notices the various objects in it, simple enough in themselves, but strangely significant by their relation to such a time and place—a vase of flowers, a little clock ticking, a bird in a cage. The flowers make him think of the symbolism of flowers—lilies they are, but faded. Lilies, the symbol of purity, in Jenny's room! But once she herself was a lily—now also morally faded. Then the clock, ticking out its minutes, hours—what

[77]

strange hours it has ticked out! He looks at the sleeping girl again, but with infinite pity. She dreams;
what is she dreaming of? To wake her would be cruel,
for in the interval of sleep she forgets all the sorrows
of the world. He thinks:

> For sometimes, were the truth confess'd,
> You're thankful for a little rest,—
> Glad from the crush to rest within,
> From the heart-sickness and the din
> Where envy's voice at virtue's pitch
> Mocks you because your gown is rich;
> And from the pale girl's dumb rebuke,
> Whose ill-clad grace and toil-worn look
> Proclaims the strength that keeps her weak.
>
> .   .   .   .
>
> Is rest not sometimes sweet to you?—
> But most from the hatefulness of man,
> Who spares not to end what he began,
> Whose acts are ill and his speech ill,
> Who, having used you at his will,
> Thrusts you aside, as when I dine
> I serve the dishes' and the wine.

Then he begins to think of the terrible life of the prostitute, what it means, the hideous and cruel part of it,
and the end of it. Here let me say that the condition
of such a woman in England is infinitely worse than it
is in many other countries; in no place is she treated
with such merciless cruelty by society. He asks himself why this should be so—how can men find pleasure
in cruelty to so beautiful and simple-hearted a creature?
Then, suddenly looking at her asleep, he is struck by
a terrible resemblance which she bears to the sweetest

Studies in Rossetti

woman that he knows, the girl perhaps that he would
marry. Seen asleep, the two girls look exactly the same.
Each is young, graceful, and beautiful; yet one is a girl
adored by society for all that makes a woman lovable,
and the other is—what? These lines best explain the
thought:

> Just as another woman sleeps!
> Enough to throw one's thoughts in heaps
> Of doubt and horror,—what to say
> Or think,—this awful secret sway,
> The potter's power over the clay!
> Of the same lump (it has been said)
> For honour and dishonour made,
> Two sister vessels. Here is one.
>
> My cousin Nell is fond of fun,
> And fond of dress, and change, and praise,
> So mere a woman in her ways:
> And if her sweet eyes rich in youth
> Are like her lips that tell the truth,
> My cousin Nell is fond of love.
> And she's the girl I'm proudest of.
> Who does not prize her, guard her well?
> The love of change, in cousin Nell,
> Shall find the best and hold it dear:
> The unconquered mirth turn quieter
> Not through her own, through others' woe:
> The conscious pride of beauty glow
> Beside another's pride in her.
>
> . . . .
>
> Of the same lump (as it is said),
> For honour and dishonour made,
> Two sister vessels. Here is one.
> It makes a goblin of the sun!

For, judging by the two faces, the two characters were
originally the same. Yet how terrible the difference
now. This woman likes what all women like; his cousin,
the girl he most loves in the world, has the very same
love of nice dresses, pleasures, praise. There is nothing
wrong in liking these things. But in the case of the
prostitute all pleasure must turn for her to ashes and
bitterness. The pure girl will have in this world all the
pretty dresses and pleasures and love that she can
wish for; and will never have reason to feel unhappy
except when she hears of the unhappiness of somebody
else. And it seems a monstrous thing under heaven that
such a different destiny should be portioned out to
beings at first so much alike as those two women. Even
to think of his cousin looking like her, gives him a
shudder of pain—not because he cruelly despises the
sleeping girl, but because he thinks of what might have
happened to his own dearest, under other chances of
life.

Yet again, who knows what may be in the future, any
more than what has been in the past? All this world
is change. The fortunate of to-day may be unfortunate in their descendants; the fortunate of long ago
were perhaps the ancestors of the miserable of to-day.
And everything may in the eternal order of change
have to rise and sink alternately. Cousin Nell is to-
day a fortunate woman; he, the dreamer at the bed-side
of the nameless girl, is a fortunate man. But what
might happen to their children? He thinks again of
the strange resemblance of the two women, and murmurs:

Studies in Rossetti

So pure,—so fall'n! How dare to think
Of the first common kindred link?
Yet, Jenny, till the world shall burn
It seems that all things take their turn;
And who shall say but this fair tree
May need, in changes that may be,
Your children's children's charity?
Scorned then, no doubt, as you are scorn'd!
Shall no man hold his pride forewarn'd
Till in the end, the Day of Days,
At Judgment, one of his own race,
As frail and lost as you, shall rise,—
His daughter, with his mother's eyes?

Then he begins to think more deeply on the great wrongs of this world, the great misery caused by vice, the cruelty of lust in itself. The ruined life of this girl represents but one fact of innumerable facts of a like kind. Millions of beautiful and affectionate women have been, and are being, and will be through all time to come, sacrificed in this way to lust—selfish and foolish and cruel lust, that destroys mind and body together. The mystery of the dark side of life comes to him in a new way. He cannot explain it—who can explain the original meaning of pain in this world? But he begins to get at least a new gleam of truth—this great truth, that every one who seeks pleasure in the way that he at first intended to seek it that night, adds a little to the great sum of human misery. For vice exists only at the cost of misery. The question is not, "Is it right for me or wrong for me to take what is forbidden if I pay for it." The real question is,

[81]

"Is it right for me or wrong for me to help in any way to support that condition of society which sacrifices lives, body, and soul, to cruelty and selfishness." We all of us in youth think chiefly about right and wrong in their immediate relations to ourselves and our friends. Only later in life, after we have seen a great deal of the red of human pain, do we begin to think of the consequences of an act in relation to the happiness or unhappiness of humanity.

Suddenly the morning comes as he is thinking thus. At once he ceases to be the philosopher, and becomes again the gentleman of the world. The girl's head is still upon his knees; he looks at the sleeping face, and wonders whether any painter could have painted a face more beautiful. But the beauty does not appeal to his senses in any passional way; it only fills him with unspeakable compassion. He does not awake her, but lifts her into a more comfortable position for sleeping, and leaves beside her pillow a present of gold coins, and then steals away without bidding her good-bye. The night has not given him pleasure, but pain only—yet a pain that has made his heart more kindly and his thoughts more wise than they had been before.

IV

Our last lecture dealt with the shorter narrative poems of Rossetti, including the ballads. There remain to be considered two other narrative poems of a much more extended kind. They are quite unique in English literature; and both of them deal with mediæval subjects. One, again, is chiefly objective in its treatment; and the other chiefly subjective—that is to say, psychological. One is a fragment, but the most wonderful fragment of its kind in existence; more wonderful, I think, than even the fragments of Coleridge, both as to volume and finish. The other is complete, a story of magic and passion entitled "Rose Mary." We may first deal with "Rose Mary," giving the general plan of the poem, rather than extracts of any length; for this narration cannot very well be illustrated by examples. We shall make some quotations only in illustration of the finish and the beauty of the work.

The subject of "Rose Mary" was peculiarly adapted to Rossetti's genius. In the Middle Ages there was a great belief in the virtue of jewels and crystals of a precious kind. Belief in the magical power of rubies, diamonds, emeralds, and opals was not confined either to Europe or to modern civilisation; it had existed from great antiquity in the Orient, and had been accepted by the Greeks and Romans. This belief was perhaps forgotten after the destruction of the Roman Empire, for a time at least, in Europe; but the Crusades revived it. Talismanic stones were brought back from Palestine by many pilgrim-knights; and as some of these were marked with Arabic characters, then supposed by the ignorant to be characters of magic, supernatural legends were invented to account for the history of not a few. Also there was a certain magical use to which precious stones were put during the Middle Ages, and to which they are still sometimes put in Oriental countries. This is called crystallomancy. Crystallomancy is the art of seeing the future in crystals, or glass, or transparent substances of jewels. The same art can be practised even with ink—a drop of ink, held in the hand, offering to the eye the same reflecting surface that a black jewel would do. In Egypt, Arabia, Persia, and India divination is still practised with ink. This is the same thing as crystallomancy. Usually in those countries a young boy or a young girl is used by the diviner. He mesmerises the boy or the girl, and bids him or her look into the crystal or the ink-drop, as the case may be, and say what he or she sees there. In this way, the future is supposed to be told. Modern investigation has taught us how the whole thing is done, though science has not been able yet to explain all that goes on in the mind of the "subject." But in the Middle Ages, when the whole process was absolutely mysterious, it was thought to be the work of spirits inside the stone, or crystal, or ink-drop. And this is the superstition to which Rossetti refers in his poem "Rose Mary."

Now there is one more fact which must be explained in connection with crystallomancy. It has always been thought that the "subject"—that is, the boy or girl who looks into the stone, crystal, or ink-drop—must be absolutely innocent. The "subject" must be virtuous. In the Catholic Middle Ages the same idea took form especially in relation to the chastity of the "subject." Chastity was, in those centuries, considered a magical virtue. A maiden, it was thought, could play with lions or tigers, and not be hurt by them. A maiden— and the word was then used for both sexes, as it is sometimes used by Tennyson in his Idylls—could see ghosts or spirits, and could be made use of for purposes of crystallomancy even by a very wicked person. But should the subject have been secretly guilty of any fault, then the power to see would be impaired. The tragedy of Rossetti's poem turns upon this fact.

In the poem a precious stone, of the description called beryl, is the instrument of divination. This beryl is round, like a terrestrial globe, and is supposed to be of the shape of the world. It is half transparent, but there are cloudings inside of it. Hidden among these cloudings are a number of evil spirits, who were enclosed in the jewel by magic. These spirits make the future appear visible to any virtuous person who looks into the stone; but they have power to deceive and to injure any one coming to consult them who is not perfectly chaste. The stone came from the East, and it was obtained only at the sacrifice of the soul of the person who obtained it. Having been brought to England, it became the property of a knightly family. This family consists only of a widow and her daughter Rose Mary. The daughter is in a state of great anxiety. She was to be married to a certain knight, who has not kept his affectionate promises. The daughter and the mother both fear that the knight may have been killed by some of his enemies. So they resolve to consult the beryl-stone. The mother does not know that her daughter has been too intimate with the absent knight. Believing that Rose Mary is all purity, the mother makes her the subject of an experiment in crystallomancy; and she looks into the beryl.

First she sees an old man with a broom, sweeping away dust and cobwebs; that is always the first thing seen. Then the inside of the beryl becomes perfectly clear, and the girl can see the open country, and the road along which her lover is expected to travel. And she sees him too. But there are perhaps enemies waiting for him. The mother tells her to look for those enemies. She looks; she sees the points of lances, in a hiding place by a roadside, and there is the evidence of what the lover has to fear in that direction. "Now look in the other direction," says the mother. The girl does so, and sees the whole road clearly, except in one place, in a valley. There she says that there is a mist; and she cannot see under the mist. This surprises the mother, and she takes away the beryl. The presence of the mist indicates that Rose Mary has committed some sin.

As a consequence the daughter confesses to the mother all that has occurred. She is not severely blamed; she is only gently rebuked, and forgiven with great love and tenderness. But it is probable that the sin must be expiated. Both are afraid. Then the expiation comes. The lover is killed by his enemies, and killed exactly on that part of the road where the mist was in the image seen in the beryl-stone. The mother goes to the dead knight's home, and examines the body. Evidently the man had died fighting bravely. The woman at first is all pity for him, as well as for her daughter. Suddenly she notices something in the dead man's breast. She takes it out, and finds that it is a package containing a love-letter, and a lock of hair. The hair is bright gold—while the hair of Rose Mary is black. This makes the mother suspicious, and she reads the letter. Then she no longer pities but abhors the dead man; for the letter proves him to have had another sweetheart, and that he had intended to betray Rose Mary.

Studies in Rossetti

When the daughter learns of her lover's death, she suffers terribly; but she makes sincere repentance for her fault, and then in her mother's absence she determines to destroy the beryl-stone, as a devilish thing. This is another way of committing suicide, because whoever breaks the stone is certain to be killed by the enraged spirits cast out of it. By one blow of a sword the stone is broken, and Rose Mary atones for all her faults by death. This is the whole of the story.

The extraordinary charm of the story is in its vividness—a vividness perhaps without equal even in the best work of Tennyson (certainly much finer than similar work in Coleridge), and in the attractive characterisation of mother and daughter. There is this great difference between the mediæval poems of Coleridge or Scott, and those of Rossetti, that when you are reading "The Lay of the Last Minstrel" or the wonderful "Christabel," you feel that you are reading a fairy-tale, but when you read Rossetti you are looking at life and feeling human passion. It is a great puzzle to critics how any man could make the Middle Ages live as Rossetti did. One reason, I think, is that Rossetti was a great painter as well as a great poet, and he studied the life of the past in documents and in museums until it became to him as real as the present. But we must also suppose that he inherited a great deal of his peculiar power. This power never wearies. Although the romance of Rose Mary is not very short, you do not get tired of wondering at its beauty until you reach the end. It is divided into three parts, which is a good thing for the student, as he can see the structure of the composition at once. It is written in stanzas of five lines, thus arranged—*a*, *a*, *b*, *b*, *b*. You would think this measure monotonous, but it is not. I give two examples. The first is the description of the magic jewel.

> The lady unbound her jewelled zone
> And drew from her robe the Beryl-stone.
> Shaped it was to a shadowy sphere,—
> World of our world, the sun's compeer,
> That bears and buries the toiling year.
>
> With shuddering light 'twas stirred and strewn
> Like the cloud-nest of the wading moon:
> Freaked it was as the bubble's ball,
> Rainbow-hued through a misty pall,
> Like the middle light of the waterfall.
>
> Shadows dwelt in its teeming girth
> Of the known and unknown things of earth;
> The cloud above and the wave around,—
> The central fire at the sphere's heart bound,
> Like doomsday prisoned underground.

I feel quite sure that even Tennyson could not have done this. Only a great painter, as well as a great observer, could have done it; and the choice of words is astonishing in its exquisiteness. Most of them have more than one meaning, and both meanings are equally implied by their use. Take, for example, the word "shadowy"; it means cloudy and it also means ghostly. Thus it is peculiarly appropriate to picture the magic stone as full of moving shadows, themselves of ghostly character. Or take the word "shuddering"; it means trembling with cold or fear, and it means also a quick trembling, never a slow motion. Just such a word might be used

[88]

to describe the strange vibration of air-bubbles enclosed
in a volcanic crystal. But we have also the suggestion
here of a ghostly motion, a motion that gives a shiver
of fear to the person who sees it. Or take the word
"freaked." "Freak" is commonly used to signify a mischievous bit of play, a wild fancy. "Fancifully
marked" would be the exact meaning of "freaked" in
the ordinary sense; but here it is likewise appropriate
as a description of the streams and streaks of colour
playing over the surface of a bubble without any apparent law, as if they were made by some whimsical spirit.
Now every verse of the whole long poem is equally
worthy of study for its astonishing finish. I shall give
a few more verses merely to show the application of
the same power to a description of pain. The girl
has just been told of her lover's murder; and the
whole immediate consequence is told in five lines.

> Once she sprang as the heifer springs
> With the wolf's teeth at its red heart-strings:
> First 'twas fire in her breast and brain,
> And then scarce hers but the whole world's pain,
> As she gave one shriek and sank again.

The first two lines might give you an undignified image
unless you understood the position of the girl when she
received the news. She was kneeling at her mother's
feet, with her mother's arms around her. On being
told the terrible thing, she tries to spring up, because of
the shock of the pain—just as a young heifer would
leap when the wolf had seized it from underneath. A
wolf snaps at the belly of the animal, close to the heart.
Therefore the comparison is admirable. As for the rest

of the verse, any physician can confirm its accuracy. The up-rush of blood at the instant of a great shock of pain feels like a great sudden heat, burning up toward the head. And in such a time one realises that certain forms of pain, moral pain, are larger than oneself—too great to be borne. Psychologically, great moral pain depends upon nervous development; and this nervous susceptibility to pain is greater than would seem fitted to the compass of one life. Moral pain can kill. It is said that in such times we feel not only our own pain, but the pain of all those among our ancestors who suffered in like manner. Thus, by inheritance, individual pain is more than individual. At all events the fourth line of the stanza I have quoted will appear astonishingly true to anybody who knows the greater forms of mental suffering.

Leaving this poem, which could not be too highly praised, we may turn to "The Bride's Prelude," the greatest of the longer compositions, therefore the greatest thing that Rossetti did. Unfortunately, perhaps, it is unfinished. It is only a fragment; death overtook the writer before he was able to complete it. Like "Rose Mary," it leads us back to the Middle Ages. But here there is no magic, nothing ghostly, nothing impossible; there is only truth, atrocious, terrible truth —a tale of cruelty, treachery, and pain related by the victim. The victim is a bride. She is just going to be married. But before her marriage, she has a story to tell her sister—a story so sad and so frightful that it requires strong nerves to read the thing without pain.

We may suppose that the incident occurred in old France, or—though I doubt it—in Norman England.

[90]

Studies in Rossetti

The scenery and the names remind us rather of Southern France. All the facts belong to the life of the feudal aristocracy. We are among princes and princesses; great lords of territory and great lords of battle are introduced to us, with their secret sorrows and shames. Great ladies, too, open their hearts to us, and prove so intensely human that it is very hard to believe the whole story is a dream. It rather seems as if we had known all these people, and that our lives had at some time been mingled with theirs. The eldest daughter of one great house, very beautiful, and very innocent, is taken advantage of by a retainer in the castle. She is foolish and unable to imagine that any gentleman could intend to do her a wrong. The retainer, on the other hand, is a very cunning villain. His real purpose is to bring shame upon the daughter of the house. Why? Because, as he is only a poor knight, he could not hope to marry into a princely family. But if he can seduce one of the girls, then perhaps the family will be only too glad to have him marry his victim, because that will hide their shame. Evidently he has plotted for this. But his plans, and everybody's plans, are affected by unexpected results of civil war. His masters, being defeated in a great battle, have to retreat to the mountains for a time; and then he deserts them in the basest manner. Meantime the unhappy girl is found to be with child. Death was the rule in those days for such a case—burning alive. Her brothers wish to kill her. But her father interferes and saves her. It is decided only that the child shall be taken from her— to be killed, probably. Everybody is forbidden to speak of the matter. Some retainers who did speak

[91]

of it are hanged for an example. Presently, by another battle, the family return into their old possessions, and enormously increase their ancient power. When this happens the scoundrel that seduced the daughter of the house and then deserted the family returns. Why does he return? Now is the time to fulfil his purpose. He has become a great soldier and a nobleman in his own right. Now he can ask for that young lady in marriage, and they dare not refuse. If they refuse, he can revenge himself by telling the story of her disgrace. If they accept him as a son-in-law, they will also be obliged to make him very powerful; and he will know how to take every advantage. The girl is not consulted at all. Her business is to obey. She thinks that it would be better to die than to marry the wicked man that had wronged her; but she must obey and she is ordered to marry him. He cares nothing about her; she is only the tool by which he wishes to win his way into power. But, cunning as he is, the brothers of the girl are even more cunning. They wish for the marriage only for the purpose of getting the man into their hands, just for one moment. He shall marry her, but immediately afterwards he shall disappear forever from the sight of men. The bride does not know the purpose of her terrible brothers; she thinks they are cruel to her when she tells her story, but they only wish to avenge her, and they are much too prudent to tell her what they are going to do. The poem does not go any further than the moment before the marriage. The first part is quite finished; but the second part was never written.

The whole of this great composition is in verses of

five lines, curiously arranged. Rossetti adopts a different form of verse for almost every one of his narrations. This is quite as unique a measure in its way— that is, in nineteeth century poetry—as was the measure of Tennyson's "In Memoriam" in elegiac poetry. Now we shall try to illustrate the style of the poem.

> Against the haloed lattice-panes
>   The bridesmaid sunned her breast;
> Then to the glass turned tall and free,
> And braced and shifted daintily
> Her loin-belt through her côte-hardie.
>
> The belt was silver, and the clasp
>   Of lozenged arm-bearings;
> A world of mirrored tints minute
> The rippling sunshine wrought into 't,
> That flushed her hand and warmed her foot.
>
> At least an hour had Aloyse,—
>   Her jewels in her hair,—
> Her white gown, as became a bride,
> Quartered in silver at each side,—
> Sat thus aloof, as if to hide.
>
> Over her bosom, that lay still,
>   The vest was rich in grain,
> With close pearls wholly overset:
> Around her throat the fastenings met
> Of chevesayle and mantelet.

Absolutely real as this seems, we know that the details must have been carefully studied in museums. Elsewhere, except perhaps in very old pictures, these things no longer exist. There are no more loin-belts of silver, no côte-hardies, no chevesayle or mantelet. I cannot explain to you what they are without pictures—further than to say that they were parts of the attire of a lady of rank about the thirteenth and fourteenth centuries. Brides do not now have their white robes "quartered in silver"—that is, figured with the family crest or arms. Why silver instead of gold? Simply because of the rule that brides should be all in white; therefore even the crest was worked in white metal instead of gold. By the word vest, you must also understand an ancient garment for women; the modern word signifies a garment worn only by men. "Grain" is an old term for texture. The description of the light playing on the belt-clasp of the bridesmaid, in the second stanza, is a marvellous bit of work, the effect being given especially by three words—"lozenged," "rippling," for the sunshine, and "minute," for the separate flushes or sparklings thrown off from the surface. But all is wonderful; this is painting with words exactly as a painter paints with colours. Sounds are treated with the same wonderful vividness:

> Although the lattice had dropped loose,
>   There was no wind; the heat
> Being so at rest that Amelotte
> Heard far beneath the plunge and float
> Of a hound swimming in the moat.
>
> Some minutes since, two rooks had toiled
>   Home to the nests that crowned
> Ancestral ash-trees. Through the glare
> Beating again, they seemed to tear
> With that thick caw the woof o' the air.

[94]

Studies in Rossetti

One must have been in the tower of a castle to feel the full force of the first stanza. The two girls are in a room perhaps one hundred and fifty or two hundred feet above the water of the moat, so that except in a time of extraordinary stillness they would not hear ordinary sounds from so far below. And notice that the poet does not tell us that this was because the air did not move; he says that the heat was at rest. Very expressive—in great summer heat, without wind, the air itself seems to our senses not air but fluid heat. And the same impression of summer is given by the description of the two crows flying to their nest and back again, and screaming as they fly. The poet does not say that they flew; he says they toiled home—because flying in that thick warm air is difficult for them. When they return he uses another word, still more impressive; he says they beat again through the glare. This makes you hear the heavy motion of the wings. And he describes the crow as seeming to tear the air, because that air is so heavy that it seems like a thing woven.

Here is a strangely powerful stanza describing the difficulty of speaking about a painful subject that for many years one has tried to forget:

> Her thought, long stagnant, stirred by speech,
>   Gave her a sick recoil;
> As, dip thy fingers through the green
> That masks a pool,—where they have been
> The naked depth is black between.

Any of you who as boys have played about a castle moat, and stirred the green water weeds covering the still water, must have remarked that the water looks black as ink underneath. Of course it is not black in itself; but the weeds keep out the sun, so that it seems black because of the shadow. The poet's comparison has a terrible exactness here. The mind is compared to stagnant water covered with water-weeds. Weeds grow upon water in this way only when there has been no wind for a long time, and no current. The condition of a mind that does not think, that dares not think, is like stagnant water in this way. Memory becomes covered up with other things, matters not relating to the past.

Now we can take four stanzas from the scene of the secret family meeting, after the shame has been confessed and is known. They are very powerful.

> "Time crept. Upon a day at length
>   My kinsfolk sat with me:
> That which they asked was bare and plain:
> I answered: the whole bitter strain
> Was again said, and heard again.

> "Fierce Raoul snatched his sword, and turned
>   The point against my breast.
> I bared it, smiling: 'To the heart
> Strike home,' I said; 'another dart
> Wreaks hourly there a deadlier smart.'

> " 'Twas then my sire struck down the sword,
>   And said, with shaken lips:
> 'She from whom all of you receive
> Your life, so smiled; and I forgive.'
> Thus for my mother's sake, I live.

Studies in Rossetti

"But I, a mother even as she,
   Turned shuddering to the wall:
For I said: 'Great God! and what would I do,
When to the sword, with the thing I knew,
I offered not one life but two!' "

This is now the most terrible part of the story; and it has a humanity about it that almost makes us doubt. Fancy the situation. The daughter of a prince unchaste with a common retainer. Now in princely families chastity was of as much importance as physical strength and will; it meant everything—honour, purity of race, the possibility of alliance. And a great house is thus disgraced. We can sympathise with the horrible mental suffering of the girl, but it is impossible not to sympathise also even with the terrible brother that wishes to kill her. He is right, she deserves death; but he is young, and cruel because young. The father sorrows, and seeing the girl smiling, thinks of the dead mother, and forgives. This is the only point at which we feel inclined to lay down the book and ask questions. Would a father in such a position have done this in those cruel ages? Would he have allowed himself to pity?—or rather, could he have allowed himself to pity? Tender-hearted men did not rule in those days. We have records of husbands burning their wives, of fathers killing their sons. All we can say is that an exception might have existed, just as Rossetti imagines. Human nature was of course not different then from what it is now, but it is quite certain that the gentle side of human nature seldom displayed itself in the families of the feudal princes; a

[97]

man who was gentle could not rule. In Italy sons who did not show the ruling character were apt to be killed or poisoned. One must understand that feudal life was not much more moral than other life.

I think we can here turn to another department of Rossetti's verse. I only hope that the examples given from the "Bride's Prelude" will interest you sufficiently to make you at a later day turn to this wonderful poem for a careful study of its beauty and power.

v

When we come to the study of the lives of the Victorian poets, we shall find that Rossetti's whole existence was governed by his passion for one woman, whom he loved in a strange mystical way, with a love that was half art (art in the good sense) and half idolatry. To him she was much more than a woman; she was a divinity, an angel, a model for all things beautiful. You know that he was a great painter, and in a multitude of beautiful pictures he painted the face of this woman. He composed his poems also in order to please her. He lost her within a little more than a year after winning her, and this nearly killed him. I may say that throughout all his poems, speaking in a general way, there are references to this great love of his life; but there is one portion of his work that we must consider as especially illustrating it, and that is the "House of Life," a collection of more than one hundred sonnets upon the subject of love and its kindred emotions. But the love of which Rossetti sings is not the love of a young man for a girl—not the love of youth and maid. It is married love carried to the utmost degree of worship. You will think this a strange subject; and I confess that it is. Very few men could be praised for touching such a subject. Coventry Patmore, you know, was an exception. He made the subject of his own courtship, wedding, and married life the subject of his poetry, and he did it so nicely and so tenderly that his book had a great success. But Rossetti did his work in an entirely different way, which I must try to explain.

Unlike Patmore, Rossetti did not openly declare that he took any personal experience for the subject of his study; we only perceive, through knowledge of his life, and through suggestions obtained from other parts of his work, that personal love and personal loss were his great inspiration. As a matter of fact, any man who sings about love must draw upon his own personal experience of the passion. Every lover thinks of love in his own way. But the value of a love poem is not the personal part of it; the value of a love poem is according to the degree in which it represents universal experience, or experience of a very large kind. It must represent to some degree a general philosophy of life. Even the commonest little love-song, such as a peasant might sing in the streets of Tokyo, as he comes in from the country walking beside his horse, will represent something of the philosophy of life if it is a good and true composition, no matter how vulgar may be the idiom of it. When we come to think about it, we shall find that all great poetry is in this sense also philosophical poetry.

Rossetti, as I have already shown you, was a true philosopher in certain directions; and he applied his

[99]

philosophical powers, as well as his artistic powers, to his own experiences, so as to adapt them to the uses of great poetry. He is never narrowly personal. And his sonnets are really very wonderful compositions —not reflecting universal experience so as to be universally understood, but reflecting universal experience so as to be understood by cultivated minds only. These productions are altogether above the range of the common mind; they are extremely subtle and elaborate, both as to thought and as to form. But their subject is not at all special. Rossetti had the idea that every phase of happiness and sorrow belonging to married life, from the hour of the wedding night to the hour of death, was worthy of poetical treatment, because married life is related to the deepest human emotions. And in the space of one hundred sonnets he treats every phase. This series of sonnets is divided into two groups. The first contains poems relating to the early conditions of love in marriage; the second group treats especially of the more sorrowful aspects of a married life—the trials of death, the pains of memory, and the hopes and fears of reuniting after death. The second part does not, however, contain all the sad pieces; there are very sad ones in the first group of fifty-nine. We have already studied one of the first group, the piece called "The Birth-Bond." There is another piece in this group, the first of four sonnets, which is exquisite as a bit of fancy. It is entitled "Willowwood."

> I sat with Love upon a woodside well,
>   Leaning across the water, I and he;
>   Nor ever did he speak nor looked at me,
> But touched his lute wherein was audible

Studies in Rossetti

The certain secret thing he had to tell:
Only our mirrored eyes met silently
In the low wave; and that sound came to be
The passionate voice I knew; and my tears fell.

And at their fall, his eyes beneath grew hers;
And with his foot and with his wing-feathers
He swept the spring that watered my heart's drouth.
Then the dark ripples spread to waving hair,
And as I stooped, her own lips rising there
Bubbled with brimming kisses at my mouth.

This is a dream of the dead woman loved. The lover
finds himself seated with the god of love, the little naked
boy with wings, as the ancients represented him, at
the edge of a spring near the forest. He does not look
at the god of love, neither does the god look at him;
they were friends long ago, but now—what is the use?
She is dead. By the reflection in the water only he
knows that Love is looking down, and he does not wish
to speak to him. But Love will not leave him alone.
He hears the tone of a musical instrument, and that
music makes him suddenly very sad, for it seems like
the voice of the dead for whom he mourns. It makes
his tears fall into the water; and immediately, magi-
cally, the reflection of the eyes of Love in the water
become like the eyes of the woman he loved. Then
while he looks in wonder, the little god stirs the surface
of the water with wings and feet, and the ripples become
like the hair of the dead woman, and as the lover bends
down, her lips rise up through the water to kiss him.
You may ask, what does all this mean? Well, it means
as much as any dream means; it is all impossible, no

doubt, but the impossible in dreams often makes us very sad indeed—especially if the dead appear to come back in them.

Another example of regret, very beautiful, is the sonnet numbered ninety-one in this collection. It is called "Lost on Both Sides."

As when two men have loved a woman well,
   Each hating each, through Love's and Death's deceit;
   Since not for either this stark marriage-sheet
And the long pauses of this wedding-bell;
Yet o'er her grave the night and day dispel
   At last their feud forlorn, with cold and heat;
   Nor other than dear friends to death may fleet
The two lives left that most of her can tell:—

So separate hopes, which in a soul had wooed
   The one same Peace, strove with each other' long,
   And Peace before their faces perished since:
So through that soul, in restless brotherhood,
   They roam together now, and wind among
   Its bye-streets, knocking at the dusty inns.

The comparison is of the hopes and aims of the artist to a couple of men in love with the same woman— bitter enemies while she lives, because of their natural rivalry, but loving each other after her death, simply because each can understand better than anybody else in the world the pain of the other. Afterward the men, once rivals, passed all their time together, wandering about at night in search of some quiet place, where they can sit down and drink and talk together. In Rossetti's time such quiet places were not to be found in the main streets, but in the little side streets called bye-streets. After this explanation, the comparison should not be obscure. The artist who loves does all his work with the thought of the woman that he loves before him; his hope to win fame is that he may make her proud of him; his aims are in all cases to please her. After he has lost her, these hopes and aims, which might have been antagonists to each other in former days, are now reconciled within him; her memory alone is now the inspiration and the theme. I hope you will notice the curious and exquisite value of certain words here: "Stark," meaning stiff, nearly always refers to the rigidness of death; it is especially used of the appearance and attitude of corpses, and its application in this poem to the cover of the marriage bed is quite enough to convey the sense of death without any more definite observation. Again the expression "long pauses," referring to the sound of the church bells, makes us understand that the bells are really ringing a funeral knell; for the ringing of wedding bells ought to be quick and joyous. It might seem a strange contradiction, this simile, but the poet has in his mind an old expression about the death of a maiden: "She became the bride of Death." Thus the effect is greatly intensified by the sombre irony of the simile itself.

We might extract a great many beauties from this wonderful collection of sonnets; but time is precious, and we shall have room for only another quotation or two. The following is one to which I should like especially to invite your attention—not only because of its strange charm, but also because of the curious legend which it recalls—a legend which we have already studied:

Pre-Raphaelite and Other Poets

BODY'S BEAUTY

Of Adam's first wife, Lilith, it is told
  (The witch he loved before the gift of Eve,)
  That, ere the snake's, her sweet tongue could deceive,
And her enchanted hair was the first gold.
And still she sits, young while the earth is old,
  And subtly of herself contemplative,
  Draws men to watch the bright web she can weave,
Till heart and body and life are in its hold.

The rose and poppy are her flowers; for where
  Is he not found, O Lilith, whom shed scent
And soft-shed kisses and soft sleep shall snare?
  Lo! as that youth's eyes burned at thine, so went
  Thy spell through him, and left his straight neck bent,
And round his heart one strangling golden hair.

The reference to the rose and the poppy may need
some explanation. The rose has been for many centuries in Western countries a symbol of love; and the
poppy has been a symbol of death and sleep from the
time of the Greeks. It is from the seeds of the poppy
that opium is extracted. The Greeks did not know the
use of opium; but they knew that the seeds of the
flower produced sleep, and might, in certain quantities,
produce death. We have the expression "poppied
sleep" to express the sleep of death.

A final word must be said about Rossetti's genius
as a translator. He has given us, in one large volume,
the most precious anthology of the Italian poets of
the Middle Ages that ever has been made—the poets of
the time of Dante, under the title of "Dante and his

Circle." This magnificent work would alone be sufficient to establish his supreme excellence as a translator of poetry; but the material is mostly of a sort that can appeal to scholars only. Rossetti is better known as a translator through a very few short pieces translated from French poets, chiefly. Such is the wonderful rendering of Villon's "Ballad of Dead Ladies," beginning

> Tell me now in what hidden way is
> Lady Flora, the lovely Roman?
> Where's Hipparchia, and where is Thais,
> Neither of them the fairer woman?
> Where is Echo, beheld of no man,
> Only heard on river and mere,—
> She whose beauty was more than human?—
> But where are the snows of yester-year?

Even Swinburne, when making his splendid translations from Villon, refrained from attempting to translate this ballad, saying that no man could surpass, even if he could equal, Rossetti's version. The burthen is said to be especially successful as a rendering of the difficult French refrain:

> *Mais ou sont les neiges d'antan?*

You will find this matchless translation almost anywhere, so we need not occupy the time further with it; but I doubt whether you have noticed as yet other wonderful translations made by this master from the French. Such is the song from Victor Hugo's drama "Les Burgraves"; you will not forget Rossetti's translation after having once read it.

Through the long winter the rough wind tears;
With their white garments the hills look wan.
    Love on: who cares?
    Who cares? Love on!
My mother is dead; God's patience wears;
It seems my chaplain will not have done!
    Love on: who cares?
    Who cares? Love on!
The Devil, hobbling up the stairs,
Comes for me with his ugly throng.
    Love on: who cares?
    Who cares? Love on.

Another remarkable translation from the same drama
is that of the song beginning:

In the time of the civil broils
Our swords are stubborn things.
A fig for all the cities!
A fig for all the kings!

and ending:

Right well we hold our own
With the brand and the iron rod.
A fig for Satan, Burgraves;
Burgraves, a fig for God!

But even more wonderful Rossetti seems when we go
back to the old French, as in the translation which has
been called "My Father's Close."

Inside my father's close
    (Fly away O my heart away!)
Sweet apple-blossom blows
    So sweet.

[106]

Studies in Rossetti

Three kings' daughters fair,
(Fly away O my heart away!)
They lie below it there
So sweet!

Now the Old French of the first stanza will show you
the astonishing faithfulness of the rendering:

Au jardin de mon père,
(Vole, mon cœur, vole!)
Il y a un pommier doux,
Tout doux.

Besides the small exquisite things, there are long translations from mediæval writers, French and Italian, of
wonderful beauty. Compare, for example, the celebrated episode of Francesca da Rimini in Dante (which
Carlyle so beautifully called "a lily in the mouth of
Hell"), as translated by Byron, and as translated by
Rossetti, and observe the immeasurable superiority of
the latter. It would be very pleasant, if we had time,
to examine Rossetti's translations more in detail; but
the year advances and we must turn to an even greater
master of verse—Swinburne.

CHAPTER II

As we are now studying Rossetti's poetry in other
hours, you may be interested in some discussion of the
merits of his prose—for this is still, so far as the great
public are concerned, almost an unknown topic. The
best of the painters of his own school, and the most
delicate poet of the Victorian period, Rossetti might
also have become one of the greatest prose writers of
the century if he had seriously turned to prose. But
ill-health and other circumstances prevented him from
doing much in this direction. What he did do, however, is so remarkable that it deserves to be very carefully studied. I do not refer to his critical essays.
These are not very remarkable. I refer only to his
stories; and his stories are great because they happen
to have exactly the same kind of merit that distin-
guishes his poetry. They might be compared with the
stories of Poe; and yet they are entirely different, with
the difference distinguishing all Latin prose fiction
from English fiction. But there is certainly no other
story writer, except Poe, with whose work that of Rossetti can be at all classed. They are ghostly stories—
one of them a fragment, the other complete. Only two
—and the outline of the third. The fragment is not
less worthy of attention because it happens to be a

[108]

Note upon Rossetti's Prose

fragment—like the poet's own "Bride's Prelude," or Coleridge's "Christabel," or Poe's "Silence." The trouble with all great fragments, and the proof of their greatness, is that we cannot imagine what the real ending would have been; and this puzzle only lends additional charm to the imaginative effect. Of the two consecutive stories, it is the fragment which has the greater merit.

The first story, called "Hand and Soul," has another interest besides the interest of narrative. It contains the whole æsthetic creed of Rossetti's school of painting,—a little philosophy of art that is well worth studying. That is especially why I want to talk about it. The so-called Pre-Raphaelite school of English painting, whereof Rossetti was the recognized chief, were not altogether disciples of Ruskin. They did not believe that art must have a religious impulse in order to be great art; and they did not exactly support the antagonistic doctrine of "Art for Art's Sake." They considered that absolute sincerity in one's own conception of the beautiful, and wide toleration of all æsthetic ideas, were axiomatic truths which it was necessary to accept without reserve. They had no detestation for any school of art; they practically banished prejudice from their little circle. I may add that they were not indifferent to Japanese art, even at a time when it found many enemies in London, and when the great Ruskin himself endeavoured to help the prejudice against it. In that very time Rossetti was making Japanese collections, and Burne-Jones and others were discovering new methods by the help of this Eastern art.

Pre-Raphaelite and Other Poets

Now the story of "Hand and Soul" is, in a small way, a history of man's experience with Painting. It is supposed to be the story of a real picture. The picture is only the figure of a woman in a grey and green dress, very beautiful. But whoever looks at that picture for a minute or two, suddenly becomes afraid—afraid in exactly the same way that he would be on seeing a ghost. The picture could not have been painted from imagination; that figure must have been seen by somebody; and yet it could not have been a living woman! Then what could have been the real story of that picture? Did the artist see a ghost; or did he see something supernatural?

The answer to these questions is the following story. The artist who painted that picture, four hundred years ago, was a young Italian of immense genius, so passionately devoted to his art that he lived for nothing else. At first he wished only to be the greatest painter of his time; and that he became without much difficulty. He painted only what he thought beautiful; and he painted beautiful faces that he saw passing by in the street, and beautiful sunsets that he saw from his window, and beautiful fancies that came into his mind. Everybody loved his pictures; and princes made him great gifts of money.

Then a sudden remorse came to this painter, who was at heart a religious man. He said to himself: "Here, God has given me the power to paint beautiful things; and I have been painting only those beautiful things which please the senses of men. Therefore I have been doing wrong. Henceforward I will paint only things which represent eternal truth, the things of Heaven."

Note upon Rossetti's Prose

After that he began to paint only religious and mystical pictures, and pictures which common people could not understand at all. The people no longer came to admire his work; the princes no longer paid him honour or brought him gifts; and he became as one forgotten in the world.

Moreover, he found himself losing his power as an artist. And then, to crown all his misfortunes, some of his most famous pictures were ruined one day by the extraordinary incident of a church fight; for two great Italian clans between whom a feud existed, happened to meet in the church porch, and a blow was struck and swords were drawn—and there was such killing that the blood of the fighters was splashed upon the paintings on the wall.

When all these things had happened, the artist despaired. He became weary of life, and thought of destroying himself. And while he was thus thinking, there suddenly entered his room, without any sound, the figure of a woman robed in green and grey; and she stood before him and looked into his eyes. And as she looked into his eyes, an awe came upon him such as he had never before known; and a great feeling of sadness also came with the awe. But he could not speak, any more than a person in a dream, who wants to cry out, and cannot make a sound. But the woman spoke and said to him, "I am your own soul—that soul to whom you have done so much wrong. And I have been allowed to come to you in this form, only because you have never been of those men who make art merely to win money. To win fame, however, you did not scruple; and that was not altogether good, although it was not

[111]

altogether bad. What was much worse was the pride
which turned you away from me—religious pride. You
wanted to do what God did not ask you to do—to work
against your own soul, and to cast away your love of
beauty. Into me God placed the desire of loveliness
and the bliss of the charm of the world. Wherefore
then should you strive against His work? And what
pride impelled you to imagine that heaven needed the
help of your art to teach men what is good? When
did God say to you, Friend, let me lean upon you, or
I shall fall down? No; it is by teaching men to seek
and to love the beautiful things in this beautiful world
that you make their hearts better within them—never
by preaching to them with allegories that they cannot
understand; and because you have done this, you have
been punished. Be true to me, your own very soul;
then you will do marvellous things. Now paint a picture of me, just as I am, so that you may know that
your power of art is given back to you."

So the artist painted a picture of his own soul in
the likeness of a woman clad in green and grey; and
all who see that picture even today feel at once a
great fear and a great charm, and find it hard to
understand how mortal man could have painted it.

That is the story of "Hand and Soul"; and it teaches
a great deal of everlasting truth. Assuredly the road
to all artistic greatness is the road of sincerity—truth
to one's own emotional sense of what is beautiful. And
just to that degree in which the artist or poet allows
himself to be made insincere, either by desire of wealth
and fame, or by religious scruples, just to that extent
he must fail. I have only given a very slight outline

Note upon Rossetti's Prose

of the tale; to give more might be to spoil your pleasure of reading it.

The second story will not seem to you quite so original as the first, though, to English minds, it probably seems stranger. It is a story of pre-existence. Now, a very curious fact is that this idea of pre-existence, expressed by Rossetti in many passages of his verse, as well as in his prose story, did not come to him from Eastern sources at all. He never cared for, and perhaps never read, any Oriental literature. His idea regarding re-birth and the memory of past lives belongs rather to certain strangely imaginative works of mediæval literature, than to anything else. Even to himself they appeared novel—something dangerous to talk about. Unless you understand this, you will not be able to account for the curious thrill of terror that runs through "St. Agnes of Intercession." The writer writes as if he were afraid of his own thought.

The story begins with a little bit of autobiography, Rossetti telling about his thoughts as a child, when he played at his father's knee on winter evenings. Of course these memories did not appear as his own; but as those of the painter supposed to tell the story. As a child this painter was very fond of picture books. In the house there was one picture book containing a picture of a saint—St. Agnes—which pleased him in such a way that he could spend hours in contemplating it with delight. But he did not know why. He grew up, was educated, became a man and became a painter; and still he could not forget the charm of the picture that had pleased him when a child. One day a young English girl, a friend of his sister's, comes to the house on a visit. He is greatly startled on seeing her, because her face is exactly like the face of the saint in the picture book. He falls in love with her, and they are engaged to be married. But before that time he paints her portrait, and as her portrait happens to be the best work of the kind that he ever did, he sends it to the Royal Academy to be put on exhibition. Critics greatly praise the picture, but one of them remarks that at Bologna in Italy there is a painting of St. Agnes that very much resembles it. Upon this he goes to Italy to find the picture, and does find it after a great deal of trouble. It is said to be the work of a certain Angiolieri, who lived some four hundred years ago. Every detail of the face proves to be exactly like that of the living face which he painted in London. Being greatly startled by this discovery, he examines the catalogue of paintings, which he bought at the door, in order to find out whether there is anything else said in it about the model from whom Angiolieri painted that St. Agnes. He cannot find any information about the model; but he finds out that in another part of the building there is a portrait of Angiolieri, painted by himself. I think you know that many famous artists have painted portraits of themselves. Greatly interested, he hurries to where the picture is hanging, and finds, to his amazement, that the portrait of Angiolieri is exactly like himself—the very image of him. Was it then possible that, four hundred years before, he himself might have been Angiolieri, and had painted that picture of St. Agnes?

A fever seizes upon him, one of those fevers only too common in Italy. While he is still under its influence, he dreams a dream. He is in a picture gallery; and on the wall he sees Angiolieri's painting hanging up; and there is a great crowd looking at it. In that crowd he sees his betrothed, leaning upon the arm of another man. Then he feels angrily jealous, and says to the strange man, tapping him on the shoulder, "Sir, I am engaged to that lady!" Then the man turns round; and as he turns round, his face proves to be the face of Angiolieri, and his dress is the costume of four hundred years ago, and he says, "She is not mine, good friend—but neither is she thine." As he speaks his face falls in, like the face of a dead man, and becomes the face of a skull. From this dream we can guess the conclusion which the author intended.

On returning to England, when the painter attempted to speak of what he had seen and learned, his family believed him insane, and forbade him to speak on the subject any more. Also he was warned that should he speak of it to his betrothed, the marriage would be broken off. Accordingly, though he obeys, he is placed in a very unhappy position. All about him there is the oppression of a mystery involving two lives; and he cannot even try to solve it—cannot speak about it to the person whom it most directly concerns. . . . And here the fragment breaks.

If this admirable story had been finished, the result could not have been more impressive than is this sudden interruption. We know that Rossetti intended to make the betrothed girl also the victim of a mysterious destiny; but he did not intend, it appears, to elucidate the reason of the thing in detail. That would have indeed destroyed the shadowy charm of the recital.

Pre-Raphaelite and Other Poets

While the causes of things remain vague and mysterious, the pleasurable fear of the unknown remains with the reader. But if you try to account for everything, at once the illusion vanishes, and the art becomes dead. It seems to me that Rossetti has given in this unfinished tale a very fine suggestion of what use the old romances still are. It was by careful study of them, combined with his great knowledge of art, that he was able to produce, both in his poetry and in his prose, the exquisite charm of reality in unreality. Reading either, you have the sensation of actually seeing, touching, feeling, and yet you know that the whole thing is practically impossible. No art of romance can rise higher than this. And speaking of that soul-woman, whose portrait was painted in the former story, reminds me of an incident in Taine's wonderful book "De l'Intelligence," which is à propos. It is actually on record that a French artist had the following curious hallucination:

He was ill, from overwork perhaps, and opening his eyes after a feverish sleep, he saw a beautiful lady seated at his bedside, with one hand upon the bed cover, and he said to himself, "This is certainly an illusion caused by my nervous condition. But how beautiful an illusion it is! And how wonderfully luminous and delicate is that hand! If I dared only put my hand where it is, I wonder what would happen. Probably the whole thing would vanish at once, and I should lose the pleasure of looking at it."

Suddenly, as if answering his thought, a voice as clear as the voice of a bird said to him, "I am not a shadow; and you can take my hand and kiss it if you

Note upon Rossetti's Prose

like." He did lift the lady's hand to his lips and felt it, and then he entered into conversation with her. The conversation continued until interrupted by the entrance of the doctor attending the patient. This is the record of an extraordinary case of double consciousness—the illusion and the reason working together in such harmony that neither in the slightest degree disturbed the other. Rossetti's figures, whether of the Middle Ages or of modern times, seem also like the results of a double consciousness. We can touch them and feel them, although they are ghosts.

As I said before, he might have been one of the greatest of romantic story tellers had he turned his attention in that direction and kept his health. No better proof of this could be asked for than the printed plans of several stories which he never had time to develop. He collected the material from the study of Old French and Old Italian poets chiefly; but that material, when thrown into the crucible of his imagination, assumed totally novel and strange forms. I may tell you the outline of one story by way of conclusion. It was a beautiful idea; and it is a great regret that it could not have been executed in the author's lifetime:

One day a king and his favourite knight, while hunting in a forest, visited the house of a woodcutter, or something of that kind, to ask for water—both being very thirsty. The water was served to them by a young girl of such extraordinary beauty that both the king and the knight were greatly startled. The knight falls in love with the maid, and afterwards asks the king's leave to woo her. But when he comes to woo, he finds out that the maid has become enamoured of the king,

[117]

whom she does not know to be the king. She says that, unless she can marry him she will never become a wife. The king therefore himself goes to her to plead for his friend. "I cannot marry you," he says, "because I am married already. But my friend, who loves you very much, is not married; and if you will wed him I shall make him a baron and confer upon him the gift of many castles."

The young girl to please the king accepts the knight; a grand wedding takes place at the king's castle; and the knight is made a great noble, and is gifted with many rich estates. Then the king makes this arrangement with the bride: "I will never visit you or allow you to visit me, because we love each other too much. But, once every year, when I go to hunt in the forest with your husband, you shall bring me a cup of water, just as on the first day, when we saw you."

After this the king saw her three times;—that is to say, in three successive years she greeted him with the cup of water when he went hunting. In the fourth year she died, leaving behind her a little daughter.

The sorrowing husband carefully brought up the little girl—or, at least caused her to be carefully brought up; but he never presented her to the king, or spoke of her, because the death of the mother was a subject too painful for either of them to talk about.

But when the girl was sixteen years old, she looked so exactly like her mother, that the father was startled by the resemblance. And he thought, "Tomorrow I shall present her to the king." And to his daughter he said, "Tomorrow I am going to hunt with the king. When we are on our way home, we shall stop at a little

[118]

Note upon Rossetti's Prose

cottage in the wood—the little cottage in which your mother used to live. Do you then wait in the cottage, and when the king comes, bring him a cup of water, just as your mother did."

So next day the king and his baron approached the cottage after their hunt; and the king was greatly astonished and moved by the apparition of a young girl offering him a cup of water—so strangely did she resemble the girl whom he had seen in the same place nearly twenty years before. And as he took the cup from her hand, his heart went out toward her, and he asked his companion, "Is this indeed the ghost of her? —or another dear vision?" But before the companion could make any answer—lo! another shadow stood between the king and the girl; and none could have said which was which, so exactly each beautiful face resembled the other—only the second apparition wore peasant clothes. And she that wore the clothes of a peasant girl kissed the king as he sat upon his horse, and disappeared. And the king immediately, on receiving that kiss and returning it, fell forward and died.

This is a vague, charming romance indeed, for some one to take up and develop. Of course the figure in the peasant clothes is the spirit of the mother of the girl. There are many pretty stories somewhat resembling this in the old Japanese story books, but none quite the same; and I venture to recommend anybody who understands the literary value of such things to attempt a modified version of Rossetti's outline in Japanese. Some things would, of course, have to be changed; but no small changes would in the least affect the charm of the story as a whole.

[119]

Pre-Raphaelite and Other Poets

In conclusion, I may observe that the object of this little lecture has not been merely to interest you in the prose of Rossetti, but also to quicken your interest in the subject of romance in general. Remember that no matter how learned or how scientific the world may become, romance can never die. No greater mistake could be made by the Japanese student than that of despising the romantic element in the literature of his own country. Recently I have been thinking very often that a great deal might be done toward the development of later literature by remodelling and reanimating the romance of the older centuries. I believe that many young writers think chiefly about the possibility of writing something entirely new. This is a great literary misfortune; for the writing of something entirely new is scarcely possible for any human being. The greatest Western writers have not become great by trying to write what is new, but by writing over again in a much better way, that which is old. Rossetti and Tennyson and scores of others made the world richer simply by going back to the literature of a thousand years ago, and giving it re-birth. Like everything else, even a good story must die and be re-born hundreds of times before it shows the highest possibilities of beauty. All literary history is a story of re-birth— periods of death and restful forgetfulness alternating with periods of resurrection and activity. In the domain of pure literature nobody need ever be troubled for want of a subject. He has only to look for something which has been dead for a very long time, and to give that body a new soul. In romance it would be absurd to think about despising a subject, because it is

Note upon Rossetti's Prose

unscientific. Science has nothing to do with pure romance or poetry, though it may enrich both. These are emotional flowers; and what we can do for them is only to transplant and cultivate them, much as roses or chrysanthemums are cultivated. The original wild flower is very simple; but the clever gardener can develop the simple blossom into a marvellous compound apparition, displaying ten petals where the original could show but one. Now the same horticultural process can be carried out with any good story or poem or drama in Japan, just as readily as in any other country. The romantic has nothing to gain from the new learning except in the direction of pure art; the new learning, by enriching the language and enlarging the imagination, makes it possible to express the ancient beauty in a new and much more beautiful way. Tennyson might be quoted in illustration. What is the difference between his two or three hundred lines of wondrous poetry entitled "The Passing of Arthur," and the earliest thirteenth or fourteenth century idea of the same mythical event? The facts in either case are the same. But the language and the imagery are a thousand times more forcible and more vivid in the Victorian poet. Indeed, progress in belles-lettres is almost altogether brought about by making old things conform to the imagination of succeeding generations; and poesy, like the human race, of which it represents the emotional spirit, must change its dress and the colour of its dress as the world also changes.

CHAPTER III

A GOOD modern critic has said that the resemblance between Shelley and Algernon Charles Swinburne is of so astonishing a kind that it tempts one to believe that Swinburne is Shelley in a new body, that the soul of the drowned poet really came back to life again, and returned to finish at Oxford University the studies interrupted by his expulsion at the beginning of the century. The fancy is pretty; and it is supported by a number of queer analogies. Swinburne, like Shelley, is well born; like Shelley, he has been from his early days at Eton a furious radical; like Shelley, he has always been an enemy of Christianity; and like Shelley, he has also been an enemy of conventions and prejudices of every description. At the beginning of the century Swinburne would certainly have been treated just as Byron and Shelley were treated, but times are changed to-day; the public has become more generous and more sensible, and critics generally recognise Swinburne as the greatest verse writer English literature produced. He will certainly have justice done him after his death, if not during his life.

If Swinburne were Shelley reborn, we should have to recognise that he gained a good deal of wisdom from the experiences of his former life. He is altogether an incomparably stronger character than Shelley. He

[122]

kept his radicalism for his poetry, and never in any manner outraged the conventions of society in such matters as might relate to his private life. He is also a far greater poet than Shelley—greater than Tennyson, greater than Rossetti, greater than Browning, greater than any other Englishman, not excepting Milton, in the mastery of verse. He is also probably one of the greatest of scholars among the poets of any country, writing poetry in English or French, in Greek and Latin. For learning, there are certainly few among the poets of England who would not have been obliged to bow before him. He is also the greatest living English dramatist—I might as well say the greatest English dramatist of the nineteenth century. Except the "Cenci" of Shelley, there is no other great drama since 1800 to be placed beside the dramas of Swinburne; and the "Prometheus Unbound" by Shelley is far surpassed by Swinburne's Greek tragedy of "Atalanta in Calydon." Another feature of Swinburne's genius is his critical capacity. He is a great critic; so great that he has been able to make his enemies afraid of him, as well as to help to distinction struggling young men of talent whose work he admires. You will perceive what force there must be in the man. Born in 1837, he has never ceased to produce poetry from the time of his University days, and he still writes, with the result that the bulk of his work probably exceeds the work of any other great poet of the century. If he be indeed the reborn Shelley, it is certain that Shelley has become a giant.

I may have surprised you by saying that Swinburne is the greatest of all our poets. But understand that I am speaking of poetry as distinguished from prose, of poetry as rhythm and rhyme, as melody and measure. By greatest of poets I mean the greatest master of verse. If you were to ask me whether Swinburne has as great a quality as Tennyson or as Rossetti or as Browning, either in the moral or philosophical sense, I should say no. Greatest of all in the knowledge and use of words, he is perhaps less than any of the three in the higher emotional, moral, sympathetic, and philosophical qualities that give poetry its charm for even those who know nothing about the art of words. And of all the Victorian poets, Swinburne will be the least useful to students of these literary classes. The extraordinary powers that distinguish him are powers requiring not only a perfect knowledge of English, but a perfect knowledge of those higher forms of literary expression which are especially the outcome of classical study. Swinburne's scholarship is one of the great obstacles to his being understood by any who are not scholars themselves in the very same direction; in this sense he would be, I think, quite as useless to you as Milton in the matter of form. In value to you he would be far below Milton in the matter of thought and sentiment.

There are several ways of studying poetry. The greater number of people who buy the books of poets, and who find pleasure in them, do not know anything about the rules of verse. Out of one hundred thousand Englishmen who read Tennyson, I doubt very much if one thousand know the worth of his art. English University students, who have taken a literary course, probably do understand very well; but a poet's reputation and fortune are not made by scholars, but by the great mass of half-educated people. They read for sentiment, for emotion, for imagination; and they are quite satisfied with the pleasure given them by the poet in this way. They are improving and educating themselves when they read him, and for this it is not necessary that they should know the methods of his work, but only that they should know its results. The educators of the great mass of any people in Europe are, in this sense, the poets.

The other way of studying a poet is the scholarly way, the critical method (I do not mean the philosophical method; that is beside our subject); we read a poet closely, carefully, observing every new and unfamiliar word, every beautiful phrase and unaccustomed term, every device of rhythm or rhyme, sound or colour that he has to give us. Our capacity to study any poet in this way depends a good deal upon literary habit and upon educational opportunity. By the first method I doubt whether you could find much in Swinburne. He is like Shelley, often without substance of any kind. By the second method we can do a great deal with a choice of texts from his best work. I think it better to state this clearly beforehand, so that you may not be disappointed, failing to find in him the beautiful haunting thoughts that you can find in Rossetti or in Tennyson or in Browning.

Here I must digress a little. I must speak of the worst side of Swinburne as well as of the best. The worst is nearly all in one book, not a very large book, which made the greatest excitement in England that had been made since the appearance of Byron's "Don Juan." It is the greatest lyrical gift ever given to

English literature, this book; but it is also, in some respects, the most immoral book yet written by an English poet. The work of Byron, at its worst, is pure and innocent by comparison with the work of Swinburne in this book. It is astonishing that the English public could have allowed the book to exist. Probably it was forgiven on account of its beauty. Some years ago, I remember, an excellent English review said, in speaking of a certain French poem, that it was the most beautiful poem of its kind in the French language, but that, unfortunately, the subject could not be mentioned in print. Of course when there is a great beauty and great voluptuousness at the same time, it is the former, not the latter, that makes the greatness of the work. There must be something very good to excuse the existence of the bad. Much of the work of Swinburne is like that French poem, valuable for the beauty and condemnable for the badness in it —and touching upon subjects which cannot be named at all. Why he did this work we must try to understand without prejudice.

First, as to the man himself. We must not suppose that a person is necessarily immoral in his life because he happens to write something which is immoral, any more than we should suppose a person whose writings are extremely moral to be incapable of doing anything of a vicious or foolish kind. Shelley, for example, is a very chaste poet—there is not one improper line in the whole of his poetry; but his life was decidedly unfortunate. Exactly the reverse happens in the case of Swinburne, who has written thousands of immoral lines. The fact is that many persons are apt to mistake

[126]

artistic feeling for vicious feeling, and a spirit of revolt against conventions for a general hatred of moral law. I must ask you to try to put yourselves for a moment in the place of a young student, such as Swinburne was at the time of these writings, and try to imagine how he felt about things. In every Western boy—indeed, I may say in every civilised boy—there are several distinct periods, corresponding to the various periods in the history of human progress. Both psychologically and physiologically the history of the race is repeated in the history of the individual. The child is a savage, without religion, without tenderness, with a good deal of cruelty and cunning in his little soul. He is this because the first faculties that are developed within him are the faculties for self-preservation, the faculties of primitive man. Then ideas of right and wrong and religious feelings are quickened within him by home-training, and he becomes somewhat like the man of the Middle Ages—he enters into his mediæval period. Then in the course of his college studies he is gradually introduced to a knowledge of the wonderful old Greek civilisation, civilisation socially and, in some respects, even morally superior to anything in the existing world; and he enters into the period of his Renaissance. If he be very sensitive to beauty, if he have the æsthetic faculty largely developed, there will almost certainly come upon him an enthusiastic love and reverence for the old paganism, and a corresponding dislike of his modern surroundings. This feeling may last only for a short time, or it may change his whole life. One fact to observe is this, that it is just about the time when a young man's passions are strongest that the story of Greek life is suddenly expounded to him in the course of his studies; and you must remember that the æsthetic faculty is primarily based upon the sensuous life. Now in Swinburne's case we have an abnormal æsthetic and scholarly faculty brought into contact with these influences at a very early age; and the result must have been to that young mind like the shock of an earth-quake. We must also imagine the natural consequence of this enthusiasm in a violent reaction against all literary, religious, or social conventions that endeavour to keep the spirit of the old paganism hidden and suppressed within narrow limits, as a dangerous thing. Finally we must suppose the natural effect of opposition upon this mind, the effect of threats, sneers, or prohibitions, like oil upon fire. For young Swinburne was, and still is, a man of exceeding courage, incapable of fear of any sort. A great idea suddenly came to him, and he resolved to put it into execution. This idea was nothing less than to attempt to obtain for English poetry the same liberty enjoyed by French poetry in recent times, to attempt to obtain the right of absolute liberty of expression in all directions, and to provoke the contest with such a bold stroke as never had been dared before. The result was the book that has been so much condemned.

We cannot say that Swinburne was successful in this attempt at reform. He attempted a little too much, and attempted it too soon. Even in his own time the great French poet Charles Baudelaire was publicly condemned in a French court for having written verse less daring than Swinburne's. The great French novelist Flaubert also had to answer in court for the production of a novel that is now thought to be very innocent. It was only at a considerably later time that the French poets obtained such liberty of expression as allowed of the excesses of writers like Zola or of poets like Richepin. Altogether Swinburne's fight was premature. He must now see that it was. But I should not like to say that he was entirely wrong. The result of absolute liberty in French literature gives us a good idea of what would be the result of absolute liberty in English literature. Extravagances of immorality were followed by extravagances of vulgarity as well, and after the novelty of the thing was over a reaction set in, provoked by disgust and national shame. Exactly the same thing would happen in England after a brief period of vicious carnival; the English tide of opinion would set in the contrary direction with immense force, and would bring about such a tyrannical conservatism in letters as would signify, for the time being, a serious check upon progress. As a matter of fact, we cannot do in English literature what can be done in French literature. Swinburne might, but there is only one Swinburne. The English language is not perfect enough, not graceful and flexible enough, to admit of elegant immorality; and the English character is not refined enough. A Frenchman can say very daring things, very immoral things, gracefully; an Englishman cannot. Only one Englishman has approached the possibility; and that Englishman is Swinburne himself.

I think you will now understand what Swinburne's purpose was, and be able to judge of it. His mistakes were due not only to his youth but also to his astonishing genius; for he could not then know how much superior in ability he actually was to any other English poet. He imagined that there were many who might do what he could do. The truth is that hundreds of years may pass before another Englishman is born capable of doing what Swinburne could do. Men of letters have long ago forgiven him, because of this astonishing power. They say, "We know the poems are improper, but we have nothing else like them, and English literature cannot afford to lose them." The scholars have forgiven him, because his worst faults are always scholarly; and a common person cannot understand his worst allusions. Indeed, one must be much of a classical scholar to comprehend what is most condemnable in the first series of the "Poems and Ballads." Their extreme laxity will not be perceived without elaborate explanation, and no one can venture to explain—I do not mean in a university class room only, I mean even in printed criticism. When this was attempted by the poet's enemies, he was able to point out, with great effect, that the explanations were much more immoral than the poems.

Now in considering Swinburne's poetry in a short course of lectures, I think it will be well to begin by explaining his philosophical position; for every poet has a philosophy of his own. As I have already said, there is less of this visible in Swinburne than in the other Victorian poets, but the little there is has a particular and beautiful interest, which we shall be able to illustrate in a series of quotations. I am presuming a little in speaking about his philosophy because there has been nothing of importance written about his philosophy, nor has he himself ever made a plain statement of it. In such a case I can only surmise, and you need not consider my opinion as definitive. Swinburne is, like George Meredith, an evolutionist, and he has something of the spiritual element in him which we notice in Meredith as a philosopher—but always with this difference, that Meredith makes evolution preach a moral law, and Swinburne does not. But here we notice that Swinburne's evolution is something totally different from Meredith's in its origin. I have said to you that Meredith expresses evolutional philosophy according to Herbert Spencer; I consider him the greatest of our philosophical poets for that very reason. Swinburne does not appear to have felt the influence of Herbert Spencer; he seems rather to reflect the opinions of Comte—especially of Comte as interpreted by Lewes, and perhaps by Frederic Harrison. He speaks of the Religion of Humanity, of the Divinity of Man, and of other things which indicate the influence of Comte. Furthermore, I must say, being myself a disciple of Spencer, that Swinburne's sociological and radical opinions are quite incompatible with evolutional philosophy as expounded by Spencer. Indeed, Swinburne's views about government, about fraternity and equality, about liberty in all matters of thought and action, are heresies for the strictly scientific mind. The great thinkers of our century have exposed and overthrown the old fallacies of the French revolutionary school as to the equality of men and the meaning of liberty and fraternity. Swinburne still champions, or appears to champion, some of the erroneous ideas of

Pre-Raphaelite and Other Poets

Rousseau. Otherwise there is little fault to be found
with his thoughts concerning the ultimate nature of
things, except in the deep melancholy that always accompanies them. Meredith is a grand optimist. Swinburne is something very like a pessimist. There is no
joy and no hope in his tone of speaking about the mystery of death; rather we find ourselves listening to the
tone of the ancient Roman Epicureans, in the time
when faith was dying, and when philosophy attempted,
without success, to establish a religion of duty founded
upon pure ethics.

An important test of any writer's metaphysical position is what he believes about the soul. Swinburne's
idea is very well expressed in the prelude to his "Songs
before Sunrise." A single stanza would be enough in
this case; but we shall give two, in order to show the
pantheistic side of the poet's faith.

> Because man's soul is man's God still,
> What wind soever waft his will
>   Across the waves of day and night
>   To port or shipwreck, left or right,
> By shores and shoals of good and ill;
>   And still its flame at mainmast height
> Through the rent air that foam-flakes fill
>   Sustains the indomitable light
> Whence only man hath strength to steer
> Or helm to handle without fear.
>
> Save his own soul's light overhead,
> None leads him, and none ever led,
>   Across birth's hidden harbour-bar,
>   Past youth where shoreward shallows are,

Studies in Swinburne

Through age that drives on toward the red
Vast void of sunset hailed from far,
To the equal waters of the dead;
Save his own soul he hath no star,
And sinks, except his own soul guide,
Helmless in middle turn of tide.

This is a very plain statement not only that man has
no god, and that he makes his own gods, but that he
never had a creator or a god of any kind. He has no
divine help, no one to pray to, no one to trust except
himself. So far this is in tolerable accord with the
teaching of the Buddha, "Be ye lights unto yourselves;
seek no refuge but in yourselves." But the question
comes, What is man's soul? Is it divine? Is it part of
the universal soul, a supreme and infinite intelligence?
There is another meaning in the first line of the first
stanza which I quoted to you about man's soul being
man's god. Some verses from the wonderful poem
called "On the Downs" will make the meaning plainer.

"No light to lighten and no rod
To chasten men? Is there no God?"
So girt with anguish, iron-zoned,
Went my soul weeping as she trod
Between the men enthroned
And men that groaned.

O fool, that for brute cries of wrong
Heard not the grey glad mother's song
Ring response from the hills and waves,
But heard harsh noises all day long
Of spirits that were slaves
And dwelt in graves.

. . . .

[133]

Pre-Raphaelite and Other Poets

With all her tongues of life and death,
With all her bloom and blood and breath,
  From all years dead and all things done,
In the ear of man the mother saith,
  "There is no God, O son,
  If thou be none."

This is the declaration of a belief in the divinity of
man, a doctrine well known to students of Comte. It
is not altogether in disaccord with Oriental philosophy; you must not suppose Swinburne to be speaking
of individual divinity, but of a universal divinity expressing itself in human thought and feeling. His view
of life is that the essential thing is to live as excellently
as possible, but we must not suppose that excellence is
used in the moral sense. Swinburne's idea of excellence
is the idea of completeness. His notions of right and
wrong are not the religious or the social notions of
right and wrong. In this respect he sometimes seems
to think very much like the German philosopher
Nietzsche. Nevertheless he does tell us that the real
spirit of the universe is a spirit of love, a doctrine at
which Huxley would certainly have laughed. But it is
beautiful doctrine in its way, even if not true, and
admirably suits the purposes of poetry.

I think that I need not say much more here about
Swinburne's philosophy; you will understand that he is
at once a pantheist and an evolutionist, and that is sufficient for our purposes. But it is necessary to remember this in order to understand many things in his
verse, and especially in order to understand some of
his extraordinary attitudes in condemning what most
men respect, and in praising what most men condemn.

Studies in Swinburne

Remember also that his judgments, like those of Nature, are never moral; they are not always the reverse, but they are founded entirely upon æsthetic perception. Those who praise him especially are men in revolt like himself. Therefore he praised Walt Whitman, at a time when Walt Whitman was being condemned everywhere for certain faults in his compositions; therefore he sang the praises of Baudelaire, as none other had done before him (and here he is certainly right); therefore he praised Théophile Gautier's "Mademoiselle de Maupin," calling it "the golden book of spirit and sense"; therefore also he wrote a sonnet praising Burton's translation of the Arabian Nights, which made a great scandal in England because it translated all the obscene passages which nobody else had ventured to put into English or French. The æsthetic judgment in all these cases is correct, but I will not venture to pronounce upon the moral judgment any further than to say this, that Swinburne delights in courage, and that literary courage in his eyes covers a multitude of sins.

Not a few, however, of these daring songs of praise are among the most wonderful triumphs of modern lyric verse. I should like, for example, to quote to you the whole of his ode to Villon, but I fear that because of its length, and the unfamiliarity of the subject, we cannot afford the time. I will quote the closing stanza as a specimen of the rest, and I am sure that you will see its beauty.

Prince of sweet songs made out of tears and fire,
A harlot was thy nurse, a God thy sire;

[135]

Pre-Raphaelite and Other Poets

Shame soiled thy song, and song assoiled thy shame.
But from thy feet now death has washed the mire,
Love reads out first at head of all our quire,
Villon, our sad bad glad mad brother's name.

Each stanza ends with this strange refrain of "sad bad glad mad," adjectives which excellently express the changeful and extraordinary character of that poor student of Paris with whose name modern French literature properly begins. He lived a terrible and reckless life, very nearly ending with the gallows; he was an associate at one time of princes and bishops, at another time of thieves and prostitutes; he would be one day a spendthrift, the next day a beggar or a prisoner; and he sang of all these experiences as no man ever sang before or since. Really Swinburne's praise in this case is not only just—it represents the best possible estimate of the singer's faults and virtues combined.

To speak in detail of the great range of subjects chosen by Swinburne is not possible within the limits of this lecture. I am going to make selections from every part of his production, except the dramatic, as well as I can, and the selections will be made with a view especially to show you the music of his verse and the brilliance of his language. Most of his poems are above the ordinary lyrical length rather than below it, and I hope that you will not be disappointed if I do not often give the whole of a poem, for the selections will contain, I am sure, the best part of the poem.

Being a descendant of great seamen, Swinburne had every reason to sing of the sea; and he has sung of it better than any one else. A great number of his poems

are sea-poems, or poems containing descriptions of the
sea in all its moods, splendours, or terrors. Sun, sea,
and wind are favourite subjects with him, and I know
of nothing in the whole of his work finer than his description of the wind as the lover of the sea. The
verses I am going to quote are from a great composition entitled "By the North Sea." The personal pro-
noun "he" in the first line means the wind personified.

> The delight that he takes but in living
>   Is more than of all things that live:
> For the world that has all things for giving
>   Has nothing so goodly to give:
> But more than delight his desire is,
>   For the goal where his pinions would be
> Is immortal as air or as fire is,
>   Immense as the sea.
>
> Though hence come the moan that he borrows
>   From darkness and depth of the night,
> Though hence be the spring of his sorrows,
>   Hence too is the joy of his might;
> The delight that his doom is for ever
>   To seek and desire and rejoice,
> And the sense that eternity never
>   Shall silence his voice.
>
> That satiety never may stifle
>   Nor weariness ever estrange
> Nor time be so strong as to rifle
>   Nor change be so great as to change
> His gift that renews in the giving,
>   The joy that exalts him to be
> Alone of all elements living
>   The lord of the sea.

[137]

Pre-Raphaelite and Other Poets

What is fire, that its flame should consume her?
More fierce than all fires are her waves:
What is earth, that its gulfs should entomb her?
More deep are her own than their graves.
Life shrinks from his pinions that cover
    The darkness by thunders bedinned;
But she knows him, her lord and her lover,
    The godhead of wind.

This titanic personification of sea and wind is sublime, but Swinburne has many other ways of personifying wind and sea, and sometimes the element of tenderness and love is not wanting. Sometimes the sea is addressed as a goddess, but more often she is addressed as a mother, and some of the most exquisite forms of such address are found in poems which have, properly speaking, nothing to do with the sea at all. A good example is in the poem called "The Triumph of Time." The words are supposed to be spoken by a person who is going to drown himself.

O fair green-girdled mother of mine,
    Sea, that art clothed with the sun and the rain,
Thy sweet hard kisses are strong like wine,
    Thy large embraces are keen like pain.
Save me and hide me with all thy waves,
Find me one grave of thy thousand graves,
Those pure cold populous graves of thine,
    Wrought without hand in a world without stain.

We shall also find great wonder and beauty in Swinburne's hymns to the sun, which is also for him, as for the poets of old, a living god, and which certainly is, in a scientific sense, the lord of all life within this

[138]

world. The best expression of this feeling is in a poem called "Off Shore," describing sunrise over the sea, and the glory of light.

> Light, perfect and visible
> Godhead of God!
> God indivisible,
> Lifts but his rod,
> And the shadows are scattered in sunder, and darkness
> is light at his nod.

> At the touch of his wand,
> At the nod of his head
> From the spaces beyond
> Where the dawn hath her bed,
> Earth, water, and air are transfigured, and rise as one
> risen from the dead.

> He puts forth his hand,
> And the mountains are thrilled
> To the heart as they stand
> In his presence, fulfilled
> With his glory that utters his grace upon earth, and
> her sorrows are stilled.
>
> .   .   .   .

> As a kiss on my brow
> Be the light of thy grace,
> Be thy glance on me now
> From the pride of thy place:
> As the sign of a sire to a son be the light on my face
> of thy face.
>
> .   .   .   .

Pre-Raphaelite and Other Poets

    Fair father of all
      In thy ways that have trod,
      That have risen at thy call,
      That have thrilled at thy nod,
Arise, shine, lighten upon me, O sun that we see to
      be God.

         .   .   .   .

      Be praised and adored of us
        All in accord,
      Father and lord of us
        Always adored,
The slayer and the stayer and the harper, the light
      of us all and our lord.

Swinburne has no equal in enthusiastic celebration of
the beauties of sky and sea and wood, of light and
clouds and waters, of sound and perfume and blossom-
ing. Indeed, one of his particular characteristics, a
characteristic very seldom found in English masterpieces, though common in the best French work, is his
art for describing odours—the smell of morning and
evening, scents of the seasons, scents also of life. We
shall have many opportunities to notice this characteristic of Swinburne, even in his descriptions of human
beauty. What the French call the *parfum de jeunesse*
or odour of youth, the pleasant smell of young bodies,
the perfume that we notice, for example, in the hair of
a healthy child, is something which English writers very
seldom venture to treat of; but Swinburne has treated
it quite as delicately at times as a French poet could do,
though sometimes a little extravagantly. You must
think of him as one whom no quality of beauty escapes,

whether of colour, odour, or motion; and as one who
believes, I think rightly, that whatever is in itself beautiful and natural is worthy of song. You will be able
to imagine, from what I have already quoted, how he
feels in the presence of wild nature. How he considers
human beauty is a more difficult matter to illustrate by
quotation, at least by quotation before a class. But I
shall try to offer some illustrations from the "Masque
of Queen Bersabe." You all know what a masque is.
The masque in question is a perfect imitation, for the
most part, of a mediæval masque, both as to form and
language. But there is one portion of it which is
mediæval only in tone, not in language, since there never
lived in the Middle Ages any man capable of writing
such verse. It is from this part that I want to quote.
But I must first explain to you that the name Bersabe
is only a mediæval form of the Biblical name Bathsheba, the wife of Uriah, whom King David caused to
be murdered. It is an ugly story. The King committed
adultery with Bathsheba; then he ordered her husband
to be put into the front rank during a battle, in such
a place that he must be killed. Afterwards the King
married Bathsheba; but the prophet Nathan heard of
the wickedness, and threatened the King with the punishment of God. This was the subject of several
mediæval religious plays, and Swinburne adopted it for
an imitation of such play. The first part of his conception is that at the command of the prophet the
ghosts of all the beautiful and wicked queens who ever
lived come before Bathsheba, to reproach her with her
sin, and to tell her how they had been punished in other
time for sins of the same kind. Each one speaks in

turn; and though I cannot quote all of what they said, I can quote enough to illustrate the magnificence of the work. Each verse is a portrait in words, uttered by the subject.

CLEOPATRA

I am the queen of Ethiope.
Love bade my kissing eyelids ope
    That men beholding might praise love.
My hair was wonderful and curled;
My lips held fast the mouth o' the world
    To spoil the strength and speech thereof.
The latter triumph in my breath
Bowed down the beaten brows of death,
    Ashamed they had not wrath enough.

. . . . . .

AHOLAH

I am the queen of Amalek.
There was no tender touch or fleck
    To spoil my body or bared feet.
My words were soft like dulcimers,
And the first sweet of grape-flowers
    Made each side of my bosom sweet.
My raiment was as tender fruit
Whose rind smells sweet of spice-tree root,
    Bruised balm-blossom and budded wheat.

. . . . . .

SEMIRAMIS

I am the queen Semiramis.
The whole world and the sea that is

[142]

Studies in Swinburne

In fashion like a chrysopras,
The noise of all men labouring,
The priest's mouth tired through thanksgiving,
  The sound of love in the blood's pause,
The strength of love in the blood's beat,
All these were cast beneath my feet
  And all found lesser than I was.

. . . . . .

I am the queen of Cypriotes.
Mine oarsmen, labouring with brown throats,
  Sang of me many a tender thing.
My maidens, girdled loose and braced
With gold from bosom to white waist,
  Praised me between their wool-combing.
All that praise Venus all night long
With lips like speech and lids like song
  Praised me till song lost heart to sing.

. . . . . .

I am the queen Alaciel.
My mouth was like that moist gold cell
  Whereout the thickest honey drips.
Mine eyes were as a grey-green sea;
The amorous blood that smote on me
  Smote to my feet and finger-tips.
My throat was whiter than the dove,
Mine eyelids as the seals of love,
  And as the doors of love my lips.

[143]

Pre-Raphaelite and Other Poets

I am the queen Erigone.
The wild wine shed as blood on me
Made my face brighter than a bride's.
My large lips had the old thirst of earth,
Mine arms the might of the old sea's girth
Bound round the whole world's iron sides.
Within mine eyes and in mine ears
Were music and the wine of tears,
And light, and thunder of the tides.

So pass the strange phantoms of dead pride and lust
and power, together with many more of whom the descriptions are not less beautiful and strange, though
much less suitable for quotation. I have made the
citations somewhat long, but I have done so because
they offer the best possible illustration of two things
peculiar to Swinburne, the music and colour of his
verse, and the peculiar mediæval tone which he sometimes assumes in dealing with antique subjects. These
descriptions are quite unlike anything done by Tennyson, or indeed by any other poet except Rossetti. They
represent, in a certain way, what has been called Pre-
Raphaelitism in poetry. Swinburne was, with Rossetti,
one of the great forces of the new movement in literature. Observe that the illustrations are chiefly made by
comparisons—that the descriptions are made by suggestion; there is no attempt to draw a clear sharp line,
nothing is described completely, but by some comparison or symbolism in praise of a part, the whole figure
is vaguely brought before the imagination in a blaze of

[144]

colour with strange accompaniment of melody. For example, you will have noticed that no face is fully pictured; you find only some praise of the eyes or the mouth, the throat or the skin, but that is quite enough to bring to your fancy the entire person. But there is another queer fact which you must be careful to notice —namely, that no comparison is modern. The language and the symbolism are Biblical or mediæval in every case. The European scholar who had made a special study of the literature of the Middle Ages would notice even more than this; he would notice that the whole tone is not of the later but of the earlier Middle Ages, that the old miracle plays, the old French romances, and the early Italian poets, have all contributed something to this splendour of expression. It is modern art in one sense, of course, but there is nothing modern about it except the craftsmanship; the material is all quaint and strange, and gives us the sensation of old tapestry or of the paintings that were painted in Italy before the time of Raphael.

Here I must say a word about the Pre-Raphaelite movement in nineteenth century literature. To explain everything satisfactorily, I ought to have pictures to show you; and that is unfortunately impossible. But I think I can make a very easy explanation of the subject. First of all you must be quite well aware that the literature of all countries seeks for a majority of its subjects in the past. The everyday, the familiar, does not attract us in the same way as that which is not familiar and not of the present. Distance, whether of space or time, lends to things a certain tone of beauty, just as mountains look more beautifully blue the further away they happen to be. This seeking for beauty in the past rather than in the present represents much of what is called romanticism in any literature.

Necessarily, even in this age of precise historical knowledge, the past is for us less real than the present; time has spread mists of many colours between it and us, so that we cannot be sure of details, distances, depths, and heights. But in other generations the mists were heavier, and the past was more of a fairy-land than now; it was more pleasant also to think about, because the mysterious is attractive to all of us, and men of letters delighted to write about it, because they could give free play to the imagination. Such stories of the past as we find even in what have been called historical novels, were called also, and rightly called, romances—works of imagination rather than of fact.

But still you may ask, why such words as romance and romantic? The answer is that works of imagination, dealing with past events, were first written in languages derived from the Latin, the Romance languages; and at a very early time it became the custom to distinguish work written in these modern tongues upon fanciful or heroic subjects, by this name and quality. The romantic in the Middle Ages signified especially the new literature of fancy as opposed to the old classical literature. Remember, therefore, that this meaning is not yet entirely lost, though it has undergone many modifications. "Romantic" in literature still means "not classical," and it also suggests imagination rather than fact, and the past rather than the present.

Studies in Swinburne

When we say "mediæval" in speaking of nineteenth century poetry, we mean of course nineteenth century literature having a romantic tone, as well as reflecting, so far as imagination can, the spirit of the Middle, Ages. But what is the difference between the Pre-Raphaelite and Mediæval? The time before Raphael, the Pre-Raphaelite period, would necessarily have been mediæval. As a matter of fact, the term Pre-Raphaelite does not have the wide general meaning usually given to it. It is something of a technical term, belonging to art rather than to literature, and first introduced into literature by a company of painters. The Pre-Raphaelite painters, in the technical sense, were a special group of modern painters, distinguished by particular characteristics.

So much being clear, I may say that there was a school of painting before Raphael of a very realistic and remarkable kind. This school came to existence a little after the true religious spirit of the Middle Ages had begun to weaken. It sought the emotion of beauty as well as the emotion of religion, but it did not yet feel the influence of the Renaissance in a strong way; it was not Greek nor pagan. It sought beauty in truth, studying ordinary men and women, flowers and birds, scenery of nature or scenery of streets; and it used reality for its model. It was much less romantic than the school that came after it; but it was very great and very noble. With Raphael the Greek feeling, the old pagan feeling for sensuous beauty, found full expression, and this Renaissance tone changed the whole direction and character of art. After Raphael the painters sought beauty before all things; previously they had sought for truth and sentiment even before beauty. Raphael set a fashion which influenced all arts after him down to our own time; for centuries the older painters were neglected and almost forgotten. Therefore Ruskin boldly declared that since Raphael's death Western art had been upon the decline and that the school of painters immediately before Raphael were greater than any who came after him. Gradually within our own time a new taste came into art-circles, a new love for the old forgotten masters of the fourteenth and fifteenth centuries. It was discovered that they were, after all, nearer to truth in many respects than the later painters; and then was established, by Rossetti and others, a new school of painting called the Pre-Raphaelite school. It sought truth to life as well as beauty, and it endeavoured to mingle both with mystical emotion.

At first this was a new movement in art only, or rather in painting and drawing only, as distinguished from literary art. But literature and painting and architecture and music are really all very closely related, and a new literary movement also took place in harmony with the new departure in painting. This was chiefly the work of Rossetti, Swinburne, and William Morris. They tried to make poems and to write stories according to the same æsthetic motives which seem to have inspired the school of painters before Raphael. This is the signification of the strange method and beauty of those quotations which I have been giving to you from Swinburne's masque. They represent very powerfully the Pre-Raphaelite feelings in English poetry.

I know that this digression is somewhat long, but

Studies in Swinburne

I believe that it is of great importance; without knowing these facts, it would be impossible for the student to understand many curious things in Swinburne's manner. Throughout even his lighter poems we find this curious habit of describing things in ways totally remote from nineteenth century feeling, and nevertheless astonishingly effective. Fancy such comparisons as these for a woman's beauty in the correct age of Wordsworth:

> I said "she must be swift and white,
> And subtly warm, and half perverse,
> And sweet like sharp soft fruit to bite,
> And like a snake's love lithe and fierce."
> Men have guessed worse.

Or take the following extraordinary description of a woman's name, perhaps I had better say of the sensation given by the name Félise, probably an abbreviation of Felicita, but by its spelling reminding one very much of the Latin word *felis*, which means a cat:

> Like colors in the sea, like flowers,
> Like a cat's splendid circled eyes
> That wax and wane with love for hours,
> Green as green flame, blue-grey like skies,
> And soft like sighs.

The third line refers to the curious phenomenon of the enlarging and diminishing of the pupil in a cat's eye according to the decrease or increase of light. It is said that you can tell the time of day by looking at a cat's eyes. Now all these comparisons are in the highest degree offences against classical feeling. The classi-

[149]

cal poet, even the half-classical poet of the beginning of
our own century, would have told you that a woman
must not be compared to a snake or a cat; that you
must not talk about her sweetness being like the sweetness of fruit, or the charm of her presence being like
the smell of perfume. All such comparisons seemed
monstrous, unnatural. If such a critic were asked why
one must not compare a woman to a snake or a cat, the
critic would probably answer, "Because a snake is a
hateful reptile and a cat is a hateful animal." What
would Ruskin or Swinburne then say to the critic?
He would say simply, "Did you ever look at a snake?
Did you ever study a cat?" The classicist would soon
be convicted of utter ignorance about snakes and cats.
He thought them hateful simply because it was not
fashionable to admire them a hundred years ago. But
the old poets of the early Middle Ages were not such
fools. They had seen snakes and admired them, because
for any man who is not prejudiced, a snake is a very
beautiful creature, and its motions are as beautiful as
geometry. If you do not think this is true, I beg of
you to watch a snake, where its body can catch the light
of the sun. Then there is no more graceful or friendly
or more attractively intelligent animal than a cat. The
common feeling about snakes and cats is not an artistic one, nor even a true one; it is of ethical origin,
and unjust. These animals are not moral according
to our notions; they seem cruel and treacherous, and
forgetting that they cannot be judged by our code of
morals, we have learned to speak of them contemptu-
ously even from the physical point of view. Well, this
was not the way in the early Middle Ages. People were

less sensitive on the subject of cruelty than they are to-day, and they could praise the beauty of snakes and tigers and all fierce or cunning creatures of prey, because they could admire the physical qualities without thinking of the moral ones. In Pre-Raphaelite poetry there is an attempt to do the very same thing. Swinburne does it more than any one else, perhaps even too much; but there is a great and true principle of art behind this revolution.

Now we can study Swinburne in some other moods. I want to show you the splendour of his long verse, verse of fourteen and sixteen syllables, of a form resurrected by him after centuries of neglect; and also verse written in imitation of Greek and Roman measures with more success than has attended similar efforts on the part of any other living poet. But in the first example that I shall offer, you will find matter of more interest than verse as verse. The poem is one of Swinburne's greatest, and the subject is entirely novel. The poet attempts to express the feeling of a Roman pagan, perhaps one of the last Epicurean philosophers, living at the time when Christianity was first declared the religion of the Empire, and despairing because of the destruction of the older religion and the vanishing of the gods whom he loved. By law Christianity has been made the state-religion, and it is forbidden to worship the other gods; the old man haughtily refuses to become a Christian, even after an impartial study of Christian doctrine; on the contrary, he is so unhappy at the fate of the religion of his fathers that he does not care to live any longer without his gods. And he prays to the goddess of death to take him out of this world, from

which all the beauty and art, all the old loved customs
and beliefs are departing. We cannot read the whole
"Hymn to Proserpine"; but we shall read enough to
illustrate the style and feeling of the whole. At the
head of the poem are the words *Vicisti, Galilæe!*—
"Thou hast conquered, O Galilean"—words uttered by
the great Roman Emperor Julian at the moment of his
death in battle. Julian was the last Emperor who tried
to revive and purify the decaying Roman religion, and
to oppose the growth of Christianity. He was, therefore, the great enemy of Christianity. His dying words
were said to have been addressed to Christ, when he
felt himself dying, but it is not certain whether he
really ever uttered these words at all.

I have lived long enough, having seen one thing, that love
    hath an end;
Goddess and maiden and queen, be near me now and be-
    friend.
Thou art more than the day or the morrow, the seasons
    that laugh or that weep;
For these give joy and sorrow; but thou, Proserpina, sleep.
Sweet is the treading of wine, and sweet the feet of the
    dove:
But a goodlier gift is thine than foam of the grapes or love.

After speaking to the goddess of death, he speaks thus
to Christ:

Wilt thou yet take all, Galilean? but these thou shalt not
    take,
The laurel, the palms and the pæan, the breasts of the
    nymphs in the brake;

[152]

Studies in Swinburne

Breasts more soft than a dove's, that tremble with tenderer
    breath;
And all the wings of the Loves, and all the joy before
    death;
All the feet of the hours that sound as a single lyre,
Dropped and deep in the flowers, with strings that flicker
    like fire.
More than these wilt thou give, things fairer than all
    these things?
Nay, for a little we live, and life hath mutable wings.
A little while and we die; shall life not thrive as it may?
For no man under the sky lives twice, outliving his day.
And grief is a grievous thing, and a man hath enough of
    his tears:
Why should he labour, and bring fresh grief to blacken his
    years?
Thou hast conquered, O pale Galilean; the world has grown
    grey from thy breath;
We have drunken of things Lethean, and fed on the fulness
    of death.

Or, in other words, the pagan says: "O Christ, you
would wish to take everything from us, yet some things
there are which you cannot take: not the inspiration of
the poet, nor the spirit of art, nor the glory of heroism,
nor the dreams of youth and love, nor the great and
gracious gifts of time—the beauty of the seasons, the
splendour of night and day. All these you cannot de-
prive us of, though you wish to; and what is better
than these? Can you give us anything more precious?
Assuredly you cannot. For these things are fitted to
human life; and what do we know about any other
life? Life passes quickly; why should we make it miserable with the evil dreams of a religion of sorrow?

[153]

Pre-Raphaelite and Other Poets

Short enough is the time in which we have pleasure, and
the world is already full enough of pain; wherefore
should we try to make ourselves still more unhappy than
we already are? Yet you have conquered; you have
destroyed the beauty of life; you have made the world
seem grey and old, that was so beautiful and eternally
young. You have made us drink the waters of forgetfulness and eat the food of death. For your religion is
a religion of death, not of life; you yourself and the
Christian gods are figures of death, not figures of life."

And how does he think of this new divinity, Christ?
As a Roman citizen necessarily, and to a Roman citizen
Christ was nothing more than a vulgar, common criminal executed by Roman law in company with thieves
and murderers. Therefore he addresses such a divinity
with scorn, even in the hour of his triumph:

O lips that the live blood faints in, the leavings of racks
    and rods!
O ghastly glories of saints, dead limbs of gibbeted Gods!
Though all men abase them before you in spirit, and all
    knees bend,
I kneel not neither adore you, but standing, look to the end!

To understand the terrible bitterness of this scorn,
it is necessary for the student to remember that a
Roman citizen could not be tortured or flogged or gibbeted. Such punishments and penalties were reserved
for slaves and for barbarians. Therefore to a Roman
the mere fact of Christ's death and punishment—for he
was tortured before being crucified—was a subject for
contempt; accordingly he speaks of such a divinity as
the "leavings of racks and rods"—that is, so much of

[154]

a man's body as might be left after the torturers and executioners had finished with it. Should a Roman citizen kneel down and humble himself before that? A little while, some thousands of years, perhaps, Christianity may be a triumphant religion, but all religions must die and pass away, one after another, and this new and detestable religion, with its ugly gods, must also pass away. For although the old Roman has studied too much philosophy to believe in all that his fathers believed, he believes in a power that is greater than man and gods and the universe itself, in the unknown power which gives life and death, and makes perpetual change, and sweeps away everything that man foolishly believes to be permanent. He gives to this law of impermanency the name of the goddess of death, but the name makes little difference; he has recognised the eternal law. Time will sweep away Christianity itself, and his description of this mighty wave of time is one of the finest passages in all his poetry:

All delicate days and pleasant, all spirits and sorrows are
    cast
Far out with the foam of the present that sweeps to the
    surf of the past:

.   .   .   .

Where, mighty with deepening sides, clad about with the
    seas as with wings,
And impelled of invisible tides, and fulfilled of unspeakable
    things,
White-eyed and poisonous-finned, shark-toothed and ser-
    pentine-curled,
Rolls, under the whitening wind of the future, the wave of
    the world.

The depths stand naked in sunder behind it, the storms flee
  away;
In the hollow before it the thunder is taken and snared as
  a prey;
In its sides is the north-wind bound; and its salt is of all
  men's tears;
With light of ruins and sound of changes, and pulse of
  years:
With travail of day after day, and with trouble of hour
  upon hour;
And bitter as blood is the spray; and the crests are as fangs
  that devour:
And its vapour and storm of its steam as the sighing of
  spirits to be;
And its noise as the noise in a dream; and its depth as the
  roots of the sea:
And the height of its heads as the height of the utmost stars
  of the air:
And the ends of the earth at the might thereof tremble, and
  time is made bare.

When the poet calls this the wave of the world, you
must not understand world to mean our planet only,
but the universe, the cosmos; and the wave is the great
wave of impermanency, including all forces of time and
death and life and pain. But why these terrible similes
of white eyes and poisonous things and shark's teeth, of
blood and bitterness and terror? Because the old philosopher dimly recognises the cruelty of nature, the
mercilessness of that awful law of change which, having
swept away his old gods, will just as certainly sweep
away the new gods that have appeared. Who can re-
sist that mighty power, higher than the stars, deeper
than the depths, in whose motion even gods are but as

Studies in Swinburne

bubbles and foam? Assuredly not Christ and his new religion. Speaking to the new gods the Roman cries:

All ye as a wind shall go by, as a fire shall ye pass and be
    past;
Ye are Gods, and behold, ye shall die, and the waves be
    upon you at last.

   .   .   .   .

Yet thy kingdom shall pass, Galilean, thy dead shall go
    down to thee dead.

Here follows a beautiful picture of the contrast between the beauty of the old gods and the uninviting aspect of the new. It is a comparison between the Virgin Mary, mother of Christ, and Venus or Aphrodite, the ancient goddess of love, born from the sea. For to the Roman mind the Christian gods and saints wanted even the common charm of beauty and tenderness. All the divinities of the old Greek world were beautiful to look upon, and warmly human; but these strange new gods from Asia seemed to be not even artistically endurable. Addressing Christ, he continues:

Of the maiden thy mother men sing as a goddess with grace
    clad around;
Thou art throned where another was king; where another
    was queen she is crowned.
Yea, once we had sight of another: but now she is queen,
    say these.
Not as thine, not as thine was our mother, a blossom of
    flowering seas,

[157]

Clothed around with the world's desire as with raiment and
    fair as the foam,
And fleeter than kindled fire, and a goddess and mother of
    Rome.
For thine came pale and a maiden, and sister to sorrow;
    but ours,
Her deep hair heavily laden with odour and colour of
    flowers,
White rose of the rose-white water, a silver splendour, a
    flame,
Bent down unto us that besought her, and earth grew sweet
    with her name.
For thine came weeping, a slave among slaves, and rejected;
    but she
Came flushed from the full-flushed wave, and imperial, her
    foot on the sea.
And the wonderful waters knew her, the winds and the
    viewless ways,
And the roses grew rosier, and bluer the sea-blue stream
    of the bays.
Ye are fallen, our lords, by what token? we wist that ye
    should not fall.
Ye were all so fair that are broken; and one more fair than
    ye all.

Why, by what power, for what reason, should the old
gods have passed away? Even if one could not believe
in them all, they were too beautiful to pass away and
be broken, as their statues were broken by the early
Christians in the rage of their ignorant and brutal zeal.
The triumph of Christianity meant much more than
the introduction of a new religion; it meant the destruction of priceless art and priceless literature, it
signified the victory of barbarism over culture and re-

finement. Doubtless the change, like all great changes, was for the better in some ways; but no lover of art and the refinements of civilisation can read without regret the history of the iconoclasm in which the Christian fanatics indulged when they got the government and the law upon their side. It is this feeling of regret and horror that the poet well expresses through the mouth of the Roman who cares no more to live, because the gods and everything beautiful must pass away. But there is one goddess still left for him, one whom the Christians cannot break but who will at last break them and their religion, and scatter them as dust—the goddess of death. To her he turns with a last prayer:

But I turn to her still, having seen she shall surely abide
    in the end;
Goddess and maiden and queen, be near me now and be-
    friend.
O daughter of earth, of my mother, her crown and blossom
    of birth,
I am also, I also, thy brother; I go as I came unto earth.

    .   .   .   .

Thou art more than the Gods who number the days of our
    temporal breath;
For these give labour and slumber, but thou, Proserpina,
    death.
Therefore now at thy feet I abide for a season in silence.
    I know
I shall die as my fathers died, and sleep as they sleep;
    even so.
For the glass of the years is brittle wherein we gaze for a
    span;
A little soul for a little bears up this corpse which is man.

Pre-Raphaelite and Other Poets

So long I endure, no longer; and laugh not again, neither
weep.
For there is no God found stronger than death; and death
is a sleep.

The third line from the end, "a little soul for a little,"
is a translation from the philosopher Epictetus. It is
the Epicurean philosophy especially which speaks in
this poetry. The address to the goddess of death as
the daughter of earth, cannot be understood without
some reference to Greek mythology. Proserpina was
the daughter of the goddess Ceres, whom the ancients
termed the Holy Mother—queen of the earth, but especially the goddess of fruitfulness and of harvests.
While playing in the fields as a young girl, Proserpina
was seized and carried away by the god of the dead,
Hades or Pluto, to become his wife. Everywhere her
mother sought after her to no purpose; and because of
the grief of the goddess, the earth dried up, the harvests
failed, and all nature became desolate. Afterwards,
finding that her daughter had become the queen of the
kingdom of the dead, Ceres agreed that Proserpina
should spend a part of every year with her husband,
and part of the year with her mother. To this arrangement the Greeks partly attributed the origin of the
seasons.

Incidentally in the poem there is a very beautiful
passage describing the world of death, where no sun
is, where the silence is more than music, where the
flowers are white and full of strange sleepy smell, and
where the sound of the speech of the dead is like the
sound of water heard far away, or a humming of bees

[160]

Studies in Swinburne

—whither the old man prays to go, to rest with his ancestors away from the light of the sun, and to forget all the sorrow of this world and its changes. But I think that you will do well to study this poem in detail by yourselves, when opportunity allows. It happens to be one of the very few poems in the first series of Swinburne's "Poems and Ballads" to which no reasonable exception can be made; and it is without doubt one of the very finest things that he has ever written. I could recommend this for translation; there are many pieces in the same book which I could not so recommend, notwithstanding their beauty. For instance, the poem entitled "Hesperia," with its splendid beginning:

Out of the golden remote wild west where the sea without
    shore is,
Full of the sunset, and sad, if at all, with the fulness of joy.

There is nothing more perfect in modern literature than the beginning of this poem, which gives us an exact imitation in English words of the sound of the Greek hexameter and pentameter. But much of this work is too passionate and violent for even the most indulgent ears; and though I think that you ought to study the beginning, I should never recommend it for translation.

The comparison of the wave in the hymn to Proserpina must have given you an idea of Swinburne's power to deal with colossal images. I know of few descriptions in any literature to be compared with that picture of the wave; but Swinburne himself in another poem has given us descriptions nearly as surprising, if not as beautiful. There is a poem called "Thalassius," a kind

[161]

of philosophical moral fable in Greek form, that contains a surprise of this kind. The subject is a young man's first experience with love. Walking in the meadows he sees a pretty boy, or rather child, just able to walk—a delicious child, tender as a flower, and apparently needing kindly care. So he takes the child by the hand, wondering at his beauty; and he speaks to the child, but never gets any reply except a smile. Suddenly, at a certain point of the road the child begins to grow tall, to grow tremendous; his stature reaches the sky, and in a terrible voice that shakes everything like an earthquake, he announces that though he may be Love, he is also Death, and that only the fool imagines him to be Love alone. There is a bit both of old and of new philosophy in this; and I remarked when reading it that in Indian mythology there is a similar representation of this double attribute of divinity, love and death, creation and destruction, represented by one personage. But we had better read the scene which I have been trying to describe, the meeting with the child:

That wellnigh wept for wonder that it smiled,
And was so feeble and fearful, with soft speech
The youth bespake him softly; but there fell
From the sweet lips no sweet word audible
That ear or thought might reach;
No sound to make the dim cold silence glad,
No breath to thaw the hard harsh air with heat,
Only the saddest smile of all things sweet,
Only the sweetest smile of all things sad.

And so they went together one green way
Till April dying made free the world for May;

And on his guide suddenly Love's face turned,
And in his blind eyes burned
Hard light and heat of laughter; and like flame
That opens in a mountain's ravening mouth
To blear and sear the sunlight from the south,
His mute mouth opened, and his first word came;
"Knowest thou me now by name?"
And all his stature waxed immeasurable,
As of one shadowing heaven and lightening hell;
And statelier stood he than a tower that stands
And darkens with its darkness far-off sands
Whereon the sky leans red;
And with a voice that stilled the winds he said:
"I am he that was thy lord before thy birth,
I am he that is thy lord till thou turn earth;
I make the night more dark, and all the morrow
Dark as the night whose darkness was my breath:
O fool, my name is sorrow;
Thou fool, my name is death."

By the term "darkness" in the third line from the end of the above quotation, we must understand the darkness and mystery out of which man comes into this world, and comes only to die. This monstrous symbolism may need some explanation, before you see how very fine the meaning is. Love, that is the attraction of sex to sex, with all its emotions, heroisms, sacrifices, and nobilities, cannot be understood by the young. To them, love is only the physical and the moral charm of the being that is loved. In man the passion of love becomes noble and specialised by the development in him of moral, æsthetic, and other feelings that are purely human. But the attraction of sex, that is behind all this, is a universal and terrible fact, a tremendous mystery, whose ultimate nature no man knows or ever will know. Why? Because if we knew the nature and origin of the forces that create, we could understand the whole universe, and ourselves, and everything that men now call mystery. But all that we certainly do know is this, that we come into the world out of mystery and go out of the world again back into mystery, and that no mortal man can explain the Whence, the Why, or the Whither. The first sensations of love for another being are perhaps the most delicious feelings known to men; the person loved seems for the time to be more beautiful and good than any one else in the world. This is what the poet means by describing the first appearance of love as a beautiful, tender child, innocent and dumb. But later in life the physical illusion passes away; then one learns the relation of this seeming romance to the awful questions of life and death. The girl beloved becomes the wife; then she becomes the mother; but in becoming a mother, she enters into the very shadow of death, sometimes never to return from it. Birth itself is an agony, the greatest agony that humanity has to bear. We come into the world through pains of the most deadly kind, and leave the world later on in pain; and what all this means, we do not know. We are only certain that the Greeks were not wrong in representing love as the brother of death. The Oriental philosophers went further; they identified love with death, making them one and the same. One cannot help thinking of the Indian statue representing the creative power, holding in his hand the symbol of life, but wearing around his neck a necklace of human skulls.

[164]

Studies in Swinburne

The poem that introduces the first volume of Swinburne's poems, as published in America, gave its name to the book, so that thousands of English readers used to call the volume by the name of this poem, "Laus Veneris," which means the praise of Venus. I do not think that there is a more characteristic poem in all Swinburne's work; it is certainly the most interesting version in any modern language of the old mediæval story. Without understanding the story you could not possibly understand the poem, and as the story has been famous for hundreds of years, I shall first relate it.

After Christianity had made laws forbidding people to worship the old gods, it was believed that these gods still remained wandering about like ghosts and tempting men to sin. One of these divinities especially dreaded by the Christian priests, was Venus. Now in the Middle Ages there was a strange story about a knight called Tannhäuser, who, riding home one evening, saw by the wayside a beautiful woman unclad, who smiled at him, and induced him to follow her. He followed her to the foot of a great mountain; the mountain opened like a door, and they went in, and found a splendid palace under the mountain. The fairy woman was Venus herself; and the knight lived with her for seven years. At the end of the seven years he became afraid because of the sin which he had committed; and he begged her, as Urashima begged the daughter of the Dragon King, to let him return for a little time to the world of men. She let him go; and he went to Rome. There he told his story to different priests, and asked them to obtain for him the forgiveness of God. But each of the priests made answer that the sin was so great that nobody except the Pope of Rome could forgive it. Then the knight went to the Pope. But when the Pope heard his confession, the Pope said that there was no forgiveness possible for such a crime as that of loving a demon. The Pope had a wooden staff in his hand, and he said, "Sooner shall this dry stick burst into blossom than you obtain God's pardon for such a sin." Then the knight, sorrowing greatly, went back to the mountain and to Venus. After he had gone, the Pope was astonished to see that the dry staff was covered with beautiful flowers and leaves that had suddenly grown out of it, as a sign that God was more merciful than his priests. At this the Pope became sorry and afraid, and he sent out messengers to look for the knight. But no man ever saw him again, for Venus kept him hidden in her palace under the mountain. Swinburne found his version of the story in a quaint French book published in 1530. He represents, not the incidents of the story itself, but only the feelings of the knight after his return from Rome. There is no more hope for him. His only consolation is his love and worship for her; but this love and worship is mingled with fear of hell and regret for his condition. Into the poem Swinburne has put the whole spirit of revolt of which he and the Pre-Raphaelite school were exponents. A few verses will show you the tone. The knight praises Venus:

> Lo, this is she that was the world's delight;
> The old grey years were parcels of her might;
>   The strewings of the ways wherein she trod
> Were the twain seasons of the day and night.

Studies in Swinburne

Lo, she was thus when her clear limbs enticed
All lips that now grow sad with kissing Christ,
   Stained with blood fallen from the feet of God,
The feet and hands whereat our souls were priced.

Alas, Lord, surely thou art great and fair.
But lo her wonderfully woven hair!
   And thou didst heal us with thy piteous kiss;
But see now, Lord; her mouth is lovelier.

She is right fair; what hath she done to thee?
Nay, fair Lord Christ, lift up thine eyes and see;
   Had now thy mother such a lip—like this?
Thou knowest how sweet a thing it is to me.

This calling upon God to admire Venus, this asking
Christ whether his mother was even half as beautiful
as Venus, was to religious people extremely shocking, of
course. And still more shocking seemed the confession
in the latter part of the poem that the knight does not
care whether he has sinned or not, since, after all, he
has been more fortunate than any other man. This
expression of exultation after remorse appeared to reverent minds diabolical, the thought of a new Satanic
School. But really the poet was doing his work excellently, so far as truth to nature was concerned; and
these criticisms were as ignorant as they were out of
place. The real fault of the poem was only a fault of
youth, a too great sensuousness in its descriptive passages. We might say that Swinburne himself was, during those years, very much in the position of the knight
Tannhäuser; he had gone back to the worship of the
old gods because they were more beautiful and more
joyous than the Christian gods; we may even say that

[167]

he never came back from the mountain of Venus. But all this poetry of the first series was experimental; it was an expression of the Renaissance feeling that visits the youth of every poet possessing a strong sense of beauty. Before the emotions can be fully corrected by the intellect, such poets are apt to offend the proprieties, and even to say things which the most liberal philosopher would have to condemn. It was at such a time that in another poem, "Dolores," Swinburne spoke of leaving

> The lilies and languors of virtue
> For the raptures and roses of vice,

—lines that immediately became famous. It was also at such a time that he uttered the prayer to a pagan ideal:

> Come down and redeem us from virtue.

But on the other hand, if all poets were to wait for the age of wisdom before they began to sing, we should miss a thousand beautiful things of which only youth is capable, wherefore it were best to forgive the eccentricities for the sake of the incomparable merits. For example, in the very poem from which these quotations have been made, we have such splendid verses as these, referring to the worship of Venus in the time of Nero:

> Dost thou dream, in a respite of slumber,
> In a lull of the fires of thy life,
> Of the days without name, without number,
> When thy will stung the world into strife;

Studies in Swinburne

When, a goddess, the pulse of thy passion
Smote kings as they revelled in Rome,
And they hailed thee re-risen, O Thalassian,
Foam-white, from the foam?

Thalassian means the sea-born, derived from the Greek
word Thalatta, the sea. Here Swinburne might be referring to the times of the Triumvirate, when Cleopatra succeeded in bewitching the great captain Cæsar
and the great captain Antony, and set the world fighting for her sake. Then we have a reference to the great
games in Rome, the splendour and the horror of the
amphitheatre:

On sands by the storm never shaken,
Nor wet from the washing of tides;
Nor by foam of the waves overtaken,
Nor winds that the thunder bestrides;
But red from the print of thy paces,
Made smooth for the world and its lords,
Ringed round with a flame of fair faces,
And splendid with swords.

The floor of the amphitheatre was covered with sand,
which absorbed the blood of the combatants. But you
will ask what had the games to do with the goddess?
All the Roman festivities of this kind were, to a certain
extent, considered as religious celebrations; they formed
parts of holiday ceremony.

There the gladiator, pale for thy pleasure,
Drew bitter and perilous breath;
There torments laid hold on the treasure
Of limbs too delicious for death;

[169]

Pre-Raphaelite and Other Poets

When thy gardens were lit with live torches;
  When the world was a steed for thy rein;
When the nations lay prone in thy porches,
  Our Lady of Pain.

When with flame all around him aspirant,
  Stood flushed, as a harp-player stands,
The implacable beautiful tyrant,
  Rose-crowned, having death in his hands;
And a sound as the sound of loud water
  Smote far through the flight of the fires,
And mixed with the lightning of slaughter
  A thunder of lyres.

The reference here in the third, fourth, and fifth lines of the first of the above stanzas is to the torture of the Christians by Nero in the amphitheatre. By "limbs too delicious for death" the poet refers to the torture of young girls. The "live torches" refers to Nero's cruelty in having hundreds of Christians wrapped about with combustible material, tied to lofty poles, and set on fire, to serve as torches during a great festival which he gave in the gardens of his palace. The second stanza represents him as the destroyer of Rome. It is said that he secretly had the city set on fire in a dozen different places, in order that he might be thereby enabled to imagine the scene of the burning of Troy, as described by Homer. He wanted to write a poem about it; and it is said that while the city was burning, he watched it from a high place, at the same time composing and singing a poem on the spectacle. The "flight of fires" refers of course to the spreading of fire through Rome. The "lightning of slaughter" means the flashing of swords in the work of killing, and is explained by the legend that Nero sent soldiers to kill anybody who tried to put out the fire. Anything was possible in the times of which Swinburne sings; for the world was then governed by emperors who were not simply wicked but mad. But what I wish to point out is that while a poet can write verses so splendid in sound and colour as those that I have quoted, even such a composition as "Dolores" must be preserved, with all its good and bad, among the treasures of English verse.

In spite of his radicalism in the matter of religion and of ethics, the Bible has had no more devoted student than Swinburne; he has not only appreciated all the beauties of its imagery and the strength of its wonderful English, but he has used for the subjects of not a few of his pieces, and his more daring pieces, Biblical subjects. The extraordinary composition "Aholibah" was inspired by a study of Ezekiel; unfortunately this is one of the pieces especially inappropriate to the classroom. "A Litany" will suit our purpose better. It consists of a number of Biblical prophecies, from Isaiah and other books of the Old Testament, arranged into a kind of dramatic chorus. God is made the chief speaker, and he is answered by his people. This is a kind of imitation of a certain part of the old church-service, in which one band of singers answers another, such singing being called "antiphonal," and the different parts, "antiphones." There is very little English verse written in the measure which Swinburne has adopted for this study, and I hope that you will notice the peculiar rhythmic force of the stanzas. We need quote only a few.

All the bright lights of heaven
I will make dark over thee;
One night shall be as seven
That its skirts may cover thee;
I will send on thy strong men a sword,
On thy remnant a rod:
Ye shall know that I am the Lord,
Saith the Lord God.

And the people answer:

All the bright lights of heaven
Thou hast made dark over us;
One night has been as seven,
That its skirt might cover us;
Thou hast sent on our strong men a sword,
On our remnant a rod;
We know that thou art the Lord,
O Lord our God.

But this submission is not enough; for the Lord replies:

As the tresses and wings of the wind
Are scattered and shaken,
I will scatter all them that have sinned,
There shall none be taken;
As a sower that scattereth seed,
So will I scatter them;
As one breaketh and shattereth a reed,
I will break and shatter them.

The antiphone is:

As the wings and the locks of the wind
Are scattered and shaken,
Thou hast scattered all them that have sinned;
There was no man taken;

[172]

Studies in Swinburne

As a sower that scattereth seed,
So hast thou scattered us;
As one breaketh and shattereth a reed,
Thou hast broken and shattered us.

Observe that, simple as this versification looks, there is nothing more difficult. With the simplest possible words, the greatest possible amount of sound and force is here obtained. There are many other stanzas, and a noteworthy fact is that very few words of Latin origin are used. Most of the words are Anglo-Saxon; perhaps that is why the language is so sonorous and strong. But when the poet does use a word of Latin origin, the result is simply splendid:

Ye whom your lords loved well,
    Putting silver and gold on you,
The inevitable hell
    Shall surely take hold on you;
Your gold shall be for a token,
    Your staff for a rod;
With the breaking of bands ye are broken,
    Saith the Lord God.

The use of the Latin adjective "inevitable" here gives an extraordinary effect, the main accent of the line coming on the second syllable of the word. But, as if to show his power, in the antiphonal response the poet does not repeat this effect, but goes back to the simple Anglo-Saxon with astonishing success:

We whom the world loved well,
    Laying silver and gold on us,
The kingdom of death and of hell
    Riseth up to take hold on us;

[173]

Pre-Raphaelite and Other Poets

> Our gold is turned to a token,
>   Our staff to a rod;
> Yet shalt thou bind them up that were broken,
>   O Lord our God.

Here the substitution of these much simpler words gives nearly as fine an effect of sound and a grander effect of sense because of the grim power of the words themselves.

Besides studies in Biblical English, the poet has made a number of studies in the Old Anglo-Saxon poets, most of whom were religious men who liked sad and terrible subjects. In the poem entitled "After Death" we have an example of this Anglo-Saxon feeling combined with the plain strength of a later form of language, chiefly Middle English, with here and there a very quaint use of grammar. It was common in Anglo-Saxon poetry to depict the horrors of the grave. Here we have a dead man talking to his own coffin, and the coffin answers him horribly:

> The four boards of the coffin lid
> Heard all the dead man did.
>
> .   .   .   .
>
> "I had fair coins red and white,
> And my name was as great light;
>
> "I had fair clothes green and red,
> And strong gold bound round my head.
>
> "But no meat comes in my mouth,
> Now I fare as the worm doth;
>
> "And no gold binds in my hair,
> Now I fare as the blind fare.

Studies in Swinburne

"My live thews were of great strength,
Now am I waxen a span's length;

"My live sides were full of lust,
Now are they dried with dust."

The first board spake and said:
"Is it best eating flesh or bread?"

The second answered it:
"Is wine or honey the more sweet?"

The third board spake and said:
"Is red gold worth a girl's gold head?"

The fourth made answer thus:
"All these things are as one with us."

The dead man asked of them:
"Is the green land stained brown with flame?

"Have they hewn my son for beasts to eat,
And my wife's body for beasts' meat?

"Have they boiled my maid in a brass pan,
And built a gallows to hang my man?"

The boards said to him:
"This is a lewd thing that ye deem.

"Your wife has gotten a golden bed;
All the sheets are sewn with red.

"Your son has gotten a coat of silk,
The sleeves are soft as curded milk.

"Your maid has gotten a kirtle new,
All the skirt has braids of blue.

[175]

Pre-Raphaelite and Other Poets

"Your man has gotten both ring and glove,
Wrought well for eyes to love."

The dead man answered thus:
"What good gift shall God give us?"

The boards answered anon:
"Flesh to feed hell's worm upon."

I doubt very much whether a more terrible effect could
be produced by any change of language. The poem is
an excellent illustration of the force of the Old English,
without admixture of any sort. Do not think that this
is simple and easy work; perhaps no other living man
could have done it equally well. It is not only in these
simple forms, however, that Swinburne shows us the
results of his Old English studies. Two of the most
celebrated among his early poems, "The Triumph of
Time" and the poem on the swallow, "Itylus," are imi-
tations of very old forms of English verse, though the
language is luxurious and new. I have already given
you a quotation from the former poem, describing the
poet's love of the sea. I now cite a single stanza of
"Itylus."

Swallow, my sister, O sister swallow,
How can thine heart be full of the spring?
A thousand summers are over and dead.
What hast thou found in the spring to follow?
What hast thou found in thine heart to sing?
What wilt thou do when the summer is shed?

Probably Swinburne found this measure in early Middle
English poetry; it was used by the old poet Hampole in
his "Prick of Conscience." After it had been forgotten

[176]

Studies in Swinburne

for five hundred years, Swinburne brought it to life again. Something very close to it forms the splendid and beautiful chorus of "Atalanta in Calydon":

> When the hounds of spring are on winter's traces,
>   The mother of months in meadow or plain
> Fills the shadows and windy places
>   With lisp of leaves and ripple of rain;
> And the brown bright nightingale amorous
>   Is half assuaged for Itylus,
> For the Thracian ships and the foreign faces,
>   The tongueless vigil, and all the pain.

Here as in all other cases, however, the poet has far surpassed his model. The measures which he revived take new life only because of the extraordinary charm which he has put into them.

Passing suddenly from these lighter structures, let us observe the great power which Swinburne manifests in another kind of revival, the sixteen syllable line. This is not a modern measure at all. It was used long ago, but was practically abandoned and almost forgotten except by scholars when Swinburne revived it. Nor has he revived it only in one shape, but in a great many shapes, sometimes using single lines, sometimes double, or again varying the accent so as to make four or five different kinds of verse with the same number of syllables. The poem "The Armada" is a rich example of this re-animation and variation of the long dead form. In this poem Swinburne describes the god of Spain as opposed to the god of England, and the most forceful lines are those devoted to these conceptions. Observe the double rhymes.

Pre-Raphaelite and Other Poets

Ay, but *we* that the wind and *sea* gird round with shelter
of storms and *waves,*
Know not *him* that ye worship, *grim* as dreams that quicken
from dead men's *graves:*
God is *one* with the sea, the *sun,* the land that nursed us,
the love that *saves.*

Love whose *heart* is in ours, and *part* of all things noble
and all things *fair;*
Sweet and *free* as the circling *sea,* sublime and kind as the
fostering *air;*
Pure of *shame* as is England's *name,* whose crowns to come
are as crowns that *were.*

Now we have, quite easily, a change in the measure.
We have sixteen syllables still, but the whole music is
changed.

But the Lord of darkness, the God whose love is a flaming
fire,
The master whose mercy fulfils wide hell till its torturers
tire,
He shall surely have heed of his servants who serve him
for love, not hire.

The double rhymes are not used here. Later on, after
the English victory and the storm, they are used again,
for the purpose of additional force. The address is to
the Spaniards and to their gods.

Lords of *night,* who would breathe your *blight* on April's
morning and August's *noon,*
God your *Lord,* the condemned, the *abhorred,* sinks hell-
ward, smitten with deathlike *swoon,*
Death's own *dart* in his hateful *heart* now thrills, and night
shall receive him *soon.*

[178]

Studies in Swinburne

God the *Devil*, thy reign of *revel* is here forever eclipsed
and *fled;*
God the *Liar*, everlasting *fire* lays hold at last on thee, hand
and *head*.

Page after page of constantly varying measures of this
kind will be found in the poem—a poem which notwithstanding its strong violence at times, represents the
power of the verse-maker better than almost any other
single piece in the work of his later years.

From what extracts we have already made, I think
you will see enough of the value and beauty of Swinburne's diction to take in it such interest as it really
deserves. We might continue the study of this author
for a much longer time. But the year is waning, the
third term, which is very short, will soon be upon us;
and I wish to turn with you next week to the study of
Browning.

CHAPTER IV

ROBERT BROWNING very much reminds us in some respects of the American thinker, Emerson. The main doctrine of Emerson is Individualism; and this happens also to be the main doctrine of Browning. By Individualism, Emerson and Browning mean self-cultivation. Both thought that the highest possible duty of every man was to develop the best powers of his mind and body to the utmost possible degree. Make yourself strong—that is the teaching. You are only a man, not a god; therefore it is very likely that you will do many things which are very wrong or very foolish. But whatever you do, even if it be wrong, do it well— do it with all your strength. Even a strong sin may be better than a cowardly virtue. Weakness is of all things the worst. When we do wrong, experience soon teaches us our mistake. And the stronger the mistake has been, the more quickly will the experience come which corrects and purifies. Now you understand what I mean by Individualism—the cultivation by untiring exercise of all our best faculties, and especially of the force and courage to act.

This Individualism in Emerson was founded upon a vague Unitarian pantheism. The same fact is true of

Studies in Browning

Browning's system. According to both thinkers, all of us are parts of one infinite life, and it is by cultivating our powers that we can best serve the purpose of the Infinite Mind. Leaving out the words "mind" and "purpose," which are anthropomorphisms, this doctrine accords fairly well with evolutional philosophy; and both writers were, to a certain degree, evolutionists. But neither yielded much to the melancholy of nineteenth century doubt. Both were optimists. We may say that Browning's philosophy is an optimistic pantheism, inculcating effort as the very first and highest duty of life. But Browning is not especially a philosophical poet. We find his philosophy flashing out only at long intervals. Knowing this, we know what he is likely to think under certain circumstances; but his mission was of another special kind.

His message to the world was that of an interpreter of life. His art is, from first to last, a faithful reflection of human nature, the human nature of hundreds of different characters, good and bad, but in a large proportion of cases, decidedly bad. Why? Because, as a great artist, Browning understood very well that you can draw quite as good a moral from bad actions as from good ones, and his unconscious purpose is always moral. Such art of picturing character, to be really great, must be dramatic; and all of Browning's work is dramatic. He does not say to us, "This man has such and such a character"; he makes the man himself act and speak so as to show his nature. The second fact, therefore, to remember about Browning is that artistically he is a dramatic poet, whose subject is human nature. No other English poet so closely

[181]

resembled Shakespeare in this kind of representation as Browning.

There is one more remarkable fact about the poet. He always, or nearly always, writes in the first person. Every one of his poems, with few exceptions, is a soliloquy. It is not he who speaks, of course; it is the "I" of some other person's soul. This kind of literary form is called "monologue." Even the enormous poem of "The Ring and the Book" is nothing but a gigantic collection of monologues, grouped and ordered so as to produce one great dramatic effect.

In the case of Browning, I shall not attempt much illustration by way of texts, because a great deal of Browning's form could be not only of no use to you, but would even be mischievous in its influence upon your use of language. In Browning every rule of rhetoric, of arrangement, is likely to be broken. The adjective is separated by vast distances from the noun; the preposition is tumbled after the word to which it refers; the verb is found at the end of a sentence of which it should have been the first word. When Carlyle first read the poem called "Sordello," he said that he could not tell whether "Sordello" was a man or a town or a book. And the obscurity of "Sordello" is in some places so atrocious that I do not think anybody in the world can unravel it. Now, most of Browning's long poems are written in this amazing style. The text is, therefore, not a good subject for literary study. But it is an admirable subject for psychological study, emotional study, dramatic study, and sometimes for philosophic study. Instead of giving extracts, therefore, from very long poems, I shall give only a summary of

[182]

the meaning of the poem itself. If such summary should tempt you to the terrible labour of studying the original, I am sure that you would be very tired, but after the weariness, you would be very much surprised and pleased.

Providing, of course, that you would understand; and I very much doubt whether you could understand. I doubt because I cannot always understand it myself, no matter how hard I try.

One reason is the suppression of words. Browning leaves out all the articles, prepositions, and verbs that he can. I met some years ago a Japanese scholar who had mastered almost every difficulty of the English language except the articles and prepositions; he had never been abroad long enough to acquire the habit of using them properly. But it was his business to write many letters upon technical subjects, and these letters were always perfectly correct, except for the extraordinary fact that they contained no articles and very few prepositions. Much of Browning's poetry reads just in that way. You cannot say that there is anything wrong; but too much is left to the imagination. Therefore he has been spoken of as writing in telegraph language.

Not to make Browning too formidable at first, let us begin with a few of his lighter studies, in very simple verse. I will take as the first example the poem called "A Light Woman." This is a polite word for courtesan, "light" referring to the moral character. The story, told in monologue, is the most ordinary story imaginable. It happens in every great city of the world almost every day, among that class of young men who

play with fire. But there are two classes among these,
the strong and the weak. The strong take life as half
a joke, a very pleasant thing, and pass through many
dangers unscathed simply because they know that what
they are doing is foolish; they never consider it in a
serious way. The other class of young men take life
seriously. They are foolish rather through affection
and pity than through anything else. They want a
woman's love, and they foolishly ask it from women who
cannot love at all—not, at least, in ninety cases
out of a hundred. They get what seems to them affection, however, and this deludes them. Then they become bewitched; and the result is much sorrow, perhaps
ruin, perhaps crime, perhaps suicide. In Browning's
poem we have a representative of each type. A strong
man, strong in character, has a young friend who has
been fascinated by a woman of a dangerous class. He
says to himself, "My friend will be ruined; he is bewitched; it is no use to talk to him. I will save him
by taking that woman away from him. I know the
kind of man that she would like; she would like such a
man as I." And the rest of the cruel story is told in
Browning's verses too well to need further explanation.

> So far as our story approaches the end,
>   Which do you pity the most of us three?—
> My friend, or the mistress of my friend
>   With her wanton eyes, or me?
>
> My friend was already too good to lose,
>   And seemed in the way of improvement yet,
> When she crossed his path with her hunting-noose,
>   And over him drew her net.

Studies in Browning

When I saw him tangled in her toils,
  A shame, said I, if she adds just him
To her nine-and-ninety other spoils,
  The hundredth for a whim!

And before my friend be wholly hers,
  How easy to prove to him, I said,
An eagle's the game her pride prefers,
  Though she snaps at a wren instead!

So I gave her eyes my own eyes to take,
  My hand sought hers as in earnest need,
And round she turned for my noble sake,
  And gave me herself indeed.

The eagle am I, with my fame in the world,
  The wren is he, with his maiden face.
You look away, and your lip is curled?
  Patience, a moment's space!

For see, my friend goes shaking and white;
  He eyes me as the basilisk:
I have turned, it appears, his day to night,
  Eclipsing his sun's disk.

And I did it, he thinks, as a very thief:
  "Though I love her—that, he comprehends—
One should master one's passions (love, in chief),
  And be loyal to one's friends!"

And she—she lies in my hand as tame
  As a pear late basking over a wall;
Just a touch to try, and off it came;
  'Tis mine,—can I let it fall?

With no mind to eat it, that's the worst!
   Were it thrown in the road, would the case assist?
'Twas quenching a dozen blue-flies' thirst
   When I gave its stalk a twist.

And I,—what I seem to my friend, you see:
   What I soon shall seem to his love, you guess:
What I seem to myself, do you ask of me?
   No hero, I confess.

'Tis an awkward thing to play with souls,
   And matter enough to save one's own:
Yet think of my friend, and the burning coals
   He played with for bits of stone!

One likes to show the truth for the truth;
   That the woman was light is very true:
But suppose she says,—Never mind that youth!
   What wrong have I done to you?

Well, anyhow, here the story stays,
   So far at least as I understand;
And, Robert Browning, you writer of plays,
   Here's a subject made to your hand!

Now let us see how much there is to study in this simple-seeming poem. It will give us an easy and an excellent example of the way in which Browning must be read; and it will require at least an hour's chat to explain properly. For, really, Browning never writes simply.

Here we have a monologue. It is uttered to the poet by a young man with whom he has been passing an hour in conversation. We can guess from the story something about the young man; we can almost see

[186]

him. We know that he must be handsome, tall, graceful, and strong; and full of that formidable coolness which the sense of great strength gives—great strength of mind and will rather than of body, but probably both. Let us hear him talk. "You see that friend of mine over there?" he says to the poet. "He hates me now. When he looks at me his lips turn white. I can't say that he is wrong to hate me, but really I wanted to do him a service. He got fascinated by that woman of whom I was speaking; she was playing with him as a cat plays with a mouse or with a bird before killing it. Well, I thought to myself that my friend was in great danger, and that it was better for me to try to save him. You see, he is not the kind of man that a woman of that class could fancy; he is too small, too feeble, too gentle; they like strong men only, men they are afraid of. So, just for my friend's sake, I made love to her one day, and she left him immediately and came to me. I have to take care of her now, and I do not like the trouble at all. I never cared about the woman herself; she is not the kind of woman that I admire; I did all this only to save my friend. And my friend does not understand. He thinks that I took the woman from him because I was in love with her; he thinks it quite natural that I should love her (which I don't); but he says that even in love a man ought to be true to his friends."

At this point of the story the young man sees that the poet is disgusted by what he has heard, but this does not embarrass him; he is too strong a character to be embarrassed at all, and he resumes: "Don't be impatient—I want to tell you the whole thing. You

[187]

see, I have destroyed all the happiness of my friend merely through my desire to do him a service. He hates me, and he does not understand. He thinks that I was moved by lust; and everybody else thinks the same thing. Of course it is not true. But now there is another trouble. The woman does not understand. She thinks that I was really in love with her; and I must get rid of her as soon as I can. If I tell her that I made love to her only in order to save my friend, she will say, 'What had that to do with your treatment of me? I did not do you any harm; why should you have amused yourself by trying to injure and to deceive me?' If she says that, I don't know how I shall be able to answer. So it seems that I have made a serious mistake; I have lost my friend, I have wantonly wronged a woman whose only fault toward me was to love me, and I have made for myself a bad reputation in society. People cannot understand the truth of the thing."

This is the language of the man, and he perhaps thinks that he is telling the truth. But is he telling the truth? Does any man in this world ever tell the exact truth about himself? Probably not. No man really understands himself so well as to be able to tell the exact truth about himself. It is possible that this man believes himself to be speaking truthfully, but he is certainly telling a lie, a half-truth only. We have his exact words, but the exact language of the speaker in any one of Browning's monologues does not tell the truth; it only suggests the truth. We must find out the real character of the person, and the real facts of the case, from our own experience of human nature.

And to understand the real meaning behind this man's words, you must ask yourselves whether you would believe such a story if it were told to you in exactly the same way by some one whom you know. I shall answer for you that you certainly would not.

And now we come to the real meaning. The young man saw his friend desperately in love with a woman who did not love that friend. The woman was beautiful. Looking at her, he thought to himself, "How easily I could take her away from my friend!" Then he thought to himself that not only would this be a cause of enmity between himself and his friend, but such an action would be severely judged by all his acquaintances. Could he be justified? When a man wishes to do what is wrong, he can nearly always invent a moral reason for doing it. So this young man finds a moral reason. He says, "My friend is in danger; therefore I will sacrifice myself for him. It will be quite gratifying both to my pride and to my pleasure to take that woman from him; then I shall tell everybody why I did it. My friend would like to kill me, of course, but he is too weak to avenge himself." He follows this course, and really tries to persuade himself that he is justified in following it. When he says that he did not care for the woman, he only means that he is now tired of her. He has indulged his lust and his vanity by the most treacherous and brutal conduct; yet he tries to tell the world that he is a moral man, a martyr, a calumniated person. Such is the real meaning of his apology.

Nevertheless we cannot altogether dislike this young man. He is selfish and proud and not quite truthful, but these are faults of youth. On the other hand we can feel that he is very gifted, very intelligent, and very brave, and, what is still better, that he is ashamed of himself. He has done wrong, and the very fact that he lies about what he has done shows us that he is ashamed. He is not all bad. If he does not tell us the whole truth, he tells a great deal of it; and we feel that as he becomes older he will become better. He has abused his power, and he feels sorry for having abused it; some day he will probably become a very fine man. We feel this; and, curiously, we like him better than we like the man whom he has wronged. We like him because of his force; we despise the other man because of his weakness. It would be a mistake to do this if we did not feel that the man who has done wrong is really the better man of the two. What he has done is not at all to be excused, but we believe that he will redeem his fault later on. This type is an English or American type—perhaps it might be a German type. There is nothing Latin about it. Its faults are of the Northern race.

But now let us take an unredeemable type, the purely bad, the hopelessly wicked, a type not of the North this time, but purely Latin. As the Latin races have been civilised for a very much longer time than the Northern races, they have higher capacities in certain directions. They are physically and emotionally much more attractive to us. The beauty of an Italian or French or Spanish woman is incomparably more delicate, more exquisite, than the beauty of the Northern women. The social intelligence of the Italian or Spaniard or Frenchman is something immeasurably superior to the same capacity in the Englishman, the Scandinavian, or the German. The Latins have much less moral stamina, but imaginatively, æsthetically, emotionally, they have centuries of superiority. The Northern races were savages when these were lords of the world. But the vices of civilisation are likely to be developed in them to a degree impossible to the Northern character. If their good qualities are older and finer than ours, so their bad qualities will be older and stronger and deeper. At no time was the worst side of man more terribly shown than during the Renaissance. Here is an illustration. We know that for this man there is no hope; the evil predominates in his nature to such an extent that we can see nothing at all of the good except his fine sense of beauty. And even this sense becomes a curse to him.

MY LAST DUCHESS

That's my last Duchess painted on the wall,
Looking as if she were alive. I call
That piece a wonder, now: Frà Pandolf's hands
Worked busily a day, and there she stands.
Will't please you sit and look at her? I said
"Frà Pandolf" by design, for never read
Strangers like you that pictured countenance,
The depth and passion of its earnest glance,
But to myself they turned (since none puts by
The curtain I have drawn for you, but I)
And seemed as they would ask me, if they durst,
How such a glance came there; so, not the first
Are you to turn and ask thus.

Let us paraphrase the above. It is a duke of Ferrara who speaks. The person to whom he is speaking is a marriage-maker, a *nakodo* employed by the prince of a neighbouring state. For the duke wishes to marry the daughter of that prince. When the match-maker comes, the duke draws a curtain from a part of the wall of the room in which the two men meet, and shows him, painted upon the wall, the picture of a wonderfully beautiful woman. Then the duke says to the messenger: "That is a picture of my last wife. It is a beautiful picture, is it not? Well, it was painted by that wonderful monk, Frà Pandolf. I mention his name on purpose, because everybody who sees that picture for the first time wants to know why it is so beautiful, and would ask me questions if they were not afraid. I have shown it to several other people; but nobody, except myself, dares draw the curtain that covers it. Yes, Frà Pandolf painted it all in one day; and the expression of the smiling face still makes everybody wonder. You wonder; you want to know why that woman looks so charming, so bewitching in the picture."

Now listen to the explanation. It is worthy of the greatest of the villains of Shakespeare:

> Sir, 'twas not
> Her husband's presence only, called that spot
> Of joy into the Duchess' cheek: perhaps‘
> Frà Pandolf chanced to say, "Her mantle laps
> Over my lady's wrist too much," or, "Paint
> Must never hope to reproduce the faint
> Half-flush that dies along her throat:" such stuff
> Was courtesy, she thought, and cause enough
> For calling up that spot of joy. She had
> A heart—how shall I say?—too soon made glad,

Studies in Browning

Too easily impressed: she liked whate'er
She looked on, and her looks went everywhere.
Sir, 'twas all one! My favour at her breast,
The dropping of the daylight in the West,
The bough of cherries some officious fool
Broke in the orchard for her, the white mule
She rode with round the terrace—all and each
Would draw from her alike the approving speech,
Or blush, at least. She thanked men,—good! but thanked
Somehow—I know not how—as if she ranked
My gift of a nine-hundred-years-old name
With anybody's gift.

The explanation at least shows us the sweet and childish character of the woman, which the speaker tries to
describe as folly: "It was not her gladness at seeing
me, her husband, that made her smile so beautifully,
that brought the rosy dimple to her cheek. Probably
the painter said something to flatter her, and she smiled
at him. She was ready to smile at anything, at anybody, she was altogether too easily pleased; she liked
everything and everybody that she saw, and she took a
pleasure in looking at everything and at everybody.
Nothing made any difference to her. She would smile
at the jewel which I gave her, but she would also smile
at the sunset, at a bunch of cherries, at her mule, at
anything or anybody. Any matter would bring the
dimple to her cheek, or the blush of joy. I do not
blame her for thanking people, but she had a way of
thanking people that seemed to show that she was just
as much pleased by what a stranger did for her, as by
the fact that she had become the wife of a man like myself, head of a family nine hundred years old." Notice

[193]

how the speaker calls the man who gave his wife a bough
with cherries upon it "an officious fool." We can begin
to perceive what was the matter. He was insanely jealous of her, without any cause; and she, poor little soul!
did not know anything about it. She was too innocent
to know. The duke does not want anybody else to
know, either; he is trying to give quite a different explanation of what happened:

> Who'd stoop to blame
> This sort of trifling? Even had you skill
> In speech—(which I have not)—to make your will
> Quite clear to such an one, and say, "Just this
> Or that in you disgusts me; here you miss,
> Or there exceed the mark"—and if she let
> Herself be lessoned so, nor plainly set
> Her wits to yours, forsooth, and made excuse,
> —E'en then would be some stooping; and I choose
> Never to stoop. Oh sir, she smiled, no doubt,
> Whene'er I passed her; but who passed without
> Much the same smile?

This means, "A man like me cannot afford to degrade
himself by showing what he feels under such circumstances; a man like me cannot say to a woman, 'I am
greatly vexed and pained when I see you smile at any
one except myself.' If I were to speak to her about
the matter at all, she might think I was jealous. Of
course she would insult me by making excuses, by saying
that she did not know, which would be nothing less than
daring to oppose her judgment to mine. To speak
about my feelings in any case would require a skill in
the use of language such as only poets or such vulgar
people possess. I am a prince, not a poet, and I shall

[194]

Studies in Browning

never disgrace myself by telling anybody, especially
a woman, that I do not like this or I do not like that.
So I said nothing. Perhaps you think that she did
not smile when she saw me. That would be a mistake;
she always smiled when I passed. But she smiled at
everybody else in exactly the same way." He found
the smile unbearable at last, and the poet lets him tell
us the rest in a very few words:

> This grew; I gave commands;
> Then all smiles stopped together.

In other words, he caused her to be killed; told somebody to cut her throat, probably, or to give her a drink
of poison, all without having ever allowed her to know
how or why he had been displeased with her. And he
is not a bit sorry. No, looking at the dead woman's
picture, in company with the marriage-maker, he coolly
expresses his admiration for it as a word of realistic art
—as much as to say, "You can see for yourself how
beautiful she was; but that did not prevent me from
killing her." Listen to his atrocious chatter:

> There she stands
> As if alive. Will't please you rise? We'll meet
> The company below, then. I repeat,
> The Count your master's known munificence
> Is ample warrant that no just pretence
> Of mine for dowry will be disallowed;
> Though his fair daughter's self, as I avowed
> At starting, is my object. Nay, we'll go
> Together down, sir. . . . Notice Neptune, though,
> Taming a sea-horse, thought a rarity,
> Which Claus of Innsbruck cast in bronze for me!

Evidently both had seated themselves in front of the picture The count says, "Now she is as if alive; and we shall go downstairs together. As for the matter of the new marriage, you can tell your master that I am quite sure so generous a man will not make any objection to my just demands for a dowry—though, of course, it is his daughter that I principally want." Here the messenger bows, to allow the duke to go first downstairs. He answers: "No, we can go down together this time." On the way, probably at a turn of the grand staircase, the count points to a fine bronze statue representing the god of the sea, and asks the man to admire it. That is all.

This is a Renaissance character, and a very terrible one But it is also very complicated. We must think a little before we can even guess the whole range and depth of this man's wickedness. Even then we can only guess, because he lets us know only so much about him as he wishes us to know. Every word that he says is carefully measured in its pride, in its falsehood, in its cruelty, in its cunning. Just this much he tells us: "I had a beautiful wife, but you must not think that I can be influenced by beauty. Look at the picture of her. You would worship a woman like that. But I cut her throat. Why did I do it? Just because I did not like her way of smiling; she was too tender-hearted to love. And I would do the same thing to-morrow to any one who displeased me. Some people will think that I am jealous; let them think so. But you had better tell the girl who now expects to become my wife what kind of person I am."

[196]

Studies in Browning

How much of this is the truth? Probably more than half. Undoubtedly the man was jealous, and he wishes to deceive us in regard to the whole extent of that jealousy. He has no shame or remorse for crime, but he has shame of appearing to be weak. Jealousy is a weakness; therefore he does not like to be suspected of being weak in that way. He gives a strong suggestion that he must not have future cause for jealousy—nothing more. But the fact that he most wishes to have understood is that his wife must be a wicked woman, a vulture among vultures. He does not want a dove. And he hated his first wife much more because she was good and gentle and loving, than because she smiled at other people. You may ask, why should he hate a woman for being good? The answer is simple. In the courts of such princes as the Borgias, a good woman could only do mischief. She could not be used for cunning and wicked purposes. She would have refused to poison a guest, or to entice a man to make love to her only in order to get that man killed; and as you will discover if you read the terrible history of the Italian republics, all these things had to be done. Morality was a hindrance to such men. Power remained only to cunning and strength; all kind-heartedness was regarded as criminal weakness. When you have become familiar with the real history of Ferrara, you will perceive the terrible truth of this poem.

The most unpleasant fact still remains to be noticed. The wickedness of this man is not a wickedness of ignorance. It is a wickedness of highly cultivated intelligence. The man is an artist, a judge of beauty, a con-

[197]

noisseur. To suppose that cultivation makes a naturally wicked man better is a great educational mistake, as Herbert Spencer showed long ago. Education does not make a man more moral; it may give him power to be more immoral. Italian history furnishes us with the most extraordinary illustrations of this fact. Some of the wickedest of the Italian princes were great poets, great artists, great scholars, and great patrons of learning. Among the monsters, we have, for example, the terrible Malatesta of Rimini, whose life was given to us some years ago by the French antiquarian Yriarte. He wrote the most delicate and tender poetry, and he committed crimes so terrible that they cannot be named When he laid his hand, however lightly, upon a horse, the animal began to tremble from head to foot. Yet he could love, and be the most devoted of gallants. Again, you know the case of Benvenuto Cellini, a splendid artist and an atrocious murderer, who actually tells us the pleasure that he felt in killing. And there were the Borgias, all of them, father, daughter, and brothers, who committed every crime and never knew remorse, yet who were beautiful and gifted lovers of art and poetry. So in this case Browning is true to life when he shows us the duke pointing out the beauty of pictures and statues, even in the same moment that he is uttering horrors. There is a strange mixture of the extremes of the bad and of the good in the higher types of the Italian race—a mingling that gives us much to think about in regard to moral problems. Probably that is why a very large number of Browning's studies are of the dark side of Italian character.

Now we can take a lighter subject. It is not black,

it is only gloomy, and the interest of it will chiefly be found in the extraordinary moral comment made by Browning. This is one of the few studies which is not all written in the first person. It is called "The Statue and the Bust." It is a tale or tradition of Florence.

The legend is that a certain duke of Florence, by name Ferdinand, attempted to captivate the young bride of a Florentine nobleman named Riccardi. But Riccardi, a very keen man, observed what was going on; and he said to his wife very quietly and firmly, "This is your room in my house; you shall stay in this room and never leave it during the rest of your life, never leave it until you are carried to the graveyard." So she had to live in that room. But the duke, who was a very handsome man, got a splendid bronze statue of himself on horseback erected in the public street opposite the window of the lady's room, so that she could always look at him. Then she had a bust of herself made and placed above the window, so that the duke could see the bust whenever he rode by. That is all the story —but not all the story as Browning tells it. Browning tells us the secret thoughts and feelings of the imprisoned wife and of the duke. At first the two intended to run away together. It would have been an easy matter. The woman would only have had to dress herself like a boy, and drop from the window, and get help from the duke to reach his palace. The duke thought to himself, "I can get this woman whenever I wish; but it will be better to wait a little while; then we can manage to live as we please without making too much trouble." So they both waited till they became old. Then the woman called an artist and said:

[199]

"Make me a face on the window there,
Waiting as ever, mute the while,
My love pass below in the square!

"And let me think that it may beguile
Dreary days which the dead must spend
Down in their darkness under the aisle,

"To say, 'What matters it at the end?
I did no more while my heart was warm
Than does that image, my pale-faced friend.' "

She thinks to console herself a moment by saying,
"What is life worth? When I was young and beautiful and impulsive, I did no more harm or good, no more
right or wrong, than the bust that resembles me. It
is a comfort to think that I did nothing wrong." But
is that enough?

"Where is the use of the lip's red charm,
The heaven of hair, the pride of the brow,
And the blood that blues the inside arm—

"Unless we turn, as the soul knows how,
The earthly gift to an end divine?
A lady of clay is as good, I trow."

Somehow or other she feels that it is no consolation not
to have done wrong. She wonders what was the use
of being so beautiful, if she could not make use of that
beauty. The bust itself lived just as much as she did.
And all this is true; but she is nearer to living than
the duke. What does he say?

"Set me on horseback here aloft,
Alive, as the crafty sculptor can,

Studies in Browning

"In the very square I have crossed so oft:
That men may admire, when future suns
Shall touch the eyes to a purpose soft,

"While the mouth and the brow stay brave in bronze—
Admire and say, 'When he was alive
How he would take his pleasure once!' "

Nothing else; he only wants to be admired after his death, to have people say, looking at his statue, "What a splendid looking man he must have been, how the women must have loved him!" And they both died, and were buried in the church near where they lived; and the English poet Browning went to that church, and heard the story, and thought about it, and gives us the moral of it. It is a startling moral and needs explanation. I think you will be shocked when you first hear it, but you will not be shocked if you think about it. The following verses are the poet's own reflections:

So! While these wait the trump of doom,
How do their spirits pass, I wonder,
Nights and days in the narrow room?

Still, I suppose, they sit and ponder
What a gift life was, ages ago,
Six steps out of the chapel yonder.

Only they see not God, I know,
Nor all that chivalry of his,
The soldier-saints who, row on row,

Burn upward each to his point of bliss—

[201]

Pre-Raphaelite and Other Poets

He condemns them. Why? Because they did not do
anything. Anything? You do not mean to say that
they ought to have committed adultery?

> I hear you reproach—"But delay was best,
> For their end was a crime." —Oh, a crime will do
> As well, I reply, to serve for a test,
>
> As a virtue golden through and through,
> Sufficient to vindicate itself
> And prove its worth at a moment's view!
>
> Must a game be played for the sake of pelf?
> .   .   .   .
>
> The true has no value beyond the sham:
> As well the counter as coin, I submit,
> When your table's a hat, and your prize, a dram.
>
> Stake your counter as boldly every whit,
> Venture as warily, use the same skill,
> Do your best, whether winning or losing it,
>
> If you choose to play!—is my principle.
> Let a man contend to the uttermost
> For his life's set prize, be it what it will!
>
> The counter our lovers staked was lost
> As surely as if it were lawful coin;
> And the sin I impute to each frustrate ghost
>
> Is the unlit lamp and the ungirt loin,
> Though the end in sight was a vice, I say.

In order to understand the full force of this strange
ethical philosophy, you must remember that the word
"counter" is here a gambling term; it is used for the

round buttons or disks of bone or ivory, not in themselves money, but representing money to be eventually received or paid. Remembering this, we can simplify Browning; this is what he says:

"These people were the most contemptible of sinners; they deliberately threw their lives away. They were afraid to commit a sin. To wish to commit a sin and to be afraid to commit it, is much worse than committing it. All their lives those two dreamed and purposed and desired a sin; they wanted to commit adultery. If they had committed the crime, there would have been some hope for them; there is always hope for the persons who are not afraid. When a young man begins to doubt what his parents and teachers tell him about virtue, it is sometimes a good thing for him to test this teaching by disobeying it. Human experience has proclaimed in all ages that theft and murder and adultery and a few other things can never give good results. It is not easy to explain the whole why and wherefore to a young person who is both self-willed and ignorant. But let him try for himself what murder means, or theft means, or adultery means, and after he has experienced the consequences, he will begin to perceive what moral teaching signifies. If he is not killed, or imprisoned for life, he will very possibly become wise and good at a later time. Now in regard to those two lovers, they wanted to have an experience; and the experience might have been so valuable to them that it would have given them a new soul—but they were afraid; they were criminals without profit; and their great sin was that of being too cowardly to commit sin. Never will God forgive such weakness as that!" Of

course all great religions teach that the man who wishes
to do wrong does the wrong in wishing as truly as if
he did it with his body; there is only a difference of
degree. Now Browning goes a little further than such
religious teaching; he tells us that only wishing under
certain circumstances may be incomparably worse than
doing, because the doing brings about its punishment
in ninety-nine cases out of a hundred, and the punishment becomes a moral lesson, forcing the sufferer to
think about the moral aspect of what he has done.
That is why Browning says, "A sin will do to serve
for a test." But only to wish to do, and not do, leaves
a person in a state of inexperience. There is an old
proverb, which is quite true: "Any man can become
rich who is willing to pay the price." With equal truth
it might be said, "You can do anything that you please
in this world, if you are willing to pay the price, but
the price of acts and thoughts is fixed by the Eternal
Powers, and you must not try to cheat them."

Philosophers will tell you that our moral laws are
not always perfect, that man cannot make a perfect
code invariably applicable to all times and circumstances. This is true. But it is also true that there
is a higher morality than human codes, and when human
law fails to give justice, a larger law occasionally steps
in to correct the failure. Browning delights in giving
us examples of this kind, extraordinary moral situa-
tions, wrong by legal opinion, right by the larger law
of nature, which is sometimes divine. A startling story
which he tells us, entitled "Ivàn Ivànovitch," will show
us how he treats such themes. Ivàn, the hero of the
story, is a wood-cutter, who works all day in his native

village, to support a large family. He is the most
highly respected of the young peasants, the strong man
of the community, a good father and a good husband.
One day, while he is working out of doors in the bitter
cold, a sledge drawn by a maddened and dying horse
enters the village, with a half dead woman on it. The
woman is the wife of Ivàn's best friend, and she has
come back alone, although she had taken her three children with her on the homeward journey. Ivàn helps
her into the house, gives her something warm to drink,
caresses her, comforts her, and asks at last for her
story. The sledge had been pursued by wolves, and
the wolves had eaten the three children, one after another. Ivàn listens very carefully to the mother's relation of how the three children were snatched out of the
sledge by the wolves. As soon as she has told every one
in her own way, Ivàn takes his sharp axe, and with one
blow cuts the woman's head off. To the other peasants
he simply observes, "God told me to do that; I could not
help it." Of course Ivàn knew that the woman had lied.
The wolves had not taken the children away from her:
she had dropped one child after another out of the sledge
in order to save her own miserable life.

At the news of the murder, the authorities of the village all hurry to the scene. There is the dead body
without its head, and the blood flowing, or rather crawl-
ing like a great red snake over the floor. The lord of
the village declares that Ivàn must be executed for this
crime. The Stàrosta, or head man, takes the same
view of the situation. But, just as Ivàn is about to be
arrested, the old priest of the village, the Pope as the
peasants call him, a man more than a hundred years

of age, comes into the assembly and speaks. He is the only man who has a word to say on behalf of Iván, but what he says is extraordinary in its force and primitive wisdom. All of it would be too long to quote. I give you only the conclusion, which immediately results in Iván's being acquitted both by law and by public opinion.

"A mother bears a child: perfection is complete
So far in such a birth. Enabled to repeat
The miracle of life,—herself was born so just
A type of womankind, that God sees fit to trust
Her with the holy task of giving life in turn.

. . . .

How say you, should the hand God trusted with life's
    torch
Kindled to light the word—aware of sparks that scorch,
Let fall the same? Forsooth, her flesh a fire-flake stings:
The mother drops the child! Among what monstrous
    things
Shall she be classed?"

Of course the old Pope is speaking from the Christian point of view when he says that perfection is complete in a birth; he refers to the orthodox belief that the soul of man is created a perfect thing of its kind, a perfect spiritual entity, to be further made or marred by its own acts and thoughts. The mother does not give birth only to a body, but to a soul also, expressly made by God to fit that body. She is allowed to repeat the miracle of creation thus far; as mother she is creator, but only in trust. She has made the vessel of the soul; her most sacred duty is to guard that little body from

all harm. A mother who would even let her child fall
to escape pain herself would be incomparably more
ignoble than the most savage of animals. The rule
is that during motherhood even the animal-mother for
the time being becomes the ruling power; the male animal then allows her to have her own way in all things.

"Because of motherhood, each male
Yields to his partner place, sinks proudly in the scale:
His strength owned weakness, wit—folly, and courage—
    fear,
Beside the female proved male's mistress—only here.
The fox-dam, hunger-pined, will slay the felon sire
Who dares assault her whelp: the beaver, stretched on fire,
Will die without a groan: no pang avails to wrest
Her young from where they hide—her sanctuary breast.
What's here then? Answer me, thou dead one, as, I trow,
Standing at God's own bar, he bids thee answer now!
Thrice crowned wast thou—each crown of pride, a child—
    thy charge!
Where are they? Lost? Enough: no need that thou en-
    large
On how or why the loss: life left to utter 'lost'
Condemns itself beyond appeal. The soldier's post
Guards from the foe's attack the camp he sentinels:
That he no traitor proved, this and this only tells—
Over the corpse of him trod foe to foe's success.
Yet—one by one thy crowns torn from thee—thou no less
To scare the world, shame God,—livedst! I hold he saw
The unexampled sin, ordained the novel law,
Whereof first instrument was first intelligence
Found loyal here. I hold that, failing human sense,
The very earth had oped, sky fallen, to efface
Humanity's new wrong, motherhood's first disgrace.

Earth oped not, neither fell the sky, for prompt was found
A man and man enough, head-sober and heart-sound,
Ready to hear God's voice, resolute to obey.

. . . .

                                          I proclaim
Ivàn Ivànovitch God's servant!"

On hearing this speech the peasantry are at once convinced; the Russian lord orders the proclamation to be
made that the murderer is forgiven, and the head man
of the village goes to Ivàn's house to bring the good
news. He expects to find Ivàn on his knees at prayer,
very much afraid of the police and coming punishment.
But on opening the door the head man finds Ivàn playing with his five children, and making for them a toy-
church out of little bits of wood. It has not even entered into the mind of Ivàn that he did anything wrong.
And when they tell him, "You are free, you will not be
punished," he answers them in surprise, "Why should
I not be free? Why should you talk of my not being
punished?" To this simple mind there is nothing to
argue about. He has only done what God told him
to do, punished a crime against Nature.

The story is a strange one; but not stranger than
many to be found in Browning. None of his moral
teachings are at discord with any form of true religion,
yet they are mostly larger than the teachings of any
creed. Perhaps this is why he has never offended the
religious element even while preaching doctrines over its
head. The higher doctrines thus proclaimed might be
anywhere accepted; they might be also questioned; but
no one would deny their beauty and power. We may

assume that Browning usually considers all incidents in their relation to eternal law, not to one place or time, but to all places and to all times, because the results of every act and thought are infinite. This doctrine especially is quite in harmony with Oriental philosophy, even when given such a Christian shape as it takes in the beautiful verses of "Abt Vogler."

Abt Vogler was a great musician, a great improviser. Here let me explain the words "improvise" and "improvisation," as to some of you they are likely to be unfamiliar, at least in the special sense given to them in this connection. An improvisation in poetry means a composition made instantly, without preparation, at request or upon a sudden impulse. In Japanese literary history, I am told, there are some very interesting examples of improvisation. For example, the story of that poetess who, on being asked to compose a poem including the mention of something square, something round, and something triangular, wrote those celebrated lines about unfastening one corner of a mosquito-curtain in order to look at the moon. Among Europeans improvisation is now almost a lost art in poetry, except among the Italians. Some Italian families still exist in which the art of poetical improvisation has been cultivated for hundreds of years. But in music it is otherwise. Improvisation in music is greatly cultivated and esteemed. Most of our celebrated musicians have been great improvisers. Those who heard such music would regret that it could not be reproduced, not even by the musician himself. It was a beautiful creation, forgotten as soon as made, because never written down.

Pre-Raphaelite and Other Poets

Now you know what Browning means by improvisation in his poem "Abt Vogler." The musician has been improvising, and the music, made only to be forgotten, is so beautiful that he himself bitterly regrets the evanescence of it. We may quote a few of the verses in which this regret is expressed; they are very fine and very strange, written in a measure which I think you have never seen before.

Would that the structure brave, the manifold music I build,
    Bidding my organ obey, calling its keys to their work,
Claiming each slave of the sound, at a touch, as when
        Solomon willed
    Armies of angels that soar, legions of demons that lurk,
Man, brute, reptile, fly,—alien of end and of aim,
    Adverse, each from the other heaven-high, hell-deep removed,—
Should rush into sight at once as he named the ineffable
    Name,
    And pile him a palace straight, to pleasure the princess
    he loved!

The musician is comparing the music that he makes to magical architecture; he refers to the Mohammedan legends of Solomon. Solomon knew all magic; and all men, animals, angels, and demons obeyed him. God has ninety-nine names by which the faithful may speak of him, but the hundredth name is secret, the Name ineffable. He who knows it can do all things by the utterance of it. When Solomon pronounced it, all the spirits of the air and of heaven and of hell would rush to obey him. And if he wanted a palace or a city built, he had only to order the spirits to build it, and they would build it immediately, finishing everything between the rising and the setting of the sun. That is the story which the musician refers to. He has the power of the master-musician over sounds; but the sounds will not stay.

> Would it might tarry like his, the beautiful building of
>   mine,
>   This which my keys in a crowd pressed and importuned
>   to raise!
> Ah, one and all, how they helped, would dispart now and
>   now combine,
>   Zealous to hasten the work, heighten their master his
>   praise!
> And one would bury his brow with a blind plunge down to
>   hell,
>   Burrow awhile and build, broad on the roots of things,
> Then up again swim into sight, having based me my palace
>   well,
>   Founded it, fearless of flame, flat on the nether springs.

The musician wishes that his architecture of sound could remain, as remained the magical palace that Solomon made the spirits build to please Queen Balkis. He remembers how beautiful his music was; he remembers how the different classes of notes combined to make it, just as the different classes of spirits combined to make the palace of Solomon. There the deep notes, the bass chords, sank down thundering like demon-spirits working to make the foundation in the very heart of the earth. And the treble notes seemed to soar up like angels to make the roof of gold, and to tip all the points of the building with glorious fires of illumination. Truly the palace of sounds was built, but it has vanished away like a mirage; the builder cannot reproduce it. Why not? Well, because great composition of any kind is not merely the work of man; it is an inspiration from God, and the mystery of such inspired composition is manifested in music as it is manifested in no other art. For the harmonies, the combinations of tones, are mysteries, and must remain mysterious even for the musician himself. Who can explain them?

But here is the finger of God, a flash of the will that can,
    Existent behind all laws, that made them, and lo, they
      are!
And I know not if, save in this, such gift be allowed to
    man,
    That out of three sounds he frame, not a fourth sound,
      but a star.
Consider it well: each tone of our scale in itself is naught:
    It is everywhere in the world—loud, soft, and all is said:
Give it to me to use! I mix it with two in my thought:
    And there! Ye have heard and seen: consider and bow
      the head!

But for the same reason that they are mysteries and cannot be understood because they relate to the infinite, they are eternal. That is the consolation. The musician need not regret that the music composed in a moment of divine inspiration cannot be remembered; he need not regret that it has been forgotten. Forgotten it is by the man who made it; forgotten it is by the people who heard it; forgotten it is therefore by all mankind. Nevertheless it is eternal, because the Universal Soul that inspired it never forgets anything. I think that the verse in which this beautiful thought is expressed—the verse that contains the whole of Browning's religion, is the most beautiful thing in all his work. But you must judge for yourselves:

All we have willed or hoped or dreamed of good shall exist;
  Not its semblance, but itself; no beauty, nor good, nor power
Whose voice has gone forth, but each survives for the melodist
When eternity affirms the conception of an hour.
The high that proved too high, the heroic for earth too hard,
  The passion that left the ground to lose itself in the sky,
Are music sent up to God by the lover and the bard;
  Enough that he heard it once; we shall hear it by and by.

By the phrase "when eternity affirms the conception of an hour," the poet means when we ourselves, in a future and higher state of being, shall see the worth of our good acts and thoughts proved by the fact that they survive along with us. Eternity affirms them—that is, recognises them as worthy of immortality by suffering them to exist. This line gives us the key to the philosophy of the rest. It is quite in harmony with Buddhist philosophy. Browning holds that all good acts and thoughts are eternal, whether men in this world remember them or not. But what of the bad acts and thoughts? Are they also eternal? Not in the same sense. Evil acts and thoughts do indeed exert an influence reaching enormously into the future, but it is an influence that must gradually wane, it is a Karma that must become exhausted. As for regretting that

[213]

nobody sees or knows the good that we do, that is very foolish. The good will never die; it will be seen again—perhaps only in millions of years, yet this should make no difference. To the dead the time of a million years and the time of a moment may be quite the same thing.

But you must not suppose that Browning lives much in the regions of abstract philosophy. He is human in the warmest way, and very much alive to impressions of sense. Not even Swinburne is at times more voluptuous, but the voluptuous in Browning is always natural and healthy as well as artistic. I must quote to you some passages from the wonderful little dramatic poem entitled "In a Gondola." You know that a gondola is a peculiar kind of boat which in Venice takes the place of carriages or vehicles of any kind. In the city of Venice there are no streets to speak of, but canals only, so that people go from one place to another only by boat. These boats or gondolas of Venice are not altogether unlike some of the old-fashioned Japanese pleasure-boats; they have a roof and windows and rooms, and it is possible to travel in them without being seen by anybody. In the old days of Venice, many secret meetings between lovers and many secret meetings of conspirators were held in such boats. The poet is telling us of the secret meeting of two lovers, at the risk of death, for if the man is seen he will certainly be killed. At the end of the poem he actually is killed; the moment he steps on shore he is stabbed, because he has been watched by the spies of a political faction that hates him. But this is not the essential part of the poem at all. The essential part of the poem is the description, of the feelings and thoughts of these two

Studies in Browning

people, loving in the shadow of death; this is very beautiful and almost painfully true to nature. We get also not a few glimpses of the old life and luxury of Venice in the course of the narrative. As the boat glides down the long canals, between the high ranges of marble palaces rising from the water, the two watch the windows of the houses that they know, and talk about what is going on inside.

> Past we glide, and past, and past!
> What's that poor Agnese doing
> Where they make the shutters fast?
> Grey Zanobi's just a-wooing
> To his couch the purchased bride:
> Past we glide!
>
> Past we glide, and past, and past!
> Why's the Pucci Palace flaring
> Like a beacon to the blast?
> Guests by hundreds, not one caring
> If the dear host's neck were wried:
> Past we glide!

It is the man who is here looking and talking and criticising. The woman is less curious; she is thinking only of love, and what she says in reply has become famous in English literature; we might say that this is the very best we have in what might be called the "literature of kissing."

> The moth's kiss, first!
> Kiss me as if you made believe
> You were not sure, this eve,
> How my face, your flower, had pursed

Its petals up; so, here and there
You brush it, till I grow aware
Who wants me, and wide ope I burst.

The bee's kiss, now!
Kiss me as if you entered gay
My heart at some noonday,
A bud that dares not disallow
The claim, so all is rendered up,
And passively its shattered cup
Over your head to sleep I bow.

Of course you know all about the relation of insects to
flowers—how moths, beetles, butterflies, and other little
creatures, by entering flowers in order to suck the
honey, really act as fertilisers, carrying the pollen from
the male flower to the female flower. It is the use of
this fact from natural history that makes these verses
so exquisite. The woman's mouth is the flower; the lips
of the man, the visiting insect. "Moth" is the name
which we give to night butterflies, that visit flowers in
the dark. What the woman says is this in substance:
"Kiss me with my mouth shut first, like a night moth
coming to a flower all shut up, and not knowing where
the opening is." The second comparison of the bee
suggests another interesting fact in the relation between insects and flowers. A bee or wasp, on finding
it difficult to enter a flower from the top, so as to get
at the honey, will cut open the side of the flower, and
break its way in. The woman is asking simply, "Now
give me a rough kiss after the gentle one." All this is
mere play, of course, but by reason of the language
used it rises far above the merely trifling into the zones

[216]

of supreme literary art. Later on, we have another comparison, made by the man, which I think very beautiful. The thought, the comparison itself, is not new; from very ancient times it has been the custom of lovers to call the woman they loved an angel. I fancy this custom is reflected in the amatory literature of all countries; it exists even in Japanese poetry. But really it does not matter whether a comparison be new or old; its value depends upon the way that a poet utters it. Browning's lover says:

> Lie back; could thought of mine improve you?
> From this shoulder let there spring
> A wing; from this, another wing;
> Wings, not legs and feet, shall move you!
> Snow-white must they spring, to blend
> With your flesh, but I intend
> They shall deepen to the end,
> Broader, into burning gold,
> Till both wings crescent-wise enfold
> Your perfect self, from 'neath your feet
> To o'er your head, where, lo, they meet
> As if a million sword-blades hurled
> Defiance from you to the world!

This is a picture painted after the manner of the Venetian school; we seem to be looking at something created by the brush of Titian or Tintoretto. I am not sure that it will seem to you as beautiful as it really is, for it is intended to appeal to the imagination of persons who have actually seen the paintings of the Italian masters, or at least engravings of them. Angels were frequently represented by those great artists as clothed with their own wings, the wings, white below, gold above, meeting over the head like two new moons joining their shining tips. What the poet means by "sword-blades" are the long narrow flashing feathers of the angel-wings, which, joined all together, look like a cluster of sword-blades. But one must have seen the pictures of the Italian masters to appreciate the skill of this drawing in words. Here I may remind you that Dante, in his vision of Paradise, uses colours of a very similar sort—blinding white and dazzling gold appear in the wings of his angels also.

The above examples of the merely artistic power of Browning will suffice for the moment; great as he always is when he descends to earth, he is most noteworthy in those other directions which I have already pointed out, and which are chiefly psychological. I want to give you more examples from the poems of the psychological kind, partly because they are of universally recognised value in themselves, and partly because it is these that make the distinction between Browning and his great contemporaries. One of these pieces, now quoted through the whole English-speaking world, is "A Grammarian's Funeral." This poem is intended to give us the enthusiasm which the students of the later Middle Ages felt for scholarship, the delight in learning which revived shortly before the Renaissance. I suppose that many of you recollect the first enthusiasm for Western studies in Japan; people then studied too hard, tried to do even more than they could do. So it was in Europe at the time of the revival of learning; men killed themselves by overstudy. In this poem Browning makes us listen to the song sung by a company of

university students burying their dead teacher; they
are carrying him up to the top of a high mountain
above the mediæval city, there to let him sleep forever
above the clouds and above the vulgarities of mankind.
The philosophy in it is very noble and strong, though
it be only the philosophy of young men.

Let us begin and carry up this corpse,
    Singing together.
Leave we the common crofts, the vulgar thorpes
    Each in its tether
Sleeping safe on the bosom of the plain,
    Cared-for till cock-crow:
Look out if yonder be not day again
    Rimming the rock-row!
That's the appropriate country; there, man's thought,
    Rarer, intenser,
Self-gathered for an outbreak, as it ought,
    Chafes in the censer.
Leave we the unlettered plain its herd and crop;
    Seek we sepulture
On a tall mountain, citied to the top,
    Crowded with culture!
All the peaks soar, but one the rest excels,
    Clouds overcome it;
No! yonder sparkle is the citadel's
    Circling its summit.
Thither our path lies; wind we up the heights;
    Wait ye the warning?
Our low life was the level's and the night's;
    He's for the morning.
Step to a tune, square chests, erect each head,
    'Ware the beholders!
This is our master, famous, calm and dead,
    Borne on our shoulders.

[219]

Pre-Raphaelite and Other Poets

Some little description will be necessary before we can go further with the poem. It was dark, before daybreak, when the students assembled for the funeral, and it is still rather dark when the funeral procession starts up the mountain. This appears from the lines, "Look out if yonder be not day again rimming the rock-row"—meaning, see if that is not daylight up there at the top of the mountains. It is not full day, but they can see, far up, the lights of the citadel. The poet wants to give us the feeling of a fortified city of the Middle Ages. You must understand that multitudes of cities, especially in France and in Germany, were then built upon mountain tops, so that they could be better fortified and defended against attack. Part of such a city would be of course on sloping ground. But the very highest place was always reserved, inside the city, for military purposes. Outside the city were walls and ditches and towers. Inside the city there was a smaller city or citadel, also surrounded by ditches and walls and towers, and occupying the highest place possible. An enemy, after capturing the city proper, would still have the citadel to capture, always a very difficult military feat. Now you will understand better the suggestions of immense height in the poem. The students are going up above the citadel to bury their teacher. They say that the place is appropriate because the air at that height is, like intellectual thought, cold and pure and full of electricity, the symbol of mental energy and moral effort. You may notice that the students are still somewhat rough in their ways. It was a rough age; they do not intend to submit to any interference on the way, nor even to any curiosity, so the ignorant "beholders" are bidden to be very careful.

At this point the poem gives us the students' account of their teacher's life. They are singing a song about it, and you must understand that all the lines in parentheses do not necessarily mean interruptions of the narrative, though some of them do. A little careful reading will make everything clear; then you will perceive how very fine the spirit of the whole thing is.

> Sleep, crop and herd! sleep, darkling thorpe and croft,
>   Safe from the weather!
> He, whom we convoy to his grave aloft,
>   Singing together,
> He was a man born with thy face and throat,
>   Lyric Apollo!
> Long he lived nameless: how should Spring take note
>   Winter would follow?
> Till lo! the little touch, and youth was gone!
>   Cramped and diminished,
> Moaned he, "New measures, other feet anon!
>   My dance is finished?"
> No, that's the world's way: (keep the mountain-side,
>   Make for the city!)
> He knew the signal, and stepped on with pride
>   Over men's pity;
> Left play for work, and grappled with the world
>   Bent on escaping:
> "What's in the scroll," quoth he, "thou keepest furled?
>   Show me their shaping,
> Theirs who most studied man, the bard and sage,—
>   Give!"—So he gowned him,
> Straight got by heart that book to its last page:
>   Learned, we found him.

Pre-Raphaelite and Other Poets

When his first students met him, they met him as a youthful and a learned man; these latest students found him old, bald, scarcely able to see—and yet he had not allowed himself any rest. In spite of the fact that he felt death was coming, he continued to study day and night, he read all the books then existing, and when he had read them all, he said only, "Now I have got to the beginning of my real studies. The material is in my hands; now I shall use it." Sickness or health made no difference to him. This life he thought of only as the commencement of eternity.

> He said, "What's Time? Leave Now for dogs and apes!
> Man has Forever!"
> Back to his books then; deeper drooped his head:
> *Calculus* racked him:
> Leaden before, his eyes grew dross of lead:
> *Tussis* attacked him.

In vain did his friends and pupils beg him to take a little rest, but he never would; he said that he must learn everything he could before dying.

> So, with the throttling hands of death at strife,
> Ground he at grammar;
> Still, through the rattle, parts of speech were rife:
> While he could stammer
> He settled *Hoti's* business—let it be!—
> Properly based *Oun*—
> Gave us the doctrine of the enclitic *De*,
> Dead from the waist down.

"Hoti" is the Greek word "that"; "Oun" is the word "then," also "now"; it has other kindred meanings.

[222]

Studies in Browning

"De" has the meaning of "toward" when enclitic; but there is another Greek word "de" meaning "but." The reference in the poem is to the rule for distinguishing the Greek "de" meaning "toward" from the Greek "de" meaning "but." "Calculus" is the disease commonly called "stone in the bladder." "Tussis" is a cough.

And now the singers have brought the body to the burial-place at the top of the mountain, and their song ends with this glorious burst:

Well, here's the platform, here's the proper place:
   Hail to your purlieus,
All ye highfliers of the feathered race,
   Swallows and curlews!
Here's the top-peak; the multitude below
   Live, for they can, there;
This man decided not to Live but Know—
   Bury this man there?
Here—here's his place, where meteors shoot, clouds form,
   Lightnings are loosened,
Stars come and go! Let joy break with the storm,
   Peace let the dew send!
Lofty designs must close in like effects:
   Loftily lying,
Leave him—still loftier than the world suspects,
   Living and dying.

We may turn from this fine poem without further comment to a piece entitled "The Patriot." There is a bit, and a very bitter bit, of the true philosophy of life in it. Nothing is so fickle, so uncertain, so treacherous as popularity. Thousands of men who tried to get the applause of the multitude, the love of the millions, and

thought that they had succeeded, found out at a later
day how quickly that applause could be turned into
roars of hate, how quickly that seeming admiration
could be changed into scorn. This fact about the insta-
bility of human favour is well known to every clear
headed person who enters into what is called the social
struggle; but it is more often illustrated in politics.
The political aspect of the matter is the most remarkable, and has therefore been chosen by Browning. I do
not know to what particular person he may be making
reference—perhaps he was thinking of Rienzi. But in
all periods of history the fact has been about the same.
You will remember, no doubt, the case of Pericles in the
history of Athens, and of many others. You may remember also how the French Revolution devoured its
own children, how the men that were one day almost
worshipped by the people like gods, would be dragged
to the guillotine the day after. And even in the history
of this country I think you must remember not a few
examples of how uncertain popular favour must always
be. In this case the victim speaks, some man who once
had been regarded as the saviour of the people, but
who is now regarded as their enemy, and who is going
to be executed as a common criminal, simply because
he happened to be unfortunate. He remembers the
past, and contrasts it with the cruel present:

> It was roses, roses, all the way,
>   With myrtle mixed in my path like mad:
> The house-roofs seemed to heave and sway,
>   The church-spires flamed, such flags they had,
> A year ago on this very day.

Studies in Browning

The air broke into a mist with bells,
    The old walls rocked with the crowd and cries.
Had I said: "Good folk, mere noise repels—
    But give me your sun from yonder skies!"
They had answered, "And afterward, what else?"

Here I may say that in Western countries from very
ancient times it has been the custom to cover with
flowers the road along which some great conqueror or
other honoured person was to come. The ancients used
especially roses and myrtles, but even to-day it is often
the custom to throw flowers on the ground before the
passing of a sovereign or other great person. "Like
mad" is an idiom used to express extreme action of any
sort; "to laugh like mad," would be to laugh unreason-
ably and extravagantly. The reference to the apparent movement of the roofs of the houses pictures the
crowding of people on the house-tops to see the hero, a
custom still kept up. And the reference to the effect
of the bells as making "mist," indicates the excessive
volume of sound; for it is said that the firing of cannon
or the making of any other great noise will often cause
rain to fall. The idea is that the people rang the bells
so hard that the rain fell, and these were what we call
"joy-bells."

"If on that day of my triumph," he says, "I had
asked them to give me the sun, they would have answered
out of their hearts, Certainly—and what else?" Now
it is very different indeed.

Alack, it was I who leaped at the sun
    To give it my loving friends to keep!

[225]

Nought man could do, have I left undone:
    And you see my harvest, what I reap
This very day, now a year is run.

There's nobody on the house-tops now—
    Just a palsied few at the windows set;
For the best of the sight is, all allow,
    At the Shambles' Gate—or, better yet,
By the very scaffold's foot, I trow.

I go in the rain, and, more than needs,
    A rope cuts both my wrists behind;
And I think, by the feel, my forehead bleeds,
    For they fling, whoever has a mind,
Stones at me for my year's misdeeds.

What he says is this: "I did not ask them for anything for myself; it was I who wanted to give them the
sun, or anything else that they wished for. Every possible sacrifice that any man could make I made for
these people, and you see what my reward is to-day—
just one year from the time when they honoured and
revered me. Nobody now stands on the house tops
to look at me; all have gone to the execution ground
to see me die, except.a few old people who cannot walk,
and who stay at the windows to see me pass, with my
hands tied behind my back. People are throwing stones
at me, and I think my face is bleeding." The last allusion is to a very cruel custom only of late years abol-
ished in England by better police regulations. In the
old times, when a prisoner was being taken to the gallows, people would often strike him, or throw stones at
him as he went by, and nobody attempted to protect

him. To-day this is not done, simply because the police do not allow it, but the natural cruelty of a mob is perhaps just as great as it ever was.

> Thus I entered, and thus I go!
> In triumphs, people have dropped down dead.
> "Paid by the world, what dost thou owe
> Me?"—God might question; now instead,
> 'Tis God shall repay: I am safer so.

These are the man's last thoughts. "I came into this city a hero, as I told you; now I am going out of it, to be executed like a vulgar criminal. How much better would it have been if I had died on the day when all the people were honouring me! I have heard that men have fallen dead from joy in the middle of such a triumph as I then had. But would it have been better if I had died happy like that? Perhaps it would not. God is said to demand a strict account in the next world from any human being who has been too happy in this. If I had died that day, God might have said to me, You have had your reward from the world; have you paid to me what you owed in love and duty? But now the world kills me; it is from God only that I can hope for justice. He is terrible, but I can trust him better than this people; I am safer with him!"

I am not sure what Browning refers to in speaking of those who have been known to drop dead in the middle of a triumph. But perhaps he is referring to the story of the Sicilian, Diagoras, which is one of the most beautiful of all Greek stories, and is fortunately quite true. Diagoras had been the greatest wrestler among the Greeks, the greatest athlete of his time, and was loved and honoured by all men of Greek blood. He had seven sons. When he was a very old man these seven sons went to contend at the great Olympic games (if I remember correctly). There were but seven prizes for all the feats of strength and skill; and these seven prizes were all won by the seven sons of Diagoras —that is to say, they had proved themselves the best men of the whole world at that time, even the boy son winning the prize given only to boys. Then the people demanded to know the name of the father of those young men, and the sons lifted him upon their shoulders to show him to all the people. The people shouted so that birds flying above them, fell down; and the old man in the same moment died of joy, as he was thus supported upon the shoulders of his sons. The Greeks said that this was the happiest death that any man ever died. Perhaps Browning was referring to this story; but I am not sure.

Kings have sometimes been accused of ingratitude, but on the whole, kings have shown more gratitude than mobs; a sovereign is apt to remember that it is good policy to repay loyalty and to encourage affection. Browning gives us a few magnificent specimens of loyal feeling toward sovereigns, feeling which it is pleasant to know was not repaid with ingratitude. I am referring to his "Cavalier Tunes," little songs into which he has managed to put all the fiery love and devotion of the English gentlemen who fought for the king against Cromwell and his Puritans, and who fought, luckily for England, in vain at that time. Right or wrong as we may think their cause, it is impossible not to admire the feeling here expressed. I shall quote the sec-

ond song first.   You must imagine that all these gentlemen are drinking the health of the king, with songs and
cheers, even at the time when the king's cause seems
hopeless.

GIVE A ROUSE!

King Charles, and who'll do him right now?
King Charles, and who's ripe for fight now?
Give a rouse: here's, in hell's despite now,
King Charles!

(*Single voice*)

Who gave me the goods that went since?
Who raised me the house that sank once?
Who helped me to gold I spent since?
Who found me in wine you drank once?

(*Chorus, answering*)

King Charles, and who'll do him right now?
King Charles, and who's ripe for fight now?
Give a rouse: here's, in hell's despite now,
King Charles!

(*Single voice*)

To whom used my boy George quaff else,
By the old fool's side that begot him?
For whom did he cheer and laugh else,
While Noll's damned troopers shot him?

(*Chorus, answering*)

King Charles, and who'll do him right now?
King Charles, and who's ripe for fight now?
Give a rouse: here's, in hell's despite now,
King Charles!

The father is reminding his friends of the brave death
of his own son, who died shouting for the king and
laughing at his executioners.   I do not think that there

is a more spirited song in English literature than this. Perhaps you may observe that the measure in the third stanza does not run smoothly like the measure of the other stanzas; it hesitates a little. But this is a great stroke of art, for it indicates the suppressed emotion of the father speaking of his dead son. The other song, the first of the three given by Browning, represents the feeling of an earlier time in the civil war, probably the time when the aristocracy and gentry first gathered together to defend the king. There is a splendid swing in it. Both songs are a little rough, because the spirit of the age was rough; the finest gentleman used to swear in those days, and to use words which we now consider rather violent. I may remark, however, that even to-day in the upper ranks of the English army and navy, something of the same scorn of conventions still remains; generals and admirals will swear occasionally in battle, just as these gentlemen of an older school swore as they advanced against the Puritan armies.

MARCHING ALONG

Kentish Sir Byng stood for his King,
Bidding the crop-headed Parliament swing:
And, pressing a troop unable to stoop
And see the rogues flourish and honest folk **droop,**
Marched them along, fifty-score strong,
Great-hearted gentlemen, singing this song.

God for King Charles! Pym and such carles
To the Devil that prompts 'em their treasonous **parles!**

Studies in Browning

Cavaliers, up! Lips from the cup,
Hands from the pasty, nor bite take nor sup
Till you're—
(*Chorus*)   Marching along, fifty-score strong,
        Great-hearted gentlemen, singing this song.

Hampden to hell, and his obsequies' knell
Serve Hazelrig, Fiennes, and young Harry as well!
England, good cheer! Rupert is near!
Kentish and loyalists, keep we not here,
(*Chorus*)   Marching along, fifty-score strong,
        Great-hearted gentlemen, singing this song.

Then, God for King Charles! Pym and his snarls
To the Devil that pricks on such pestilent carles!
Hold by the right, you double your might;
So, onward to Nottingham, fresh for the fight,
(*Chorus*)   March we along, fifty-score strong,
        Great-hearted gentlemen, singing this song.

The names in this poem are all of them great names
of the Civil War. Hampden, you know, was Parliamentary leader in the movement against the king. He
was killed in battle, and his place as leader was taken
by Pym. The other names are of members of the Long
Parliament—except Rupert. Rupert, or Prince Rupert, as he is more generally known, was the leader of
the Royal cavalry, one of the most brilliant cavalry
leaders of history. He was never beaten seriously until
he met Cromwell's Puritan cavalry. A reference may
be necessary in regard to Nottingham. There was no
fight exactly at Nottingham; but it was at Nottingham
that the cavalry gathered round the king's standard

before the battle of Edgehill, near Banbury, a drawn battle, not decided either way.

So much for the references. As for the song itself, something remains to be said. I think that the two songs are about the most spirited in English literature. They are so for many reasons, especially because of the fiery emotion which the poet has flung into them, and because of their absolute truth to the feeling of the seventeenth century, both as to form and as to tone. But I wonder whether any of you have noticed what it is that gives such uncommon force to the verses. To a great degree, it is the use of triple rhymes. In both songs the rhymes are triple, while the measure is short, and the result is something of that rough strength which characterises the old Northern poetry. For instance:

> Hold by the *right,* you double your *might,*
> So onward to Nottingham, fresh for the *fight.*

> King Charles, and who'll do him *right* now?
> King Charles, and who's ripe for *fight* now?
> Give a rouse: here's, in hell's *despite* now,
> King Charles!

You see that very great effects may be produced by very simple means. In "Marching Along," the "swing" or "lilt" is partly due to the fact that the three rhymes follow each other not in regular but in irregular succession, a rhymeless measure alternating between the second and the third rhymes, as will be plainly seen if we write the verses in another form:

Studies in Browning

Kentish Sir *Byng*
Stood for his *king,*
Bidding the crop-headed
Parliament *swing.*

But I want to explain the spirit rather than the workmanship of Browning; and I have turned aside here to the subject of measure only because the instances happened to be very extraordinary. The beauty of the work is really in the glow and strength of the loyal feeling that peals through it.

Do not suppose, however, that the poet picks out by preference the noble or the attractive side of human feeling in any form of society, for his subject. Quite the contrary. Most often he paints the ugly side, even in speaking of kings and courts, nobles and princes. In the splendid poem "Count Gismond," which I dictated last year, you may have seen one very beautiful side of knightly character, but there were horrible phases of human nature exhibited in the story. Browning made the shadows very heavy, with the result that the lights appeared more dazzling Sometimes we have no lights—all is shadow, and sometimes a shadow of hell. Such is the case in the horrible poem called "The Laboratory," depicting the feelings of a jealous courtlady, as she stands in the laboratory of a chemist who is selling her a poison with which she intends to poison her rival in the favour of the king. The story is laid in the time of Louis XIV, probably, when such things did actually occur in France. A still blacker shadow, a still more infernal picture of humanity's dark side, is "The Heretic's Tragedy," portraying the wicked

[233]

feelings of a superstitious person while watching a heretic being burned alive. Another frightful thing is "The Confessional," a story of the Inquisition in Spain, showing how the inquisitors succeeded in seizing, convicting, and burning alive a young man, by taking advantage of the innocence of his sweetheart, who was made to betray him through confession without knowing it. Another piece that is ugly psychologically, is "Cristina and Monaldeschi." Cristina was a queen of Sweden, and one of the most learned women of her time, but very masculine; she liked to wear men's clothes and to follow the amusements of men. She abdicated her throne, merely in order to feel more free in her habits. It is believed that she secretly loved her private secretary, and that he was dishonourable enough to tell other people of his relation to her. At all events, one day she ordered him to come into her room, and after upbraiding him with treachery to her, she had him killed in her presence. The fact shocked Europe a great deal at the time. Browning tries to make us understand Cristina's feeling, and he forces us to sympathise a little with her anger. There are multitudes of poems of this class in Browning. He wants us to know all the strange possibilities of the human soul, bad or good, and he never hesitates because a subject may be shocking to weak nerves. It is just because he does not care about public feeling, ignorant public opinion, upon these matters, that he manages to give us such exact truth; he is not afraid. For a little bit of truth thus exemplified—this is not ugly—let us take a little piece entitled "Which?" Here is another picture of the manners of the old French court, a very corrupt court and very luxurious. You must read Taine's "Ancien Régime" to understand what its morals were. But let us turn to the little picture. Three great ladies are talking with a priest about love—a fashionable priest, a priest of the old age, ready to make love or to say mass just according as it suited his private interest. A very good priest could scarcely have existed in the court; one had to be very clever and very subtle to live there. The conversation of these four persons gives us a hint of the feeling of the age. Only one woman really seems to say what she thinks; and she says what she thinks only because she is the most clever of the three.

So, the three Court-ladies began
   Their trial of who judged best
In esteeming the love of a man:
Who preferred with most reason was thereby confessed
Boy-Cupid's exemplary catcher and cager;
An Abbé crossed legs to decide on the wager.

First the Duchesse: "Mine for me—
   Who were it but God's for Him,
And the King's for—who but he?
Both faithful and loyal, one grace more shall brim
His cup with perfection: a lady's true lover,
He holds—save his God and his king—none above her."

"I require"—outspoke the Marquise—
   "Pure thoughts, ay, but also fine deeds:
Play the paladin must he, to please
My whim, and—to prove my knight's service exceeds
Your saint's and your loyalist's praying and kneeling—
Show wounds, each wide mouth to my mercy appealing."

[235]

Then the Comtesse: "My choice be a wretch,
　Mere losel in body and soul,
　Thrice accurst! What care I, so he stretch
Arms to me his sole saviour, love's ultimate goal,
Out of earth and men's noise—names of 'infidel,' 'traitor,'
Cast up at him? Crown me, crown's adjudicator!"

And the Abbé uncrossed his legs,
　Took snuff, a reflective pinch,
　Broke silence: "The question begs
Much pondering ere I pronounce. Shall I flinch?
The love which to one and one only has reference
Seems terribly like what perhaps gains God's preference."

The answer of the priest, giving the victory to the
Comtesse, is clever and double-edged. He probably
knows everything that goes on in the court: he knows
how many lovers the Duchesse has had, and the Marquise. He knows that their talk about religion and
loyalty as the perfections of man, are not quite
sincere. Indeed, the Marquise is much more sincere
than the Duchesse; but if she were altogether sincere,
she would have recognised that her wish—her expressed wish, at least—must appear as pure pride,
not anything else. But the Comtesse tells a bitter
truth by pointing out that if it is a question of real
love, the place and station of the man can signify
nothing at all; love should be a thing of the heart,
not a thing of rank and fashion. And the priest,
in supporting her claim and in saying that a true
love can have reference only to one person, really
suggests to his audience, whose love relations have
doubtless been very numerous, what he thinks to be the

opinion of God on the subject. But "perhaps," as the priest utters the word, is terrible irony. "Perhaps gains God's preference," means "I know, of course, that in the society to which we belong, love only for one's husband is not considered fashionable; yet the opinions of God may not be the same as the opinions of our society. It would not be polite of me to say directly that your opinions and God's opinions are different, but I just hint it." It was a very queer age. Taine, in his history of the time, tells a story about a nobleman who, on entering his wife's room suddenly and finding her making love to another man, took off his hat and saluted her, saying, "Oh, my dear, how can you be so careless! Suppose it had not been your husband who opened the door!" You must understand all this, to understand the mockery of the poem. Then, again, you must understand the desire of the Comtesse even for the love of a "wretch," a mere losel, as meaning that here is a woman who deserves to be loved, but is not loved by her husband, and who has learned that real love has a value in this world beyond all value of rank or money or influence.

If you ask me why I have talked so much about so short a poem, the answer is that nearly all of Browning's short poems mean a great deal, and force us to think and to talk about them. The reason is that the characters in these poems are really alive; they impress us exactly as living persons do, and excite our curiosity in precisely the same way. Accordingly, notwithstanding their many faults of construction and obscure English, they have something of the greatness of Shakespeare's dramas.

[237]

Pre-Raphaelite and Other Poets

It is now time to turn to the study of the greatest of all Browning's poems. Perhaps I should not call it a poem. It is rather an immense poetic drama. As printed in this single volume it represents four hundred and seventy-seven pages of closely printed small text. It is, therefore, even considered as a dramatic composition, many times larger than any true drama. But no true drama, except Shakespeare's, is more real or more terrible. Besides, it is a purely psychological drama. There is no scenery, no narrative in the ordinary sense. Everything is related in the first person. The whole is divided into twelve parts, each of which is a monologue. Nearly all of the monologues are spoken by different persons. The first monologue is the author's own, in which he tells us the meaning of the title and the story of the drama.

It is a true story of Italian life in the seventeenth century, the chief incident having really occurred in the year 1698. The poet one day found in an old Italian book shop a little book for sale, which was the history of a celebrated criminal trial. Besides the book, which included the speeches of the lawyers on both sides, and the evidence given before the court, there was a good deal of old manuscript—papers probably prepared by some lawyer of the time in connection with the case. Browning was able to buy the whole thing for eight pence; that small sum furnished him with material for the most enormous poem in the English language. When he read the facts of the trial, he said he could actually see all the characters as plainly as if they were alive, and could even hear them speak. He soon formed in his mind the plan for his poem; but it was a

[238]

Studies in Browning

peculiar plan. The plan is indicated by the title of "The Ring and the Book." In Italy there is a great deal of beautiful light gold work made—for rings especially, which looks so delicate that at first sight you cannot understand how it was made. In a gold ring there are leaves and flowers and fruits and insects, so lightly made that even if you let the ring fall they would be injured and destroyed. Gold is very soft. In order to cut the gold in this way, the goldsmith uses a hard composition with which he covers the gold work, and after the carving and engraving have been done, this composition is melted off, so that only the pure gold is left, with all the work upon it. Browning says that he made his book somewhat in the same way that the Italian goldsmith makes his ring—by the use of an alloy. The facts of history and of law represent the gold in this case, and the poet mixes them with an alloy of imagination, emotion, sympathy, which helps him to make the whole story into a perfectly rounded drama, a complete circle, a Ring. This is the meaning of the title.

I shall first tell you the story briefly, according to the historical facts. About the year 1679 there was a family in Rome of the name of Comparini. The family consisted only of husband and wife; but it happened that the fact of their being without children proved a legal obstacle in the way of obtaining some money which they greatly desired. The wife, Violante, knew that her husband was too honest to wish to cheat the law, so she determined to try to get the money without letting him know her deceit in the matter. She pretended to have given birth, unexpectedly, to a child, but the child had really been bought from a woman of loose life—it was a very pretty female child, and was called Francesca Pompilia. Little Pompilia was supposed to be the real child of the Comparini; and the much desired money thus passed into their hands. This is the first act of the tragedy.

Pompilia grew up into a wonderfully beautiful girl; and when she was thirteen years old, many people wished to marry her. Guido Franceschini, Count of Arezzo, noticed the girl's beauty, and heard that she was rich. He determined to marry her if possible, chiefly for the sake of her money. He was a wicked old man, between fifty and sixty years of age, ugly, cunning, and poor. But he had immense influence, both among the nobility and among the church dignitaries, on account of his family relations; and he was himself of high rank. The marriage was negotiated successfully. Pompilia, a child of thirteen, could not naturally have wished to marry this horrible old man, but she had been taught to obey her parents as she obeyed Almighty God, and when she was told to marry him she married him without one word of complaint. By this marriage the wicked Count got into his hands all the property of the Comparini family, but it had been promised that the parents of the girl were to live in the palace of the Count, and to be taken care of for the rest of their lives. Nevertheless, as soon as the Count had everything in his hands, he turned the old parents out of his house, in a state of absolute destitution; he had taken from them their daughter and all their money, everything that they had in the world. This is the second act of the tragedy.

Studies in Browning

Naturally the Comparini family were very angry. The mother of the girl was so angry that she told her husband all about the trick which she had played in passing off Pompilia for her own child. Pompilia, you know, was not her real child at all. This changed the legal aspect of the matter. Old Comparini went to the Count and said, "You took our money, and thought that you were taking our daughter. But you must give back that money. The girl is not our daughter; the money does not belong to her: it will have to be given back to the government that we deceived." This is the third act of the tragedy.

The Count was equal to the occasion. He understood the law; but he understood it much better than the Comparini people. So long as he kept Pompilia as his wife, he knew that he could keep the money. If he divorced her, on the ground that she was of vulgar origin, then he would have to give up the money. But this was not the only alternative. There was a third possibility. If Pompilia committed adultery, then he could either kill her or get rid of her and keep the money notwithstanding. Pompilia was a weak child only thirteen years old. He was a wicked and terrible man, with half a century of experience, diabolical cunning, diabolical cruelty, and ferocious determination. He would make her commit adultery. That would be the simplest possible solution of the difficulty. But, strange to say, this terrible man could not conquer that delicate child of thirteen. First he tried to appeal to her passions, to excite her imagination in an immoral way. But her heart was too pure to be corrupted. There was in her no spur of lust. She was a

[241]

simple good pure wife, too pure for any wicked ideas to be planted in her mind. Then he tried force, atrocious cruelty, horrible menace, always without letting her know what he really intended. What he really intended was to force her to run away from him. She could not run away except in the company of a protector. If she ran away with a protector, then he could kill both her and the man and claim that he had detected the two in adultery. After having tortured the girl hideously, in every moral and immoral way, he did succeed in getting her to ask for protection. She first asked protection from priests and bishops. The priests and bishops were afraid of the Count, and told her, like the cowards that they were, that they could not help her. She wanted to become a nun. The nuns were afraid of the Count, and refused her prayer. At last she did find one priest, a brave man, who was willing to save her if possible. He said, "You must run away with me, though it will look very bad; there is no other way to help you." She ran away with him. Within twenty-four hours the pair were overtaken by the Count and his company of armed men. The opportunity to kill Pompilia and her "lover" had come; but the so-called "lover," although only an honest poor priest, showed fight, and protected Pompilia against the Count and all his followers. The priest refused to surrender Pompilia except to the Church. The Church arrested both. Pompilia was put into a convent for safe keeping. The priest was tried for adultery, and acquitted. But he had done wrong by breaking the law of the Church even for a good purpose; therefore he was sentenced to banishment for a certain num-

ber of years. This is the fourth act of the tragedy.
The Count finds that all his plans have failed. He
has not been able to convict his wife of adultery, although he has been able to injure her reputation in
the opinion of the public. He cannot get rid of her,
and keep her money too, except by killing her. But
she is in the convent. While he is thinking what to
do, another event happens which upsets all his calculations. Pompilia gives birth to a child of which he
certainly is the father. The money question, the legal
aspect of it, is still more complicated by the birth of
the child. At once the Count determines to kill Pompilia and her parents, out of revenge. He knows that
on certain days she goes to visit her parents. He
watches for such an occasion, and with the help of some
professional murderers, he kills the Comparini, and
stabs Pompilia twenty-two times with a dagger. He
imagined that this could be done so as to remain un-
discovered; he thought that the crime could not be
proved upon him. But poor Pompilia is very hard to
kill. Although her slender body was thus stabbed
through and through by a powerful man, she did not
die at once; her wonderful youth kept her alive long
enough to tell the police what had happened. The
Count and his hired murderers were arrested and
thrown into prison. This is the fifth act of the tragedy.

It is one thing to find the author of a crime, and
put him into prison; it is a very different thing to
convict and punish him. The Count was very powerful with the army, with the nobility, with the Church;
everybody in his native city was more afraid of him
than of the devil. Nothing is so hard to get in this

world as justice. The Count's powerful friends and relations all united to defend him. Dukes and great captains, cardinals and bishops and abbots and priests, rich merchants, influential statesmen, all combined to secure his acquittal. They obtained the services of great lawyers. They used money and threats to corrupt witnesses or to terrify them. Yet there was one thing necessary to secure his acquittal—evidence that the deed, which he cannot deny, was justified by adultery. An attempt was made to blacken the character of the murdered wife. But this evidence was overthrown in the court, and the judges pronounced sentence of death. Thereupon all the Count's friends made an appeal to the Pope; the Pope can save the Count, if pressure be brought of a sufficient sort upon his judgment. But the Pope happened to be a good man, and a keen man. He examines the evidence. He sees the truth. He understands the innocence and beauty of the character of the murdered Pompilia; he comprehends also the innocence and the courage of the priest who tried to defend her. He sends word to the prison that the Count must be executed immediately. So justice is obtained, at least so far as the punishment of murder can be called justice. But what becomes of the money? The nuns of the convent in which Pompilia died, they get the money by very discreditable means, and they keep it. The terrible Franceschini family cannot try to get that money from the convent; for the convent means the power of the Church; and the power of the Church is even more terrible than the power of the Franceschini. Of course the Pope knows nothing of this matter; the Pope is the finest character in the

Studies in Browning

whole story. Historically this Pope was Innocent XII, but his character, as drawn in the study of Browning, is much more like the character of one of his predecessors, Innocent XI.

Now I have told you the story, or rather the history of the real tragedy, which happened something more than two hundred years ago. You can imagine how complicated the whole thing is, from the very short summary which I have made. Now if you had to treat a story like this dramatically, how would you do it? where would you begin? in what way could you hope to make artistic order out of such confusion? The task might have puzzled even Shakespeare. It puzzled Browning for more than a year before he felt how the thing was possible to manage. When I tell you the way in which he treated the whole material of the case, I think you will perceive that only a genius could have thought of the way.

As I have said, Browning divides his poem into twelve parts; and each part is a monologue. I shall now give you in paragraphs as brief as possible, the subject of each monologue. You had better follow the order of the book, using Roman numerals at the beginning of each paragraph, and putting the title of the book in Italic letters:

I. *The Ring and the Book.* Interpretation of the title, and history of the crime and the trial as told in the ancient legal documents. This monologue represents the author's speaking only.

II. *Half-Rome.* Public opinion is always divided upon any extraordinary event. Browning here tries to give us one side of public opinion in the year 1698, upon

[245]

the Franceschini murder. The monologue represents the ideas of a man of the society of that time.

III. *The Other Half-Rome.* This monologue represents the contrary opinion on the subject. But it is a curious fact that neither form of public opinion even approaches the truth. Both sides are absolutely mistaken, and very unjust to poor Pompilia.

IV. *Tertium Quid* (i.e., "a third somebody" or "party"). This opinion is quite different from that of the two halves of Rome, but it is equally far from the truth.

V. *Count Guido Franceschini.* Notice that although the three forms of opinion previously expressed all contradict each other, and all are untrue, nevertheless every one of them seems true while you read it. So does the story of Count Guido Franceschini, the murderer, in his own defence. Although you have been prejudiced against him from the beginning, when you first read his side of the story you cannot help thinking that it is a very reasonable and very true story. He says in substance that he made a great mistake in marrying so young a girl, that she disliked him, that he did everything in his power to obtain her affection and to make her happy, that she ran away from his house with a monk, that even after that he was willing to make every allowance for her, but that at last it was impossible for him, without losing all self-respect, not to punish her crimes, and those of her infamous parents. He makes an excellent speech, this Count Guido Franceschini.

VI. *Giuseppe Caponsacchi.* This is the good priest, the true loyal man that tried to save Pompilia. He tells his story with perfect truthfulness and simplicity, and you know that it is true. But at the same time you feel that no one can believe it. The evidence is against the priest. Although he is innocent, everybody laughs at his protestations of innocence.

VII. *Pompilia.* This is the most horrible part of the book. It is a monologue by Pompilia telling of the cruelty and the atrocious wickedness of her husband. It makes your blood run cold to read it, but you know that nobody would believe that story in a court of justice. It is too terrible, too unnatural. Those who hear it only think that Pompilia is a very cunning wicked woman, trying to make people' hate her husband, in order to excuse her own adultery.

VIII. *Dominus Hyocinthus de Archangelis, Pauperum Procurator.* The speech of the lawyer for the defence, very cautious, very learned, very cunning. It was in those days the custom to argue such cases partly in Latin, and the papers were made out in Latin. "Dominus," "lord," was the Latin title of lawyer. "Pauperum Procurator" means the advocate or counsel of the poor; persons without money enough to procure legal services in the ordinary way, might be furnished with a lawyer employed by the state.

IX. *Juris Doctor Johannes-Battista, Bottinius, &c.* The speech of the lawyer on the other side, equally learned, equally cunning, and equally cautious. The reader is forced to the conclusion that neither of these lawyers really understands the truth of the case. Both are telling untruth, and both are afraid of the truth. But you will notice that the lawyer who should speak in favour of Pompilia really does her more harm than the lawyer whose duty it is to speak against her. This is the result of cowardice and self-interest on both sides.

X. *The Pope*. A beautiful study of character. For the first time we learn the truth in this tenth monologue, so that we feel it is all there, and not to be mistaken by any one who hears it.

XI. *Guido*. Horrible. The murderer's confession of his own character.

XII. *The Book and the Ring*. Conclusion, and moral commentary.

I believe there is only part of this whole drama that has been seriously called into question by critics—the last line of the eleventh monologue, where Guido cries out, "Pompilia, will you let them murder me?" The question is whether the poet is right in representing this terrible man in such a passion of fear that he calls to his dead wife to help him. Certainly it is a general rule that the man capable of studied cruelty to women and children—to the weak, in short—is a coward at heart. But there are exceptions to this rule, and a great many remarkable Italian exceptions. Again many tribes of savages contradict the rule, being at once brave and cruel. I think that the criticism in this case may have been largely inspired by the history of certain Italian families, who were cruel indeed, but ferociously brave as well. However, Browning studied the facts for his characters very closely, and he may be right in representing Guido as a coward. He has been proved to be both treacherous and avaricious by the evidence in the case, and although prudence may sometimes be mistaken for cowardice, there were some facts brought out by witnesses that seem to show the man to have been as much of a coward as he was a miser.

Now observe the immense psychological work that this treatment of the story involves—the study of nine or ten completely different characters, no one of whom could resemble a character of the nineteenth century, not at least in the matter of thought and speech. To create these was almost as wonderful as to call the dead of two hundred years ago out of their graves, a veritable necromancy. This work alone would make the book a marvellous thing. But the book is more than marvellous; it is in the highest degree philosophically instructive. Almost anything that happens in this world is judged somewhat after the fashion of the judgments delivered in "The Ring and the Book." For example, let us suppose an episode in Tokyo to-day, rather than an episode in Italy two hundred years ago, a case of killing. At first when the mere fact of the killing is known, there is a great curiosity as to the reason of it, and different newspapers publish different stories about it, and different people who knew both parties express different opinions as to the why and how. You may be sure that none of these accounts is perfectly true—they could not be true, because those from whom the accounts come have no perfect knowledge of the antecedents of the crime. But presently the case comes before the criminal court, with lawyers on both sides, to prosecute and to defend. Each does his duty the very best he can, one trying to convict, one trying to secure acquittal. But do these know the real story from beginning to end? Probably not. It is very seldom indeed that a lawyer can learn the inside, the psychological, history of a crime. He learns only the naked facts, and he must theorise largely from these facts. Finally the judge pronounces judgment. Does the judge know all about the matter? Almost certainly not. His duty is fixed by law in rigid lines, and he cannot depart from those lines; he can sentence only according to the broad conclusions which he draws from the facts. And after the whole thing is over, still the real secrets of the two parties, of the criminal and the victim, remain forever unknown in a majority of cases. Now what does this prove? It proves that human judgment is necessarily very imperfect, and that nothing is so difficult to learn as the absolute truth of motives and of feelings, even when the truth of the facts is unquestionable. Browning's book tells us more than this; it shows us that in some cases, where power and crime are on one side, and poverty and virtue upon the other, the chances against truth being able to make itself heard are just about a thousand to one. Of course the world is a little better to-day than two hundred years ago; murder is less common, justice is less corrupt. But allowing for these things, the chances of a man persecuted by a rich corporation, without reason, perhaps with monstrous cruelty, to obtain even a hearing, would be scarcely better than those of Pompilia in the story of "The Ring and the Book."

So much for the teaching. There is more than teaching, however; there are studies of character truly Shakespearian. Pompilia is quite as sweet a woman as Shakespeare's Cordelia. Her sweetness is altogether shown by a multitude of details, little words and thoughts and feelings, that we find scattered through

her account of her terrible sufferings. The author
never interrupts his speakers; he makes them describe
themselves. In the case of the Pope, we are brought into
the presence of a very superior intellect—one-sided,
perhaps, but immensely strong in the direction of moral
judgment; the mind of an old man whose entire life has
been spent in the finest study of human nature from
an ethical point of view, of human nature in its mani-
festations of good and evil. Nothing but this long experience helps him to see exactly how matters stand.
The evidence brought before him is hopelessly confused,
and where not confused, the facts are against Pompilia
and strongly in favour of the murderer. Moreover, the
murderer is powerful in the Church, with all the influence
of clergy and nobility upon his side. But the old man
can see through the entire plot; he cuts it open, gets
to the heart of it, perceives everything that was hidden.
What is the lesson of his character? I think it is this,
that a pure nature obtains, simply by reason of its
unselfishness and purity, certain classes of perceptions
that very cunning minds never can obtain. Very cunning people are peculiarly apt to make false judgments,
because they are particularly in the habit of looking
for selfish motives. They judge other hearts by their
own. A pure nature does not do this; it considers the
motive in the last rather than the first place, preferring
to judge kindly so long as the evidence allows it. Intellectual training cannot always compensate for purity
of character.

The studies of Guido himself, which are very horrible, are especially studies of the man of the Renaissance. We have had other studies of this kind in other

poems of Browning, some of which I have already quoted to you. But there is a special moral in this study of Guido, the moral that a really wicked man must hate a really good woman, simply for the reason that she is good. Then we have in the two lawyers two pictures of conflicting selfish interests, of selfishness and falsehood combined to defeat the truth, not because truth is necessarily unpleasant to the lawyer, but because he wants to make no enemies by exposing it. This is the way of the world to-day, and although these men speak the language of the sixteenth or seventeenth century, their feelings are those of the shrewd and selfish modern man of society, the man who has no courage in the face of wrong, if his pocket happens to be in danger. We like only three characters in the whole drama—Pompilia, the Pope, and Caponsacchi. Yet there is nothing very remarkable about Caponsacchi, except in the way of contrast. He is the one character who, although his life and interests and reputation are at stake, boldly risks everything simply for a generous impulse. Happily he is not extraordinary; if he were, one would lose faith in so terrible a world. Happily we know that wherever and whenever a great wrong is done, there will always be a Caponsacchi to speak out and to do all that is possible against it. But Caponsacchi is crushed; and even the Pope is obliged to punish him for doing what is noble. This is one of the moral problems of the composition. The man who wants to do right, and cannot do right except by disobedience to law, may be loved for doing right, but he must be punished nevertheless for breaking the law. Does this mean that he is punished for doing right? I think we should not look at it in that way. The truth is that the observance of discipline must be insisted upon even in exceptional cases, because it regards the happiness of millions. We cannot allow men to decide for themselves when discipline should be broken. Caponsacchi is thus a martyr in the cause of individual justice. He has to pay, justly, the penalty of setting a dangerous example to thousands of others. But he is not on that account less estimable and lovable, and even the Pope, in punishing him, gives him words of warm praise.

The consideration of this huge poem ought also to tempt some of you at a later day to try some application of its method to some incident of real life. I do not now mean in poetry, but in prose. If you know enough about human nature to make the attempt, there is no better way of telling a story. It was a pure invention on the part of Browning, and we may call it a new method. But of course one must have a very great power of reading character to be able to do anything of the same kind.

This is the most colossal attempt in psychology made by Browning, but a large number of his longer poems are worked out in precisely the same manner as single monologues. "The Bishop Orders his Tomb," another Italian study, gives us all the ugly side of the Renaissance character—its selfishness, lust, hypocrisy, and ambition, together with that extraordinary sense of art which gave a certain greatness even to very bad men. "Bishop Blougram's Apology" (which is said to be a satire upon a famous English Cardinal) is quite modern, but it is almost equally ugly. It shows us a very powerful mind arguing, with irresistible logic and merciless cleverness, in an absolutely unworthy cause. The bishop has heard a young free thinker observe that the bishop could not believe the doctrines of the church, he was too clever a bishop for that. So he calls the young man to him, and utterly crushes him by a very clever lecture, in which he proves that belief or unbelief are equally foolish, that right and wrong are interchangeable, that black may be white or white black, that common sense and a knowledge of the world represent the highest wisdom, and that the free thinker is an absolute fool because he tells the world that he is a free thinker. We know that the bishop is morally wrong the whole way through, that every statement which he makes is wrong; yet it would take a clever man to prove him wrong. The logic is too well managed. Few psychological studies are comparable to this. "Mr. Sludge, 'the Medium,' " said to be a satire upon the great Scottish spiritualist and humbug, Home, shows us another kind of quackery; a man who lives by imposture explains to us how he can practise imposture with a good moral conscience, and under the belief that imposture is a benefit to mankind. He talks so well that he obliges even the person who has detected his imposture to lend him or give him a considerable sum of money—in short, he can trick even those who know his trickery. But see how different these beings are from each other, and how different the studies of their character must necessarily prove. Yet Browning seems never to find any difficulty in painting the mind of a man, whether good or bad, whether of to-day or of the Middle Ages. "Paracelsus," for example, is a mediæval character; Browning makes him tell us the story of his researches into alchemy and magic, makes him impart to us the secret ambition that once filled him, and the consequences of disappointment and of failure. "Sordello," again, is of the thirteenth century; you will find his name in the great poem of Dante. Sordello was a poet and troubadour, who tried to succeed socially and politically by the exercise of a brilliant talent, and almost did succeed. Browning's poem on him is the whole story of a human soul; only, it is the man himself who tells it. And the moral is that suffering and sorrow bring wisdom. How various and how wonderful is this range of character-study! Yet I have mentioned only a few out of scores and scores of compositions. I cannot insist too much upon this quality of versatility in Browning, this display of Shakespearian power. In all Tennyson you will find scarcely more than twenty really distinct characters; and some of these are but half drawn. In Rossetti you will find scarcely more than half a dozen, mostly women. In Swinburne there is no character whatever, except the poet's own, outside of that grand singer's dramatic work. But in Browning there are hundreds of distinct characters, and there is nothing at all vague about them; they speak, they move, they act with real and not with artificial life. Sometimes a character may occupy a hundred pages, sometimes it may be drawn in half a dozen lines, but the drawing is equally distinct and equally true. And there is scarcely any kind of human nature of which we have no picture. Even the lowest type of savage is drawn, the primitive savage, for "Caliban upon Setebos" gives us the thoughts and feelings of such a savage about God—God being figured in the savage mind, of course, as only a much stronger and larger kind of savage, possessing magical power.

In all his poems, as I said, Browning is essentially dramatic. Quite rightly has he grouped several collections of short poems under titles which suggest this fact, such as "Dramatic Idyls," "Dramatis Personæ," "Men and Women." Sometimes the poet himself is the only speaker and actor, giving us his own particular feelings of the moment; but in the most noteworthy cases of this kind he is talking, not to the reader, but to ghosts. For instance, "Parleyings with Certain People of Importance in Their Day," are imaginary conversations which Browning holds with the ghosts of men long dead—writers, philosophers, statesmen, priests. It is in this collection that you will find the remarkable verses on the great poem of Smart, which revived Smart's work for modern readers after a hundred years of oblivion. I cannot find time to tell you about the other personages of these imaginary conversations; but I may mention that Mandeville is the subject of a special conversation, and that you will find the whole germ of Mandeville's philosophy in this composition. But let us turn to some consideration of Browning's work in the true dramatic form—in plays, tragedies or comedies, and in translations of plays from the Greek.

It would require several lectures to give a summary of Browning's plays; and they do not always represent his best genius. For it is a curious fact that this man who, as a simple poet, was the greatest of English dramatists after Shakespeare, was rarely quite successful when he attempted the true dramatic form. He was great in the monologue; he was not great upon the stage. Some of his plays were acted, such as "Strafford" and "The Blot on the 'Scutcheon"; but they did not prove to be worthy of great success. "In a Balcony," which could not be put upon the stage at all, is much better; and perhaps it is better because it consists only of two monologues, or rather of a conversation between two persons; for the part taken by the other actors is altogether insignificant. "The Return of the Druses" and "Luria," like Tennyson's dramas, are excellent poetry, but they are not suited for the stage. The best of all Browning's dramas, the only one that I really want you to read, is "A Soul's Tragedy." I may say a word about the plot of this. It is a story of friendship between two young men, patriots and statesmen. In a political crisis one of the young men stabs a political enemy, and has fled from the country. But before fleeing, he trusts all his interests and his property to his friend, and asks the friend also to take care of his betrothed. What does the friend do? Exposed to great temptation, he betrays his trust. He sees a chance to obtain political power by pretending to be the man who really stabbed the politician on the other side—the tyrant of an hour. The people acclaim him as their saviour, make him dictator. Then he goes further in his treachery, by making love to his friend's sweetheart. At last a Roman statesman, Ogniben, appears upon the scene, with power to crush the revolution, or to do anything that he pleases. But Ogniben is a terribly clever man, and he does not want bloodshed; he knows the character of the new dictator, and

[257]

determines to play with him, as a cat with a mouse.
First he flatters him enough to make him betray all
his weaknesses, his vanities, his fears. Then, at quite
the unexpected moment, he summons the young man
who had run away, I mean the friend betrayed, and
brings him face to face with the treacherous dictator.
The result is of course a moral collapse; that is the
real Soul's Tragedy. I am giving only a thin skeleton
of the plot. But you ought to read this play, if only
for the wonderful studies of character in it, not the
least remarkable of which is the awful Ogniben, far-
seeing, cunning beyond cunning, strong beyond force,
who can unravel plots with a single word and pierce
all masks of hypocrisy with a single glance; but whom
you feel to be, in a large way, generous and kindly, and
so far as possible, just. I think not only that this
is Browning's greatest play, but that as a play it is
psychologically superior to anything else which has been
done in Victorian drama. It is not fit for the stage,
and it is not even very great as poetry—indeed half of
it or more is prose, and rather eccentric prose; but it
offers wonderful examples of analytical power not surpassed in any other contemporary poet or dramatist.

About Browning's translations from the Greek poets,
I scarcely know what to say. Most critics of authority
acknowledge that Browning has made the most faithful
metrical translation of the "Agamemnon" of Æschylus.
But they also declare that in spite of its exactness,
the Greek spirit and feeling have entirely vanished
under Browning's treatment. My own feeling about
the matter is that you would do much better to read
the prose translation of Æschylus. Yet I could not

Studies in Browning

say this in regard to Browning's translation of the "Alkestis" of Euripides, which you will find embodied in the text of "Balaustian's Adventure." Balaustian is a Greek dancing girl. She is taken prisoner with many Athenian people at the time of the disastrous Greek expedition to Syracuse, which you must have read about in history. To please her captors, she repeats for them the wonderful verses of Euripides, by which they are so much affected that they pardon both her and her companions. This incident is founded upon fact, and Browning uses it very well to introduce his translation. Perhaps the genius of Euripides was closer to the genius of Browning than that of Æschylus; for this translation is incomparably better from an emotional point of view than the other. It is very beautiful indeed; and even after having read the Greek play in a good prose translation, I think that you would find both pleasure and profit in reading Browning's verses.

The important thing now for you to get clearly into your minds is one general fact about this enormously various work of Browning. Suppose somebody should ask you what is different in the work of Browning from that of all other modern poets, what would you be able to answer? But unless you can answer, the whole value of this lecture would be lost upon you. Browning himself has excellently answered, in a little verse which forms the prologue to the second series of the Dramatic Idyls.

> "You are sick, that's sure,"—they say:
> "Sick of what?"—they disagree.

Pre-Raphaelite and Other Poets

" 'Tis the brain,"—thinks Doctor A;
" 'Tis the heart,"—holds Doctor B.
"The liver—my life I'd lay!"
"The lungs!" "The lights!"
                Ah me!
So ignorant of man's whole
Of bodily organs plain to see—
So sage and certain, frank and free,
About what's under lock and key—
      Man's soul!

That is to say, even the wisest doctors cannot agree
about the simple fact of a man's sickness, notwithstanding the fact that they have studied anatomy and
physiology and osteology, and have examined every
part of the body. Yet, although the wisest men of
science are obliged to confess that they cannot tell you
everything about the body, which can be seen, even
ignorant persons think that they know everything about
the soul of a man, which cannot be seen at all, and about
the mind of a man, to which only God himself has the
key. Now all the purpose of Browning's work and life
has been to show people what a very wonderful and
complex and incomprehensible thing human character is
—therefore to show that the most needful of all study
is the study of human nature. He is especially the poet
of character, the only one who has taught us, since
Shakespeare's time, what real men and women are, how
different each from every other, how unclassifiable according to any general rule, how differently noble at
their best, how differently wicked at their worst, how
altogether marvellous and infinitely interesting. His
mission has been the mission of a great dramatic psy-

chologist. And if anybody ever asks you what was Robert Browning, you can answer that he was the great Poet of Human Character—not of character of any one time or place or nation, but of all times and places and peoples of which it was possible for him to learn anything.

Here we must close our little studies of Victorian poets—that is to say, of the four great ones. I hope that you will be able to summarise in your own mind the main characteristic of each, as I have tried to indicate in the case of Browning. Remember Tennyson as the greatest influence upon the language of his mother country, because of his exquisiteness of workmanship and his choice of English subjects in preference to all others. He is the most English of all the four. Remember Rossetti as being altogether different in his personality and feeling—a man of the Middle Ages born into the nineteenth century, and in the nineteenth century still the poet of mediæval feeling. And think of Swinburne—the greatest musician of all, the most perfect master of form and sound in modern poetry—as an expounder of Neo-Paganism, of another Renaissance in the world of literature.

CHAPTER V

WILLIAM MORRIS suffers by comparison with the more exquisite poets of his own time and circle. Nevertheless he is quite great enough to call for a special lecture. I am not sure whether I shall be able to make you much interested in him; but I shall certainly try to give you a clear idea of his position in English poetry as something entirely distinct, and very curious.

A few words first about the man himself—in more ways than one the largest figure among the Romantics. He was the great spirit of the Pre-Raphaelite coterie; he was the most prolific poet of the century; and he was in all respects the nearest in his talent and sentiment to Sir Walter Scott. All these reasons make it necessary to speak of him at considerable length.

He was born in 1834 and died in 1896, so that he is very recent in his relation to English poetry. There was nothing extraordinary in the incidents of his life at school or in his university career. In this man the extraordinary gift was altogether of the mind. Without the eccentricity of genius, he was also without the highest capacity of genius; but in his life as well as in his poetry he was always correct and always charming in a certain gentle and dreamy way. He had the stature and strength of a giant, perfect health, and immense working capacity, and did very well whatever

[262]

William Morris

he tried to do. Fortunately for his inclinations, he was the son of a rich man and never knew want; so that when he took to literature as a profession, he never had to think about pleasing the public, nor to care how much money his books might bring. After leaving Oxford University he devoted his life to art and literature, becoming equally well known as a painter and a poet. At a later day he established various businesses for an æsthetic purpose. For example, he thought that the early Italian printers and Venetian printers had done much better work and produced much more wonderful books than any modern printer; and he founded a press for the purpose of producing modern books in the same beautiful way. Then he thought that a reform in the matter of house furniture was possible. The furniture of the sixteenth and seventeenth centuries had been good, solid, costly, and beautiful; but the later furniture had become both cheap and ugly. Morris's artistic interests had led him to study furniture a great deal; he became familiar with the furniture of the Middle Ages, of the Elizabethan Age, and of later times, as scarcely any man of the day had become. It occurred to him that the best and most beautiful forms of mediæval and later furniture might be reintroduced, if anybody would only take pains to manufacture them. The ordinary manufacturers of furniture would not do this. Morris and a few friends established a factory, and there designed and made furniture equal to anything in the past. This undertaking was successful, and it changed the whole fashion of English house furnishing. Only a decorative artist like Morris would have been capable of imagining and carrying out such a plan; and it was carried out so well that almost every rich house in England now possesses some furniture designed by him.

Thus you will see that he must have been a very busy man, occupied at once with poetry, with romance (for he wrote a great many prose romances), with artistic printing, with house furniture, with designs for windows of stained glass, and with designs for beautiful tiling— also with a very considerable amount of work as a decorative artist. All this would appear almost too much for any one person to attempt. But it was rendered easy to Morris by the simple fact that the whole of his various undertakings happened to be influenced by exactly the same spirit and motive, the artistic feeling of the Middle Ages, and of the period ending with the eighteenth century. Whether Morris was making books of poetry or books of prose, whether he was translating sagas from the Norse or writing stories in imitation of the early French romances, whether he was casting Italian forms of type for the making of beautiful books or designing furniture for some English palace, whatever he was doing, he had but one thought, one will—to reproduce the strange beauty of the Middle Ages. There was almost nothing modern about the man. The whole of his writings, comprising a great many volumes, contained scarcely ten pages having any reference to modern things. Even the language that he used has been correctly described by a great critic as eighteenth century English, mixed with Scandinavian idioms and forms. Thus there were two men among the Pre-Raphaelites who actually did not belong to their own century—Rossetti and Morris. Both were painters as

William Morris

well as poets, and though the former was the greater in both arts, the practical influence of Morris counted for much more in changing English taste both in literature and in æsthetics.

We have chiefly to consider his writing, and, of that writing, especially the poetry. As a poet I have already mentioned him as having points of resemblance with Sir Walter Scott. But he also had even more points of resemblance with Chaucer. He was like Scott in the singular ease and joyous force of his creative talent. Scott could sit down and write a romance in verse beautifully, correctly, without any more difficulty than other men write prose. Byron, you know, used to write his poetry straight off, without even taking the trouble to correct it; as a consequence it is now becoming forgotten. But Scott took very great trouble to make his verse quite correct, without trying to be exquisite, and his verse will always count as good, stirring English poetry. Morris had almost exactly the same talent, the talent that can give you a three-volume story either in verse or prose, just as you may prefer. And he wrote in verse on a scale that astonishes, a scale exceeding that of any modern poet. To find his equal in production we must go back to the poets of those romantic Middle Ages which he so much loved, the poets who wrote vast epics or romances in thirty or forty thousand lines. Eleven volumes of verse and fifteen volumes of prose represent Morris's production; and the extraordinary thing is that all his production is good. It does not reach the very highest place in literature; no man could write so much and make his work of the very highest class. But it is good as to form, good as to feeling, much beyond mediocrity at all times; and sometimes it rises to a level that is only a little below the first class.

I am not going to give selections from his larger works, so I can only mention here what the large works signify and how he is related to Chaucer through one of them. The most successful, in a popular sense, of all his poems is the "Earthly Paradise," originally published in five volumes, now published in four—and the volumes are very thick. This vast composition is much on the plan of the "Canterbury Tales"; and Morris and Chaucer both followed the same method, and were filled with the same sense of beauty. Both found in the legends of the Middle Ages and in the myths of antiquity, material for their art in the shape of stories; and as these stories had no inter-relation, belonging even to widely different epochs of human civilisation, it was necessary to imagine some general plan according to which all could be brought harmoniously together, like jewels, upon a single tray. This plan of uniting heterogeneous masses of fiction or legends into one artistic circle was known to the East long before it was known in Europe; the great Indian collections of stories, such as the Panchatantra and the Kathâ-sarit-sâgara, are perhaps the oldest examples; and the huge Sanskrit epics show something of the same design, afterwards adopted by Arabian and Persian story-tellers. But Chaucer was the first to make the attempt with any success in English literature. His plan was to have the stories told by pilgrims travelling on their way to Canterbury, every man or woman of the company being obliged to tell one or two stories. The plan was so

good that it has been followed in our own day; Long-
fellow's "Tales of a Wayside Inn" are constructed
upon precisely the same principle. But Chaucer made
a plan so large that he had not the strength nor the
time to carry it to completion; Morris, upon a scale
nearly as large, brought his work to a happy conclusion
with the greatest ease. He makes a company of exiled
warriors tell the stories of a foreign court, as results
of their experience or knowledge obtained in many different countries. There are twenty-four stories, twelve
mediæval or romantic and twelve classical; and each
pair of these corresponds with one of the twelve months,
the first two stories being told in January, the second
two in February, and so forth. The division neatly
partitions the great composition into twelve books,
with the regular prologues and epilogues added. The
English are not apt to trouble themselves to read very
long poems these days; but Morris was able actually
to revive the mediæval taste for long romances. Tens
of thousands of his books were sold, notwithstanding
their costliness, and the result was altogether favour-
able for the new development of romantic feeling, not
only in literature, but in art and decoration. One
might suppose that such composition was enough to
occupy a lifetime, but Morris threw it off quite lightly
and set to work upon a variety of poetical undertakings
nearly as large. He translated Homer and Virgil into
the same kind of flowery verse; and he put the grand
Scandinavian epic of Sigurd the Volsung into some of
the finest long-lined poetry produced in modern times.
This epic seems to me the better work of the two long
productions by which Morris is best known; later on

some lines from it may be quoted. But Morris was scarcely less attracted by Greek myths than by the old literature of Scandinavia; and he also produced a long epic poem upon the story of Jason and Medea, the story of the Golden Fleece. Nevertheless, I can much better illustrate to you what Morris is in literature and what his influence and his objects were, by means of his still earlier and shorter poems. There are several volumes of these, now published in more compact form under the titles of "Poems by the Way" and "Love is Enough" and "The Defense of Guinevere." From the last, originally dedicated to Rossetti, I will make some quotations that will show you how Morris tried to revive the Middle Ages.

One of the most remarkable things in the late Mr. Froude's charming account of a voyage which he made to Norway, is his statement of a sudden conviction that there came to him about the character of the ancient Vikings. He felt assured, he said, that the modern Norwegian and the ancient Norwegian were very much the same; that modern customs, religion, and education had produced only differences of surface; and that if we could go back against the stream of time to the age of the sea kings, we should find that they were exactly like the men of to-day in all that essentially belongs to race character. Now Morris, while studying mediæval romances and loving them for their intrinsic curious beauty, came to a very similar conclusion. It is true, he thought, that the Middle Ages were much more cruel, more ignorant, more savage than the ages before them or after them; but after all, the men and women of those times must have felt about many things just like

modern men and women. Why should we not feel
enough of this to study their fashions, joys, and feelings under the peculiar conditions of their terrible society? And this is what he did. You may say that,
except for some difference in the home speech, the talk
of these people in the poems of Morris is the talk of
modern men and women. There is some difference as
to sentiment. But you cannot say that it is not natural, not likely; in fact, the seeming pictures often have
such force that you cannot forget them. That is a
test of truth.

They are very brief pictures, like sudden glimpses
caught during a flash of lightning: a glimpse into an
arena where two men are about to fight to the death in
presence of their king, according to the code of the
day; a knight riding through a flooded country in order
to take a castle by surprise; a woman driven to madness by the murder of her lover; a woman at the stake
about to be burned alive, when the sound of the hoofs
of the lover's horse is heard, as he gallops to her rescue;
ladies in the upper chamber of a castle, weaving and
singing; the capture of a robber and his vain pleading
for life; also some fairy tales of weird and sensuous
beauty, told as people of the Middle Ages must have
felt them. To me one of the most powerful pictures
is the story of "The Haystack in the Floods." -We are
not told how the tragedy began, nor how it ended; and
this is great art to tell something without beginning
and without end, so well that the reader is always thereafter wondering what the beginning was and what the
end might have been. The poem begins with the
words:

Pre-Raphaelite and Other Poets

> Had she come all the way for this
> To part at last without a kiss?
> Yea, had she borne the dirt and rain
> That her own eyes might see him slain
> Beside the haystack in the floods?

We know from this only that the woman referred to is a woman of gentle birth, accustomed to luxurious things, so that it was very difficult for her to travel in rainy weather and cold, and that she thought it was a great sacrifice on her part to do so even for a lover. If she thought this, we have a right to suspect that she is a wanton—though we are not quite sure about it. The description of her does not explain anything further than the misery of the situation.

> Along the dripping leafless woods,
> The stirrup touching either shoe,
> She rode astride as troopers do;
> With kirtle kilted to her knee,
> To which the mud splashed wretchedly;
> And the wet dripp'd from every tree
> Upon her head and heavy hair,
> And on her eyelids broad and fair;
> The tears and rain ran down her face.

The delicate woman has also the pain of being lonesome on her ride; for the lover, the knight, cannot ride beside her, cannot comfort her; he has to ride far ahead in order to see what danger may be in the road. He is running away with her; perhaps he is a stranger in that country; we shall presently see.

Suddenly, nearby in the middle of a flooded place the

enemy appears, a treacherous knight who is the avowed lover of the woman and the enemy of the man. She counts the number of spears with him—thirty spears, and they have but ten. Fighting is of no use, the woman says, but Robert (now we know for the first time the name of her companion) is not afraid—believes that by courage and skill alone he can scatter the hostile force, and bring his sweetheart over the river. She begs him not to fight; her selfishness shows her character—it is not for him she is afraid, but for herself.

> But, "O!" she said,
> "My God! my God! I have to tread
> The long way back without you; then
> The court at Paris; those six men;
> The gratings of the Chatelet; . . ."

And worse than the gratings of the Chatelet is the stake; at which she may be burned, or the river into which she may be thrown, if her lover is killed; there is only one way to secure her own safety—that is to accept the love of another man whom she hates, the wicked knight Godmar, who is now in front of them with thirty spearsmen. Evidently this is no warrior woman, no daughter of soldiers; she may love, but like Cleopatra she is afraid of battle. Her lover Robert, like a man, does not answer her tearful prayers, but gives the command to his men to shout his war-cry, and boldly charges forward. Then, triple sorrow! his men stand still; they refuse to fight against three times the number, and in another moment Robert is in the p

of his enemy, disarmed and bound. Thereupon Godmar
with a wicked smile observes to the woman:

> "Now, Jehane,
> Your lover's life is on the wane
> So fast, that, if this very hour
> You yield not as my paramour,
> He will not see the rain leave off."

He does more than threaten to kill her lover; he
reminds her of what he can further do to her. She has
said that if he takes her into his castle by force, she
will kill either herself or him (we may doubt whether
she would really do either); and he wants a voluntary
submission. He talks to her about burning her alive;
how would she like that? And the ironical caressing
tone of his language only makes it more implacable.

> "Nay, if you do not my behest,
> O Jehane! though I love you well,"
> Said Godmar, "would I fail to tell
> All that I know?" "Foul lies," she said.
> "Eh? lies, my Jehane? by God's head,
> At Paris folks would deem them true!
> Do you know, Jehane, they cry for you:
> Jehane the brown! Jehane the brown!
> Give us Jehane to burn or drown!
> Eh!—gag me Robert!—sweet my friend,
> This were indeed a piteous end
> For those long fingers, and long feet,
> And long neck, and smooth shoulders sweet;
> An end that few men would forget
> That saw it. So, an hour yet:
> Consider, Jehane, which to take
> Of life or death!"

William Morris

She considers, or rather tries to consider, for she is almost too weary to speak, and very quickly falls asleep in the rain on the wet hay. An hour passes. When she is awakened, she only sighs like a tired child, and answers, "I will not." Perhaps she could not believe that her enemy and lover would do as he had threatened; and in spite of the risk of further angering him, she approaches the prisoner and tries to kiss him farewell. Immediately,

> With a start
> Up Godmar rose, thrust them apart;
> From Robert's throat he loosed the bands
> Of silk and mail; with empty hands
> Held out, she stood and gazed, and saw
> The long bright blade without a flaw
> Glide out from Godmar's sheath, his hand
> In Robert's hair; she saw him bend
> Back Robert's head; she saw him send
> The thin steel down; the blow told well,
> Right backward the knight Robert fell,
> And moaned as dogs do, being half dead,
> Unwittingly, as I deem: so then
> Godmar turn'd grinning to his men,
> Who ran, some five or six, and beat
> His head to pieces at her feet.

The knight groans involuntarily, in the death struggle only, and probably the sound of his pain pleases Godmar, but in order to make sure that he cannot recover again, he makes a sign to his followers to finish the work of murder; so they beat in his skull— an ugly thing for a woman to see done. There were rough-hearted men in those days who could see a woman

[273]

burned alive and laugh at her suffering. You have read, I think, the terrible story about Black Fulk, who made a great holiday on the occasion of burning his young wife alive, and took his friends to see the show, himself putting on his best holiday attire. This Godmar seems to be nearly as harsh a brute, judging from what he next has to say.

> Then Godmar turn'd again and said:
> "So, Jehane, the first fitte is read!
> Take note, my lady, that your way
> Lies backward to the Chatelet!"
> She shook her head and gazed awhile
> At her cold hands with rueful smile,
> As though this thing had made her mad.
>
> This was the parting that they had
> Beside the haystack in the floods.

Notice the brutal use of the word "fitte" (often spelled fytte). This was an old name for the divisions of a long poem, romance, or epic. Later the Italian term "canto" was substituted for it. Godmar refers to the woman's love as her romance, her poem: "Now the first canto of our love-romance has been read—only the first, remember!" The second fitte will be perhaps the burning of the woman when she is brought back to the castle prison from which she fled. It all depends upon circumstances. If she has really become mad, she may escape. The poem ends here, leaving us in doubt about the rest. We can only imagine the termination. I think that she has not really become mad, that she is too selfish and weak to bear or even to feel the real emotional shock of the thing; and that when they are half way to the prison she is likely to yield to Godmar's will. If she does so, he will probably keep her in his castle until he tires of her, and finds it expedient to end her existence with as little scruple as he showed in killing Robert. But, as an actual fact, it is difficult to be sure of anything, because we know neither the beginning nor the end of the affair. We have only a glimpse of the passion, suffering, selfishness, cruelty— then utter darkness. And this method of merely glimpsing the story causes it to leave a profound impression upon the imagination. Please do not forget this, because it is the most important art in any kind of narrative literature, whether of poetry or of prose.

A second example of the same device is furnished by another terrible poem called "The Judgment of God." The Judgment of God is an old name for trial by single combat. It was a superstitious law, a foolish and wicked law, but it served a purpose in the Middle Ages, and it afforded an opportunity for many noble and courageous deeds. Browning took up this subject in his stirring poem of "Count Gismond." The law was this: when one knight was accused by another of some evil, cruel, or treacherous act, he was allowed to challenge the man who brought the charge against him to fight to the death—*a l'outrance*, as the old term expressed it. The combat took place in the presence of the lord or king and before a great assembly, according to fixed rules. If the man who brought the charge lost the fight, then it was thought that he had proved himself a liar. If the person accused won the battle, then he was declared to be innocent. For it was thought that

Pre-Raphaelite and Other Poets

God would protect the truth in such cases; and therefore these combats were called the "judgment of God." Nevertheless you will perceive that a very skilful knight might be able to kill a great number of accusers, and lawfully "prove" himself innocent of a hundred crimes. That was a great defect of the system.

The "Judgment of God" is a monologue, quite as good in its way as many of the short monologues of Browning. It is the knight against whom accusation has been brought that tells us the feelings and impressions of the moment that he enters the lists to fight. In this case we are more moved to sympathy than in the former stories, because we know that the man, whether otherwise bad or good, has saved a woman from the stake, and killed the lords who were about to burn her. So we are inclined to think of him as a hero. We have just one sudden vision of a man's mind, as he stands in the face of death, with no sympathy about him except that of his old father, who comes to give him advice about fighting, because he is to be matched against a very skilful knight.

> "Swerve to the left, son Roger," he said,
> "When you catch his eyes through the helmet-slit,
> Swerve to the left, then out at his head,
> And the Lord God give you joy of it!"

The old man knows how to fight, has probably won many a battle, and he has observed the way that the light is falling. So he tells his son, "When you begin to fight, don't turn to the right—turn to the left; then you will be able to see his eyes through the helmet, and immediately that you see them, strike straight for

William Morris

his head, and may God help you to kill him." He has just heard these words from his father when the prologue begins.

> The blue owls on my father's hood
>   Were a little dimm'd, as I turned away;
> This giving up of blood for blood
>   Will finish here somehow to-day.
>
> So when I walked from out the tent,
>   Their howling almost blinded me;
> Yet for all that I was not bent
>   By any shame. Hard by, the sea
>
> Made a noise like the aspens where
>   We did that wrong, but now the place
> Is very pleasant, and the air
>   Blows cool on any passer's face.
>
> And all the throng is gather'd now
>   Into the circle of these lists—
> Yea, howl out, butchers! tell me how
>   His hands were cut off at the wrists;
>
> And how Lord Roger bore his face
>   A league above his spear point, high
> Above the owls, to that strong place
>   Among the waters—yea, yea, cry!

The owls on the crest are the emblem of the family. The knight has been waiting in his tent according to rule, until the signal is given; and his father and his retainers probably helped to arm him there. He feels no emotion except at the moment of bidding his father good-bye, and then he knows that there are tears in his own eyes, because the owl crest on his father's hood

[277]

suddenly appears dim. Then, as the signal is given, he walks out of the tent into the lists, only to hear a roar of hatred and abuse go up from all the circles of seats. The friends of the dead are evidently in great force, and he has no friend except his father and his retainers. And they shout at him, his enemies, telling him what he has done—how he cut off the hands of the knight and cut off his head and carried it upon the top of a spear for three miles, carried it above his own banner to his own castle. This was indeed considered an unknightly thing in those days, for such was the treatment given to common people in war, not to knights or men of rank.

Then he sees the man with whom he must fight, waiting for him, all in armour, with white linen over his arm, to indicate that he is fighting for the cause of truth. At this Roger can very well laugh; and he remarks that the face of the champion's lady looks even whiter than the linen upon her lord's arm. She has reason, perhaps, to be afraid for him. And though he has not much time for thinking, Roger remembers his own beloved, waiting for him, remembers even how he first met her. Addressing her in thought, he says:

> And these say: "No more now my knight,
>   Or God's knight any longer"—you
> Being than they so much more white,
>   So much more pure and good and true,
>
> Will cling to me forever—there,
>   Is not that wrong turn'd right at last
> Through all these years, and I wash'd clean?
>   Say, yea, Ellayne; the time is past,

William Morris

Since on that Christmas-day last year
Up to your feet the fire crept;
And the smoke through the brown leaves sere
Blinded your dear eyes that you wept;

Was it not I that caught you then
And kiss'd you on the saddle-bow?
Did not the blue owl mark the men
Whose spears stood like the corn a-row?

Evidently she has reason to love him and his house; did he not save her from the fire?—did he not come with his spearmen and crush her enemies, and take her away upon his horse to safety? And was not that enough to atone for whatever other wrong he might have done? But he has only a moment in which to think all this, for the trumpet is about to sound for the fight, and there are other things to think about. One of these is that his antagonist is a very good man, difficult to overcome; the other is that there is danger for him even if he conquers, because there are so many present who hate him.

This Oliver is a right good knight,
And needs must beat me, as I fear,
Unless I catch him in the fight,
My father's crafty way—John, here!

Bring up the men from the south gate,
To help me if I fall or win,
For even if I beat, their hate
Will grow to more than this mere grin.

If the reader could imagine the result of the combat, the real effect of the poem in its present form

[279]

would be lost. No man can imagine it. The challenged knight acknowledges his antagonist to be a better man —indeed, he says that he can only hope to conquer him by the cunning trick taught him by his old father. But the really dangerous man never underrates the capacity of an enemy; and we may suspect that the forces are at least even. So, as I have said, no man can guess the result of the battle, and the reader is forced to keep wondering what happened. He will always wonder, but he will never be able to feel convinced. And to leave the mind of the reader thus interested and unsatisfied is a great stroke of literary art. The same book contains a number of mediæval pieces of the same sort, showing how very unimportant it is whether you begin a story in the middle or whether you leave it without an end. The greatest French story-tellers of modern times have made almost popular the form of art in fiction to which I refer. Take, for example, the late Guy de Maupassant, many of whose short stories have, I am told, been translated into Japanese. No one modern prose writer ever succeeded better in telling a story without any beginning or without any end. Positively no beginning and no end is necessary, in many cases; and remember, this method of representing only the middle of things is exactly true to life. We never see or hear of the whole of any incident that happens under our eyes. We see only a fact, without knowing what caused it to come about, and without knowing what will be the consequences of it. Outside of our own homes we do not see much of other people's lives, and never the whole of any one's life.

Among other pieces in the book I should call your

William Morris

attention to "The Little Tower," "Sir Peter Harpdon's End," "The Wind," "The Eve of Crecy," "In Prison," and "The Blue Closet." They are very different in idea, but I think that you will find them all extremely original. "The Little Tower" has no beginning and no end. It only describes faithfully the feelings of a knight riding over an inundated country, swimming his horse along the side of bridges under water, and thinking to himself of the joy of capturing an enemy's castle by surprise, killing the lord and burning the lady. It is brutal in a certain way, but supremely natural. The story of "Sir Peter Harpdon's End" is not a monologue; it is a very dramatic narrative in which a number of men of different character play their parts. It has no beginning, but the end is plainly suggested —and this shows the tender side of human nature in the Middle Ages. Sir Peter is brave, kindly, and true. Therefore, when he has his enemy at his mercy, instead of killing him, he only cuts off his ears. As a consequence he is afterwards himself destroyed; the obvious moral of the narrative is that a merciful heart was a dangerous possession in those times. The good men were easily trapped by playing upon their feelings of pity or sympathy. "The Wind" represents the madness of a very old knight, alone in his castle. The sound of the wind makes him think of the voices of the dead whom he knew, and brings him back to the memories of his youth, and of a woman that he loved. And at last the ghosts of forgotten friends enter and glide about him. This has no beginning and no end, and it remains very strongly impressed upon the memory. We should like to know the story of that woman,

[281]

the story of the madness of the old man, but we shall never know. "The Eve of Crecy" represents the state of mind of a young French knight just before the fatal battle, when the flower of the French chivalry was destroyed by a mere handful of English soldiers driven to bay. You may remember that before the battle the English prepared themselves very thoroughly and made fervent prayers to heaven for success. But the French spent the night in carousing and jesting, never dreaming that they could lose the fight. Here Morris shows us one of the young noblemen thinking only about his sweetheart, some girl of noble rank whom he hopes to win. He is going to do great deeds the next day, then the king will smile upon him, and he will not be afraid to ask the father of that girl to permit him to become his son-in-law. And so the poem abruptly breaks off. The end here we can guess—a corpse riddled with English arrows, and trampled under the feet of thousands of horses. "In Prison," among the others, represents the emotions of a knight confined in a mediæval dungeon. "The Blue Closet" is a fantasy, a wild mediæval fairy tale, put into a dramatic form that reminds one singularly of the later work of Maeterlinck. It is, however, a noteworthy composition as poetry, and attained immediate popularity among all those who looked for beauties of colour and sound rather than reflections of life.

Those notes will give you an idea of the variety of the book. And the mediæval pieces are worth thinking about, if any of you should care to attempt authorship in a similar direction, whether in poetry or in prose. There was a period in Japanese feudalism, a period of constant civil wars and baronial quarrels, which would have produced a very similar condition of things to that described in certain of these poems, and I even think that more startling effects could be produced by a judicious handling of Japanese themes in the same way, that is, without attempting any beginning or suggesting any end.

But observe that I am not holding up these poems to you as great masterpieces of verse. I mean only that they suggest how great masterpieces might be made. And please to note especially one phase of the art of them, its psychological quality. Morris was not so great a psychologist as Browning, who came nearest to Shakespeare in this respect of all English poets. But Morris has considerable ability in this way, and the most striking effects in his short poems are produced by making us understand the feelings of persons in particular moments of pain or terror or heroic effort. For example, how natural and horrible is the soliloquy of Guinevere in the long poem with which the book opens. You know that Tennyson did not follow the original account of Malory in regard to the more cruel episodes of the old story. He felt repelled by such an incident as the preparations for burning the queen alive. In the real story she is about to be burned when Lancelot comes and saves her, not without killing half the knights present and some of his own relations into the bargain. But Morris saw in this episode an opportunity for psychological work, and took it, just as Browning might have done. He makes the queen express her thought:

Pre-Raphaelite and Other Poets

> . . . "I know
> I wondered how the fire, while I should stand,
> And burn, against the heat, would quiver so,
> Yards above my head."

This startles, because it is true. The quotations which I gave you from "The Haystack in the Floods" contain several passages of an equally impressive sort. We can best revive the past in literature not by trying to describe the details of custom and of costume then prevalent, but by trying to express faithfully the feelings of people who lived long ago. And this can be managed most effectively either by monologue or dialogue.

The only other collection of short poems written by Morris is now compressed into a companion volume entitled "Poems by the Way." All of it is later work, but it is not more successful than the youthful productions which we have been considering. Nevertheless it excels in greater variety. You have here dramatic pieces of several kinds, ballads and translations of ballads, fairy tales and translations of fairy tales, mediæval and Norse stories, and strangely mixed with these a number of socialist poems—for Morris believed in the theories of socialism, in the possibility of an ideal communism.

The bulk of the pieces in the volume, however, are Scandinavian, and the general tone of the book is Northern. Morris was a tremendous worker in the interest of Scandinavian literature. He loved the mediævalism of the pagan Norse even more than the corresponding period of the Christian and chivalrous South. He helped the work of those great Oxford professors who brought out the Corpus Poeticum Boreale,

William Morris

translating in conjunction with one of them several ancient Sagas. And as a poet he did a great deal to quicken English interest in Norse literature, as we shall see later on. In this book we have only short pieces, but they are good, and a number of them have the value of almost literal translations. As for the style, a good example is furnished by the story of the killing of the Hallgerd (or Hallgerda) by Hallbiorn the Strong. The story is taken from an old Icelandic history, and is undoubtedly true. Hallbiorn wedded a daughter of a man called Odd, on account of his odd character. She was very beautiful. Her father insisted that Hallbiorn should spend the whole next season, winter, with him, and said that he might take his bride away in the spring for the summer. During the winter Hallgerda had a secret intrigue with a blood relation called Snæbiorn. The husband did not know, he only felt a little suspicious at times. When the summer came, and he asked Hallgerda to go with him to the house which he had built for her, she did not answer. He asked her twice, still she did not answer. The third time she refused. Then he killed her. Then Snæbiorn, her lover, attacked him, and after a terrible fight in which eight or nine men were killed, Hallbiorn was cut down. Snæbiorn then left the country vowing that he would never speak to man again, and settled in Greenland, where he died. The incidents are not wonderful, but the simple and terrible way in which they are told by the Icelandic chronicle makes them appeal greatly to the imagination. And Morris did justice to the style of the old Landnámabok, as it is called. The following lines relate to the tragedy only:

[285]

Pre-Raphaelite and Other Poets

. . . But Hallbiorn into the bower is gone
And there sat Hallgerd all alone.
She was not dight to go nor ride,
She had no joy of the summer-tide,
Silent she sat and combed her hair,
That fell all round about her there.
The slant beam lay upon her head
And gilt her golden locks to red.
He gazed at her with hungry eyes
And fluttering did his heart arise.
"Full hot," he said, "is the sun to-day,
And the snow is gone from the mountain-way,
The king-cup grows above the grass,
And through the wood do the thrushes pass."
Of all his words she hearkened none
But combed her hair amidst the sun.
"The laden beasts stand in the garth,
And their heads are turned to Helliskarth."
The sun was falling on her knee,
And she combed her gold hair silently.
"To-morrow great will be the cheer
At the Brother's Tongue by Whitewater."
From her folded lap the sunbeam slid;
She combed her hair, and the word she hid.
"Come, love; is the way so long and drear
From Whitewater to Whitewater?"
The sunbeam lay upon the floor;
She combed her hair and spake no more.
He drew her by the lily hand:
"I love thee better than all the land."
He drew her by the shoulders sweet,
"My threshold is but for thy feet."
He drew her by the yellow hair,
"Oh, why wert thou so deadly fair?
Oh, am I wedded to death?" he cried,
"Is the Dead-strand come to Whitewater side?"

William Morris

In order to know how terrible all this is, we must understand the character of the Norse woman. Like the will of the man, her will is iron; she cannot be broken, she cannot be made to bend, except by love, and when she refuses to bend there is nothing to be done but to kill her. All the facts stated here in rhymed verse are even more terrible and more simple in the prose chronicle. Throughout Norse history we repeatedly hear of women being killed under like circumstances. These ferocious men would not beat or abuse their women; that would have been no use. But they insisted upon being obeyed; to refuse obedience was to court death. In the present true story, however, the refusal to obey means much more than to court death; it means a bold confession by the bride that she has loved and still loves another man than her husband, and that is the reason of his sudden and terrible question, "Oh, am I wedded to death? Is the Dead-strand come to this place?" The Dead-strand or Corpse-strand was, in Norse mythology, the name of a part of Hel, the region of the dead, the Hades of old Norse, so his question really means, "Have the evil dead come here for us both?" for good men and women did not go to the Dead-strand. Now hear her answer. When he speaks at last, she sings in his face her secret lover's favourite song, which is just the same thing as to say, "I am glad to be killed for my lover's sake." And to kill a Norse woman meant, of course, death for the man who slew her, for her kindred were bound to avenge her. So she is defying him in every way.

The sun was fading from the room,
But her eyes were bright in the change and the gloom,

"Sharp Sword," she sang,—"and death is sure,
But over all doth love endure."
She stood up shining in her place
And laughed beneath his deadly face.
Instead of the sunbeam gleamed a brand,
The hilts were hard in Hallbiorn's hand.

The last line contains a phrase from old Northern war poetry. To say that the hilt of a man's sword was hard in his hand, signifies that he was a terrible swordsman, accustomed to mighty blows. But Morris here makes a little departure from the original chronicle. He makes Hallbiorn pass his sword through the woman's body. As a matter of fact he did nothing of the kind; he simply cut her head off at a single blow. Very dramatic, however, is his telling of the subsequent flight of Hallbiorn, and the pursuit by Snæbiorn. Hallbiorn's men are surprised at the fact that he does not hold his ground, for they know nothing of what happened in the house, and one of them says, "Where shall we sleep to-night?" Hallbiorn answers grimly, "Under the ground." Then his retainers know for the first time that they are going to be attacked. The attacking party consists of twelve men. Hallbiorn's retainers urge their master to hasten forward; it is still possible, they think, to escape. But he stops his horse and leaps down, exclaiming:

"Why should the supper of Odin wait?
Weary and chased I will not come
To the table of my father's home."

That is a fine expression about the supper of Odin, referring to the hope of every brave man to enter, at

his death, into Valhalla, the hall of Odin, and to sup
with the gods. And to enter there one had to be killed
in battle. So you can see the fierce humour of Hallbiorn's remark that he does not want to come late to the
supper of the gods, and to keep the feast waiting.
Snæbiorn does not speak. Hallbiorn only laughs. He
kills five men; then one of his feet is cut off, but he
rushes forward upon the bleeding stump, and kills two
more before he is overpowered. It was a terribly savage
world, the old Norse world; but we like to read about
it, and we cannot help loving the splendid courage of
the men and women who passed their lives among such
tragedies, fearing nothing but loss of honour.

Several other Norse subjects have been treated by
Morris with equal success; and one is remarkable for
the strange charm of a refrain used in it, a refrain from
the Norse. It is called "The King of Denmark's Sons,"
and it is the story of a fratricide. King Gorm of Denmark had two sons, Knut and Harald:

> Fair was Knut of face and limb,
> As the breast of the Queen that suckled him;
> But Harald was hot of hand and heart
> As lips of lovers ere they part.

In history Knut was called the beloved. All men
loved him, he was the heir; and the old king loved him
so much that he one day said, "If any one, man or
woman, ever tells me that my son Knut is dead, that
person has spoken the word which sends him or her to
Hel." But this great love only made the younger
brother jealous. Harald was a Viking; he voyaged
southward and eastward, ravaging coasts in the Medi-

terranean or desolating provinces nearer home. His name was a terror in England at one time. But his father never praised him as he praised his brother. So one day at sea he attacked his brother, overcame all resistance, and killed him. Then he went home and told his mother what had been done. But who dare tell the King? The mother imagined a plan. During the night she decked the palace hall all in black, taking away every ornament. So in the morning, when the King entered the hall, he asked, "Who has dared to do this?" the Queen answered, "We, the women of the palace, have done it." "Then," said the King, "tell me that my son Knut is dead!" "You yourself have said the word," the Queen made answer. And therewith the old king died as he sat in his chair; and the wicked son became king. This is the simple history, and Morris has not departed from historic truth in his version of it. The refrain excellently suits the ballad measure chosen; from the very first stanza, the tone of it suggests all the tragedy that is going to follow.

> In Denmark gone is many a year,
> *So fair upriseth the rim of the sun,*
> Two sons of Gorm the King there were,
> *So grey is the sea when the day is done.*

Sunrise symbolises happiness, joy; grey is the colour of melancholy; and nothing is so lonesome, so sad looking, as the waste of the sea when it turns to grey in the twilight. The refrain reminds one of a famous line by an American poet, Bryant, who certainly never saw this ballad:

[290]

William Morris

Old ocean's grey and melancholy waste.

Besides the above Norse subjects, I might call your attention to the following titles: "The Folk-Mote by the River," "Knight Aagen and Maiden Else," "Hafbur and Signy," "The Raven and the King's Daughter." All these are well worth reading. So are the purely fairy tales. Northern fairy tales had a great charm for Morris. He chose them as subjects, perhaps because he saw a way of putting into them a new charm, a charm not suited for child readers, but attractive to the adult public. I suppose you know that fairy tales, as written for children, are written so as to appeal chiefly to the imagination, and to those simple emotions of which children are capable. But originally such stories were told for the amusement of grown up people, and a great deal of love sentiment figures in some of them. Morris, remembering this, took several charming stories and infused them with a new artistic sensuousness, making love the motive and the principal sentiment. In the other volume of which I spoke, the old story of "Rapunzel" is treated in this way; in the volume now under consideration we have the story "Goldilocks and Goldilocks." It is the wildest, the most impossible kind of fairy tale (so, for that matter, is Coleridge's "Christabel"), but he gave it a very human charm by putting delightful little bits of human nature into it—such as the passage where the enchanted maiden, who never saw a man before, meets the handsome knight for the first time:

> But the very first step he made from the place
> He met a maiden face to face.

Face to face, and so close was she,
That their lips met soft and lovingly.

Sweet-mouthed she was, and fair he wist;
And again in the darksome wood they kissed.

Then first in the wood her voice he heard,
As sweet as the song of the summer bird.

"O thou fair man with the golden head,
What is the name of thee?" she said.

"My name is Goldilocks," said he,
"O sweet-breathed, what is the name of thee?"

"O Goldilocks the Swain," she said,
"My name is Goldilocks the Maid."

He spake, "Love me as I love thee,
And Goldilocks one flesh shall be."

She said, "Fair man, I wot not how
Thou lovest, but I love thee now."

And they go on talking together, like two children,
in their eighteenth century English—she full of wonder at the beauty of the stranger of another sex, he
full of loving pity for her supreme innocence. And
then all kinds of magical dangers and troubles come
to separate them, but love conquers all. The story is
known by many children, but not as Morris tells it.
His principal purpose is to picture a character of perfect innocence and perfect trust; and he does this so
delightfully that we cease to care whether the tale is

William Morris

a fairy one or not. It stirs most agreeably something which is true in everybody's heart; we love what is beautiful in the character of the child or the supremely innocent young girl.

As a single work in one key, the greatest production of Morris is the "Story of Sigurd"; indeed, we might call it the masterpiece of the poet, but for the fact that it is not original in the true sense. It is little more than a magnificent translation in swinging verse of the Volsunga Saga. But in more ways than one, it has become a literary work of extreme importance. It was through this metrical version that the Volsunga Saga first became known to English readers in a general way. Since then we have had prose translations.

I want to speak about this Saga, because the subject is of extreme literary importance. To-day you can scarcely open a literary periodical or any volume of essays on literary subjects without finding there some reference to the famous Northern story. It is one version of an epic which in various forms belongs to the whole Northern race; and one of the forms best known is the Nibelungenlied of Germany. Through German musical art the latter form of the story has in our own time become universally known in all great cities of the West, for Wagner made it the subject of a magnificent composition; the greatest of all modern operas, dramatically at least, is certainly his musical presentation of the epic cycle.

A word now about the place of this story in European literature. Mediæval Europe produced four great epics. Each of these represents the beginning of a vast national literature. The great English epic is the story

[293]

of Beowulf, and I am sorry to say that it is not the best. The great French epic is the story of Roland. The great Spanish epic is the story of the Cid. And the great German epic is the Nibelungenlied or Nibelunge Nôt, as it has also been called. Of these four the German epic is the grandest. Its date is not exactly known. But the best critics assert that it cannot be older than the middle of the twelfth century, and not later than the middle of the thirteenth. Therefore the date must be somewhat between 1150-1250.

But the German epic is by no means the oldest form of the story. The older forms are Norse. There are poetical fragments of the story to be found in the ancient Scandinavian literature (you can find them in the library in the Corpus Poeticum Boreale), and there is a splendid prose version of the story in the old Icelandic—this is the Volsunga Saga, from which Morris took his poetical materials. Between the versions of the German and the North, there are great differences of narrative, but perhaps not great differences of merit. If we could have the whole of the old Norse epic, we should perhaps find it even grander than the German. But only fragments have been preserved of the poetry, and we can only imagine from the prose Saga how magnificent the lost poetry may have been. And now a word about the story itself.

When Herbert Spencer, some years ago, criticised certain English translations issued by the Japanese department of education, he stated that the story of the great swordsman Musashi was not a proper subject for the admiration of the youth, because it is a story of vengeance. He was speaking from the standpoint of ideal education, and from that standpoint his criticism is not disputable. But ideal education, in the present state of humanity, he himself would acknowledge to be impossible. It is only something toward which we can all work a little, slowly and patiently. In the meantime, the same objection made to the story of Musashi might equally well be made to all the epic poems of the Western world, and to nearly all the great romances of the past. To begin with, the grand poems of Homer, both the Iliad and the Odyssey, are epics of vengeance. The great story of King Arthur is a narrative full of incidents of revenge and even of crime. We can scarcely mention any great composition which is not full of vengeance, and which is not also admired. But I wonder what could Mr. Spencer say of the Volsunga Saga or the Nibelungenlied. For all stories of vengeance ever told, whether in verse or prose, pale before the immense quarrel and cruelty of these. They are terrible stories, and the Volsunga version is even more terrible than the German.

The story takes its name from the great family of the Volsung. It opens with an account of the might and power of King Volsung, the heroism of his sons and the beauty of his only daughter Signy. These rule in the far North. After a time the King of the Goths in the South, hearing of the wonderful beauty of Signy, asks for her hand in marriage, and obtains it. He goes to the country of the Volsung to wed her, and during the wedding he becomes jealous of the splendour and strength of the Volsung family. When he takes his bride South with him there is an evil purpose in his heart—the purpose to destroy the family of his bride by treachery whenever opportunity offers. What follows does not belong to the German story at all; it is only to be found in the Norse.

Siggeir, the Gothic king, next year invites the King Volsung and his sons to come South and pay him a visit. The sons of King Volsung suspect treachery, and they advise their father not to go without a great army. But the old king wants to see his daughter, and he thinks that it would be showing fear to go with a great army, so he tells his sons that they must go as invited, with only a small following. They go. But the suspicion of the sons was justified by events. In the middle of the festival of welcome, King Volsung and his party are attacked by an immense force, and nearly all the followers of the king are killed. The sons are taken prisoners and left in a wood tied to trees for the wolves to devour. Only one escapes, Sigmund. He hides in the forest and becomes a hunter, and dreams of vengeance.

But the real avenger is Signy, the daughter of the dead King Volsung and the wife of the murderer. Signy knows that her brother Sigmund is alive. But that makes only two Volsungs; and two young people alone cannot hope to destroy a king and an army. But Signy believes that three can do it. Secretly she keeps her brother supplied with provisions and weapons, and she resolves to raise up sons to avenge the wrong. When her first son is born she begs to train him, and when he is old enough to begin to learn what war means, she sends him to her brother in the wood that he may teach the lad.

Sigmund does not much like the boy. He thinks that

he talks too much to be really brave. He tests the lad's courage in different ways, telling him, among other things, to bake and knead cake in which a poisonous snake has been hidden. The boy is afraid of the snake. Sigmund sends him back to Signy, saying that he will not do.

Signy almost despairs. Must her sons be cowards because they have a coward father? Suddenly a strange idea comes to her. "I shall do as the Gods did in ancient times," she said; "only my brother can produce such a child as I wish for, and I shall have a child by him." She goes to a witch, who changes her body, transforms her so completely that her brother can have no suspicion of what has taken place. Then by him she has a son, Sinfiotli. When he is old enough she sends the boy to Sigmund.

Sigmund is astonished by the extraordinary fierceness and sullenness of the child. "Is it possible," he wonders, "that my sister can have such a child by her husband?" The boy scarcely speaks at all, but does whatever he is told, and is afraid of nothing. Sigmund gives him flour to knead and bake containing a poisonous snake. Instead of being afraid of the serpent, the child breaks and crushes the creature in his fingers and rolls the poisonous body in the flour, and makes the whole thing into cakes. Sigmund is delighted. He sends word to his sister, "This boy will do."

The rest of this part of the story you can imagine. The boy grows up a giant, and is trained in all arts by Sigmund. On a certain day these two unexpectedly force their way into the palace of the King Siggeir, slaughter his people and himself, and set fire to the palace. Thus King Volsung is avenged. But Signy, after having told her brother the story of Sinfiotli, goes back into the burning house of the king, and voluntarily dies. She has done her duty, but she does not care to live any longer. This ends the great episode of the Volsung Saga.

The next part contains the story of the dragon Fafnir. Here we have no more Sigmund. Sinfiotli has been poisoned, Sigmund has been killed in battle. But there is still one child of the Volsung blood alive in the world. This is Sigurd (the Siegfried of the German story). Sigurd is kindly brought up by a foster father, a Viking, who teaches him all the arts of seamanship and war. One of the teachers who helped the Viking in the work is a strange old man called Regin, who much resembles the Merlin of the story of King Arthur. Sigurd wants a sword, a magical sword, that will not break in his hand; for he is so strong that common swords are of no use to him. Regin alone knows the art. But he does not wish to give Sigurd such art. He makes in succession a number of swords. Sigurd takes each one of them and strikes the anvil with it, whereupon the blade flies into pieces. He threatens Regin so terribly that the latter at last is obliged to make the magical sword. When he finishes, Sigurd strikes the anvil with the blade, and the anvil is cut in two pieces. In the musical presentation of the story by Wagner, the finest episode is this forging of the sword. If you ever see that performed in a great theatre, you will not easily forget it. But in the German story it is not Regin but the hero himself who makes the blade. The anvil is placed upon the stage

[298]

and all the forging is really done there. When the anvil is cut in two, a flash as of lightning follows the blade of the sword; the spectacle is very grand.

But to return to the Volsung legend. Sigurd needs the sword in order that he may perform great deeds in the world, and the first great deed that he wishes to perform is to secure a magical hoard of wealth, belonging to the Dwarfs of the underworld and guarded by the terrible dragon Fafnir. He goes with Regin to the place of the hoard, and meets the dragon, and kills him. Regin then says to him, "Give me his heart—cut it out and roast it." Sigurd obeys, cuts out the heart of the dragon, and begins to roast it over the fire. But while roasting it, some grease gets upon his fingers, and he licks it off with his tongue. Immediately a wonderful thing happens—he can understand the language of birds and animals. In the trees above him he hears the birds speaking, and they give him warning that Regin intends to kill him. Thereupon he kills Regin. This story of the dragon's heart is very famous in European literature, and you will find many references to it in the poetry and prose of to-day.

The next part of the story is one of the finest—the meeting of Sigurd and Brynhild, the first love episode. Brynhild is half human, half divine. Though born among men, she had been taken to heaven by Odin and made a Valkyria, one of the celestial virgins called the "Choosers of the Slain." But for a fault which she committed she had been sent back to earth again, to suffer pain and sorrow. In an enchanted sleep she was left upon the summit of a mountain, and all about her sleeping-place towered a wall of never-dying fire. "Only the man brave enough to ride through the fire shall have this maiden"—so spake Odin.

Sigurd rides through the fire, and the fire, although roaring like the sea, does not hurt him, because he is brave. Entering the enchanted circle, he there sees a human figure lying, all in golden armour not made by any human smith. He tries to awake the sleeper, but cannot. He tries to take off the armour, but he cannot unfasten it. Then he takes his wonderful sword and cuts open the armour as easily as if it were silk. Then he finds that the sleeper is a woman, more beautiful than any woman of earth. She opens her eyes and looks at him. They fall in love with each other, and pledge themselves to become man and wife. Probably this part of the story is one of the sources from which the beautiful fairy tale of the Sleeping Beauty came into our child literature. But the idea is also found in very ancient Eastern literature.

The third part of the great story treats of the history of Brynhild especially. Being a Valkyria, she has power to see much of the future; she can foretell things in a dim way. She warns Sigurd that there is danger for him if he should ever be untrue to her. Sigurd accepts the warning in the noblest spirit. But the Fates are against him. He goes upon a warlike expedition to the kingdom of Niblung in the North. The Niblung family, after a great battle which Sigurd has helped them to win, wish to adopt him as a son, and the beautiful daughter of the King falls in love with him. Her father and her brothers wish Sigurd to marry the girl, whose name is Gudrun. But Sigurd remembers his promise to Brynhild. Then the wicked Queen Grimhild, the mother of Gudrun, gives Sigurd a poisonous drink that causes him to forget the past; and while he is under the influence of this magical drink he is persuaded to marry Gudrun.

But this is not the worst thing that he is obliged to do through the magical arts of Grimhild. He is obliged to go to Brynhild, and persuade her to become the wife of young Gunnar, the brother of Gudrun. He rides through the fire again, and persuades Brynhild to become the wife of Gunnar. She obeys his will, but the result is the destruction of Sigurd and all concerned. For the two women presently begin to quarrel. Brynhild loves Sigurd with a supernatural love, and he knows that he has been deceived. Gudrun also loves Sigurd fiercely, and her jealousy quickly perceives the secret affection of Brynhild. In short, the result of the quarrel between the women is that the brothers of Gudrun resolve to kill Sigurd while he sleeps. One of them stabs him in the middle of night. Sigurd, awakening, throws his sword after the escaping murderer with such force that the man is cut in two. But Sigurd dies of his wound, and Brynhild then kills herself, and the two are burnt upon the same funeral pyre.

The last part of the story is the revenge of Gudrun, one of the most terrible characters in all Northern stories. She lives only to avenge Sigurd. On finding that her brothers have caused his murder, she curses her house, her family, her people, and vows that they shall all suffer for the wrong done her. Her brothers, who know her character, are afraid, but there is a hope that time will make her heart more gentle. At all events she cannot remain always a widow. Presently she is

Pre-Raphaelite and Other Poets

asked for in marriage by Atli, king of the Goths. Her
brothers wish for this marriage, all except one, who
is against it. Gudrun marries Atli. This gives her
power to plan her longed-for revenge. She persuades
her husband that the great treasures which Sigurd got
by killing the dragon are worth securing even at the
cost of the lives of her brothers and father. She does
not lie to the King; she frankly tells him that she hates
her people, and he believes her. By treachery, all the
Niblungs are allured to Atli's hall. In the middle of
the day of their arrival, they are suddenly attacked.
They make a great fight, but all their followers are
killed, and they themselves are taken prisoners—that
is, the brothers, the father having died before the oc-
currence. During the fight Gudrun is present and the
blood spurts upon her dress and hands, but the expression of her face never changes. This is one of the most
awful scenes in the poem.

When all the brothers are dead but two, Hogni and
Gunnar, the King says to Gunnar, "Give me the treasure of the Niblungs, and I will spare your life." Gunnar
answers: "I must first see the heart of my brother
Hogni cut out of his breast and laid upon a dish." The
King's soldiers take among the prisoners a tall man
whom they imagine to be Hogni, but who is really only
a slave, and they cut out the man's heart and put it
upon a dish and bring it to Gunnar. Gunnar looks at
it and laughs and says, "That is not my brother's
heart; see how it trembles—that is the heart of a slave!"
Then the soldiers kill the real Hogni and cut out his
heart and bring it upon a plate. This time Gunnar
does not laugh. He says, "That is really my brother's

[302]

heart. It does not tremble. Neither did it ever tremble in his breast when he was alive. There were only two men in the world yesterday who knew where the treasure of the Niblungs is hidden, my brother and myself. And now that my brother is dead, I am the only one in the world who knows. See if you can make me tell you. I shall never tell you." He is tortured and killed, but he never tells.

There is only one of the whole Niblung race still alive, Gudrun. She has avenged her husband upon her own brothers, but that does not satisfy her. By the strange and ferocious Northern code she must now avenge her kindred, though they be her enemies, upon the stranger. She has used Atli in order to destroy her brothers; but, after all, they were her brothers and Atli only her husband. She sets fire to the palace, kills Atli with her own hands, and then leaps into the sea. Thus all the characters of the story meet with a tragic end. There is no such story of vengeance in any other literature. Yet this epic, or romance, is the greatest of mediæval compositions, and every student ought to know something about it, either in its Scandinavian or its German form. In the German form the character of Gudrun—she is there called Kriemhild—is much less savage; and the German story is altogether a more civilised expression of feeling. But any form of the story (and there are several other forms besides those of which I have spoken) shows the moving passion to be vengeance; and to return to the subject of Mr. Spencer's criticism, we may say that there is no great tale, Western or Eastern, in which this passion has no play.

Pre-Raphaelite and Other Poets

The values of the story are in the narration, in the descriptions of battles, weapons, banquets, weddings, in the heroic emotions often expressed in speeches or pledges, and in the few chapters of profound tenderness strangely mingled among chapters dealing only with atrocious and cruel passions; all these give perpetual literary worth to the composition, and we cannot be tired of them. The subject was a grand one for any English poet to take up, and Morris took it up in a very worthy way. He has put the whole legend into anapestic verse of sixteen syllables, a long swinging, irregular measure which has a peculiar exultant effect upon the reader. To give an example of this work is very difficult. Any part detached from the rest, loses by detachment—for Morris, although a good poet, and a correct poet, and a spiritual poet, is not an exquisite poet. He does not give to his verses that supreme finish which we find in the compositions of the greater Victorian poets. However, I shall attempt a few examples. I thought at first of reading to you some passages regarding the forging of the sword; but I gave up the idea on remembering how much better Wagner has treated the same incident where the hero chants as he strikes out the shape of the blade with his hammer, and at last, with a mighty shout lifts up the blade and cuts the anvil in two. Perhaps a better example of Morris's verse may be found in these lines:

By the Earth that groweth and giveth, and by all the
    Earth's increase
That is spent for Gods and man-folk, by the sun that
    shines on these;

William Morris

By the Salt-Sea-Flood that beareth the life and death of
men;
By the Heaven and Stars that change not, though Earth
die out again;

   ·   ·   ·   ·   ·   ·   ·

I hallow me to Odin for a leader of his host,
To do the deeds of the Highest, and never count the cost;
And I swear, that whatso great-one shall show the day and
the deed,
I shall ask not why nor wherefore, but the sword's desire
shall speed:
And I swear to seek no quarrel, nor to swerve aside for
aught
Though the right and the left be blooming, and the straight
way wend to nought,
And I swear to abide and hearken the prayer of any thrall,
Though the war-torch be on the threshold and the foemen's
feet in the hall:
And I swear to sit on my throne in the guise of the kings
of the earth,
Though the anguish past amending, and the unheard woe
have birth:
And I swear to wend in my sorrow that none shall curse
mine eyes
For the scowl that quelleth beseeching, and the hate that
scorneth the wise.
So help me Earth and Heavens, and the Under-sky and
Seas,
And the Stars in their ordered houses, and the Norns that
order these!
And he drank of the cup of Promise, and fair as a star he
shone,
And all men rejoiced and wondered, and deemed Earth's
glory won.

[305]

Pre-Raphaelite and Other Poets

This will serve very well to show you the ringing spirit of the measure. Here is an example of another kind taken from the pages describing the first secret love of the maiden Gudrun for Sigurd. It is true to human nature; the Northern woman is apt to be most cruel to the man whom she loves most, and these few lines give us a dark suggestion of the character of Gudrun long before the real woman reveals herself— immensely passionate and immensely strong in self-control.

But men say that howsoever all other folk of earth
Loved Sigmund's son rejoicing, and were bettered of their
    mirth,
Yet ever the white-armed Gudrun, the dark haired Niblung
    Maid,
From the barren heart of sorrow her love upon him laid;
He rejoiceth, and she droopeth; he speaks and hushed is
    she;
He beholds the world's days coming, nought but Sigurd
    may she see.
He is wise and her wisdom falters; he is kind, and harsh
    and strange
Comes the voice from her bosom laden, and her woman's
    mercies change.
He longs, and she sees his longing, and her heart grows
    cold as a sword.
And her heart is the ravening fire, and the fretting sorrows'
    hoard.

A great deal is said in these lines by the use of suggestive words and words of symbolism. Paraphrased these verses mean much more. "No matter how much all other people showed their love and admiration for

Sigurd by making festival and public rejoicing, feeling happier and better for having seen him, all their affection was as nothing to the love that Gudrun secretly felt for him, out of her lonesome heart; and great was her secret grief at the thought that he might not love her. Then she acted with him after the manner of the woman resolved to win. Whenever she saw him rejoice she became sad. Whenever he spoke to her, she remained silent. Many things Sigurd knew—so wise he was that he could see even the events of the future; but she saw nothing and knew nothing thereafter except Sigurd, nor did she wish to see or to know anything else. And when he showed himself wise, she acted as a foolish child. And when he tried to be kind to her she answered him with a strange and harsh voice, and suddenly became without pity. And at last when he began to long for love, and she perceived it, then her heart became cold as a sword. So was the soul of this woman in the time of her passion—now like ravening fire, now again desolate with all the sorrows that corrode and destroy."

Because she sees still that love is not for her, the whole scene of the courting—this is one of the cases where the maiden woos the man without ever losing her dignity as a maiden—is of consummate skill, showing Gudrun at one moment simple and sweet as a child, revealing suddenly, at another time, the strange height and depth of her, many things terrible in her, capable of the making or the ruin of a kingdom.

I am not going to quote, but I hope that you will notice particularly the fine scene of the death of Brynhild. There is a grand thought in it. I did not tell you, in the brief epitome of the plot which I gave you, about the second wooing of Brynhild. When Sigurd wooed her for King Gunnar, he lay down beside her at night; but he placed his naked sword between them. This episode is famous in Western literature. So he brought her chaste to her bridegroom. And when afterwards Brynhild kills herself, in order that she may be able to join him in the spirit world, she shows her admiration of Sigurd's action by saying, "When you put my dead body on the funeral pyre beside the dead body of Sigurd, put his naked sword again between us, as it was put between us when he wooed me long ago, for the sake of King Gunnar." The suicide chapter is very grand. And the ending of the long tragedy has also a peculiar grandeur, when Gudrun leaps into the sea.

The sea-waves o'er her swept;
And their will is her will henceforward; and who knoweth
    the deeps of the sea
And the wealth of the bed of Gudrun, and the days that
    yet shall be?

A finer simile could not be imagined than this sudden transformation of a passionate woman's will into the vast motion and unimaginable depths of the sea. The idea is, "Deep and wide was her soul like the sea; and the strength of her and the depth of her are now the strength and depth of the ocean; and who knows what her spirit may hereafter accomplish?"
In concluding this little study of the romance, I may say that some of its incidents are probably im-

[308]

William Morris

mortal because they contain perpetual truth. I am not now speaking particularly of Morris's work, but only of the legend of Sigurd. The studies in it of evil passions need not demand our praise, but the stories of heroism, like that of the naked sword laid between the man and the maid, will always seem to us grand. Symbolically we may say that the wealth of the world is still guarded by dragons as truly as in the story of Sigurd; formidable and difficult to overcome are the powers opposing success in the struggle of life, and the acquisition of the prize can be only for the hero, the strong man mentally or morally. Again that strange fancy of Brynhild ringed about in her magical sleep with a wall of living fire—I do not know how it may seem to the far Eastern reader, but to the Western it is the symbol of a real truth, that beauty, the object of human desire, is still truly ringed about by fire, in the sense that the winner of it must risk all possible dangers of body and soul before he succeeds. Still in Northern countries the finest woman is for the best man; only the hero can truly ride through the fire of the gods.

I have said enough about the great poems of Morris; I do not think that it will be necessary to say anything about "The Life and Death of Jason." If you like his other work, probably you will like that book also. But I think that the story of Jason is more charmingly told by Charles Kingsley in his Greek fairy tale, and that Morris was at his best, so far as long narrative poems are concerned, in Norse subjects. I have already told you about his strong personal interest in Norse literature, and about his work as a prose

[309]

Pre-Raphaelite and Other Poets

translator. In this connection I may mention a queer
fact. Morris, who claimed to have Norse blood in
his own veins, became so absorbed by the Norse subjects that his character seems to have been changed in
later life. He became stark and grim like the old
Vikings, even to his friends. But if he offended in this
wise, he certainly made up for the fault by that tremendous energy which he appeared to absorb from the
same source. No man ever worked harder for romantic
literature and romantic art, and few men have made
so deep an impression upon the æsthetic sentiments
of the English public.

CHAPTER VI

At the present time (1900) scarcely any English poet is more in vogue than George Meredith. His popularity is comparatively new, but it is founded upon solid excellence of a very extraordinary kind. George Meredith is an exception to general rules—even to the rule that a great poet is scarcely ever a great prose writer; for he was known to the public as a novelist for half a century before he began to be known as a poet. To-day he is so often quoted from, so often referred to, that we cannot ignore him in the course of lectures upon English literature.

He is now nearly seventy-two years old, having been born in 1828. He studied mostly in Germany, and studied law, but he had scarcely left his university when he resolved to abandon law and devote his life to literature. Returning to England he published his first book, a volume of poems, in 1851. It attracted no notice at all. In 1856 his next book appeared, called "The Shaving of Shagpat," a wonderful fairy-tale, written in imitation of the Arabian Nights with Arabian characters and scenery. It remains the best thing of the kind ever done by any European writer, but the kind was not popular, and only a few of the great poets and critics noticed what a wonderful book it

[311]

was. After that Meredith took up novel writing, studying English life and character in an entirely new way. But he was not at first able to attract much attention. His novels were too scholarly and too psychological. Ten years from the date of his first volume of poems, in 1862, he published another book of verses, entitled "Modern Love." This attracted the notice of Swinburne, but of scarcely anybody else, and Meredith went back to novel writing. Twenty years later, in 1883, a third volume of poems appeared, "Poems and Lyrics of the Joy of Earth." This book obtained some critical praise, but only the cultivated men of letters appreciated it. More novels followed, and in 1887 and 1888 appeared the last volumes of poems, "Ballads and Poems of Tragic Life," and "A Reading of Earth." Since then Meredith has chiefly written novels, but occasionally he writes poems. Success came to him only in old age—within the last twenty years. It is not within the purpose of this lecture to speak of his novels at all; we shall deal only with his poetry.

At the first sight of such poetry a good judge would naturally exclaim, "How is it that I never heard of this wonderful poet before?" But a further examination will easily furnish the reason. Meredith is uncommonly difficult as well as uncommonly deep. He has the obscurity of Browning, and yet a profundity exceeding Browning's; he is essentially a psychological poet, but he is also an evolutional philosopher, which Browning scarcely was. He did not study in Germany for nothing, and he alone of all living Englishmen really expresses the whole philosophy of the modern

The Poetry of George Meredith

scientific age. Now such a man necessarily found himself in a peculiar position. The older thinkers of his own time could scarcely understand him; he was uttering new thoughts, and uttering them often in a German rather than in an English way. The younger thinkers of the period were still at school or in the university when he began to express himself. His audience was therefore extremely small at first. Now it is very large, and he is known as well in France and Germany as at home, but we may say that he gave his whole life for this success.

A word now about his philosophy. Meredith is a thinker of the broadest and most advanced type, but he is essentially optimistic—that is, he considers all things as an evolutionist, but also as one who believes that the tendency of the laws which govern the universe is toward the highest possible good. He believes the world to be the best possible world which man could desire, and he thinks that all the unhappiness and folly of men is due only to ignorance and to weakness. He proclaims that the world can give every joy and every pleasure possible to those who are both wise and strong. Above all else he preaches the duty of moral strength—the power to control our passions and impulses. He has, however, very little compassion in him; he is a terribly stern teacher, never pitying weakness, never forgiving ignorance. He never talks of any theological God—not at least as a God to believe in; but you get from all his poetry the general impression that he considers the working of the universe divine. It will not be necessary to say more here about his opinions, because we shall find them better expressed in his poems than they could be in any attempt at a brief *résumé*.

I think that it will be better to take some of his simpler poems first, for study; indeed the longer ones are very difficult and would require much explanation as well as paraphrasing. The shorter ones will better serve the first purpose of showing you how different this man's poetry is from that of any other English poet of the time. The first example will be from "Ballads and Poems of Tragic Life." I need not explain to you the meaning of the word "Tragic." But the tragedies in which Meredith is interested are never tragedies of mere physical pain. There may be some killing in them, but the shedding of blood does not mean the tragedy. "King Harald's Trance" is a good illustration of this.

Harald—a name common in Scandinavian history—we may suppose to be a Norwegian Viking. The Vikings of old Norway were the most terrible men that ever lived, but they were also among the grandest and noblest. Their trade was war, their religion was war, their idea of happiness after death was still war—eternal war in heaven, ghostly fighting on the side of the gods. Such an idea of life requires many great qualities as well as natural fearlessness and great physical strength. These men had to learn from childhood not only how to fight, but how to control their passions, for in fighting, you know that the man who first gets angry is almost certain to get beaten. The Norse character was above all things a character of great self-mastery, and the finer qualities of it are those which have also made the finer qualities of both

[314]

The Poetry of George Meredith

the German and the English speaking races of the
modern world. It occurred to the poet Meredith to
study such a character among its ancient surroundings, and among the most trying possible circumstances.
What could break down such mighty strength? What
could conquer such iron hearts? We are going to see.

I

Sword in length a reaping-hook amain
Harald sheared his field, blood up to shank;
    'Mid the swathes of slain
    First at moonrise drank.

II

Thereof hunger, as for meats the knife,
Pricked his ribs, in one sharp spur to reach
    Home and his young wife,
    By the sea-ford beach.

III

After battle keen to feed was he:
Smoking flesh the thresher washed down fast,
    Like an angry sea
    Ships from keel to mast.

IV

Name us glory, singer, name us pride
Matching Harald's in his deeds of strength;
    Chiefs, wife, sword by side,
    Foemen stretched their length!

V

Half a winter night the toasts hurrahed,
Crowned him, clothed him, trumpeted him high,
  Till awink he bade
  Wife to chamber fly.

Mightily Harald, as a reaper in a field of corn mows
down the grain, with his scythe-long sword moved down
the enemy—standing in blood up to his ankles. All
day he slew, and when the battle was finished after
dark and the dead lay all about him, like the swathes
of grain cut down by reapers, then for the first time
he was able to drink, as the moon began to rise.

Then the great effort and excitement of the battle
left him hungry. His hunger pricked him like a knife
—impelled him to mount his horse and gallop straight
home at full speed to where his young wife was waiting for news of him.

He always ate prodigiously after fighting; to see
him eating roast meat and washing it down his great
throat with drinks of ale after a battle, made one
think of the spectacle of a stormy sea swallowing
ships.

Then came the customary banqueting and singing
and drinking. Professional singers sang songs in praise
of his fighting that day, while he sat enthroned among
his warriors, with his sword by his side, and his young
wife seated at his right hand. All his enemies were
dead.

For half the night the drinking and singing continued. Harald had to sit there and hear himself
praised, and drink whenever his own health was drunk

[316]

The Poetry of George Meredith

to—such was the custom. But when the strong men had begun to show the influence of liquor too much, the king made a sign to his wife to withdraw to her own room. When the warriors drank too much, it was not a time for women to be present.

This is the substance of the first part of the poem. Observe that Harald is never spoken of as having been fatigued by his battle; fighting only makes him hungry. This is a giant and probably a kindly giant in his way; we see that he is fond of his young wife. But he cannot retire from the banquet according to the custom of his people. He must drink with everybody after the great victory. And he drinks so much that he remains like a dead man for three days. Only after that, his great strength is to be tried.

VI

Twice the sun had mounted, twice had sunk,
Ere his ears took sound; he lay for dead;
    Mountain on his trunk,
    Ocean on his head.

VII

Clamped to couch, his fiery hearing sucked
Whispers that at heart made iron-clang;
    Here fool-women clucked,
    There men held harangue.

VIII

Burial to fit their lord of war,
They decreed him: hailed the kingling: ha!
    Hateful! but this Thor
    Failed a weak lamb's baa.

[317]

Pre-Raphaelite and Other Poets

IX

King they hailed a branchlet, shaped to fare,
Weighted so, like quaking shingle-spume,
When his blood's own heir
Ripened in the womb!

Twice the sun had risen and had set, yet Harald had
not stirred. His hearing returned; but he could not
move, could not speak, could not open his eyes. Upon
his breast there seemed to be a weight like the weight
of a mountain keeping him down; above his head it
seemed to him that there was a whole ocean—in his
head there was the sound of it.

But soon other sounds came to his ears, as he lay
upon his bed, as if fixed to it with bands of iron. He
heard whispers that made a disturbance at his heart.
He heard women cluttering like hens; he heard also
men making speeches.

What were they making speeches about? About
him. He heard them say that he was dead; that he
must be grandly buried like a great warrior and
king. And he heard them talk of the new king—
rather, of the kingling. Why did they appoint so
weak a man to be king? How quickly he could stop
all that with a word. But although he had been as
strong and terrible as the God Thor, he could not now
even make a noise like the bleat of a lamb.

Still he listened, he heard more. This king that was
to be was only very distantly related to him. Such
a man never could have force of will to rule the men
of that country. He would have no more power than

[318]

The Poetry of George Meredith

sea foam on a beach of rocks. But why should a king
have been elected at all? Was not his own wife soon
to become a mother? His child would be a man fit to
rule. While the child was still a child, the chiefs could
govern. Why did they elect that other?

He is going to learn why—and this is the beginning
of the terrible part of the poem.

X

Still he heard, and doglike, hoglike, ran
Nose of hearing till his blind sight saw:
    Woman stood with man,
    Mouthing low, at paw.

XI

Woman, man, they mouthed; they spake a thing
Armed to split a mountain, sunder seas:
    Still the frozen king
    Lay and felt him freeze.

XII

Doglike, hoglike, horselike now he raced,
Riderless, in ghost across a ground
    Flint of breast, blank-faced,
    Past the fleshly bound.

Still the King listened in his trance, and he listened
until his hearing acted for him as a dog acts for the
hunter, or as a wild hog acts, following the scents of
the roots that he wants even under the surface of the
ground. Alone by his hearing he perceived what was

[319]

going on; his eyes could not see, but his mind saw even more clearly than eyes. His young wife had been false to him; she was talking to another man even there within his own house; they were kissing each other, they were touching each other, they were speaking wickedness, such wickedness as would have power to split a mountain or to separate the waters of the sea—crime as would destroy the world. But he, the giant they betrayed, the King they betrayed, the husband, he could not move. Coldness of death is about him; he feels his blood freezing. O! for the days when he could renew his strength in a moment merely by filling his great lungs with the sea winds. "If I could only breathe the sea wind for one second," he thinks, "then I could rise up." And the ghost of him really seeks the shore of the sea, the flint-breasted naked rocks of the beach—racing like a horse in order to get strength from the sea wind to awaken the great inert body. When the ghost gets in, then the King can wake.

XIII

Smell of brine his nostrils filled with might,
Nostrils quickened eyelids, eyelids hand;
    Hand for sword at right
    Groped, the great haft spanned.

XIV

Wonder struck to ice his people's eyes;
Him they saw, the prone upon the bier,
    Sheer from backbone rise,
    Sword uplifting peer.

[320]

The Poetry of George Meredith

XV

Sitting did he breathe against that blade,
Standing kiss it for that proof of life:
Strode, as netters wade,
Straightway to his wife.

Here the scene has suddenly changed. We are on
the sea shore. But you will remember that in the last
of the verses before paraphrased, we were in the house,
and the man imagined himself moving as a ghost on
the sea shore in search of strength. Before we paraphrase again, it is necessary to understand this. First
I must tell you that Meredith does not believe in ghosts,
and does not want us to imagine that the man's spirit
was really moving outside of his body. He has been
describing only the feeling and imagination of the
warrior, in the state between life and death. It was
the custom to burn the dead body of a great sea-king
on the sea shore, and you must imagine that the body
has been carried down to the shore to be burnt. Then
the smell of the sea really revived him. And this
explanation is further required by the fact that later
on, Harald is represented in full armour, with his helmet
upon his head and his sword laid by his side. It was
a custom to burn the warrior with his arms and armour. All we have been reading about the ghost represents only what Harald felt, just before his awakening. Now we will paraphrase: The smell of the sea
came to him; he breathed the sea wind, and, as he
breathed it, it seemed to fill him with strength. He
opened his eyes, he saw; at once he felt at his right

[321]

hand for his sword, which he knew ought to be there. He felt the handle, grasped it.

Then he sat up on the bier, and his men were utterly astonished, for they had thought him dead; but lo! he had risen up straight to a sitting posture. They stared motionless, as if their eyes had been frozen.

Sitting up, Harald still doubted whether he was really alive. He lifted the blade of his sword to his lips, and breathed upon it. Seeing his own breath on the great steel, he kissed the sword affectionately, out of gratitude to find himself alive again. Then standing up he advanced toward his wife—slowly, slowly,—as a fisherman or a bird catcher advances, wading in water, against a current.

XVI

Her he eyed: his judgment was one word,
Foulbed!—and she fell; the blow clove two.
    Fearful for the third,
    All their breath indrew.

XVII

Morning danced along the waves to beach;
Dumb his chiefs fetched breath for what might hap,
    Glassily on each
    Stared the iron cap.

XVIII

Sudden, as it were a monster oak
Split to yield a limb by stress of heat,
    Strained he, staggered, broke
    Doubled at their feet.

The Poetry of George Meredith

He looked upon her face, judged her guilt, expressed that judgment by the single word "Adulteress"—and struck. His blow killed two, for she was about to become a mother. Whom would he kill next? Who was the guilty man? Evidently he was not there; or perhaps Harald did not know yet who he was. Everybody waited in silent terror.

The sun rose, sending his gold light dancing over the waves from the East. And still the men stood there in silent fear. Harald said nothing, did not move; but he looked at each man with a glassy stare, with the look of one who does not find what he is waiting for.

Then suddenly, like a great oak tree, too large to be cut with the ax and therefore possible only to split by the use of fire, the giant seemed to make a sudden effort, he moved, he staggered, he fell dead at their feet.

What is the deeper meaning of this terrible poem, founded upon an historical fact? Simply that moral pain is much more powerful than physical pain—that it is capable of breaking down any strength. Harald could not be killed in battle under ordinary circumstances; fighting could not even tire him, it only made him hungry and thirsty. No physical excess could injure that body of iron. His vast eating and drinking only gave him a heavy sleep. But when he was wounded in his affections, by the treachery of the only being whom he could love and trust, then his heart burst. He dies in the poem magnificently, even like a moral hero, containing himself perfectly until death takes him away. But the teaching of the story is very awful as well as very true.

Pre-Raphaelite and Other Poets

The remarkable thing to notice about this poetry is its compression, a compression that only seems to make the colour more vivid and the emotion more forceful. In order to paraphrase it intelligibly one must use two or three times as many words as the poet uses. Browning has the same strange power, and in many ways Meredith strongly resembles Browning. But he is much more philosophical, as we see later on.

Of ballads written in the true ballad form, there are not more than three or four in the whole book, notwithstanding the title, "Ballads and Poems." Another ballad more famous than that which I have quoted is called "Archduchess Anne," a title which at once makes us think of various episodes in Austrian history. It is a splendid piece of psychological study, but less suitable for quotation than the poem on King Harald, for it is very long. The object of the poet is to show the consequences of a foolish act on the part of a person ruling the destiny of a nation. Anne is practically a queen; and she is married. But she takes a strong fancy to a handsome man among her courtiers, Count Louis. In other words, she falls in love with him. He takes every advantage of the situation, because he is both diplomatic and selfish. The Archduchess rules her own cabinet; but the Count soon learns how to rule her; consequently he gets all the power of the government into his hands. And when he has done this, he shows his selfishness. She immediately reassumes her power, and then there is a political quarrel. The state is divided in two parties. Count Louis then does what no gentleman under the circumstances could very well do, he marries a young

[324]

wife, and brings her to the court. Of course, when
there is, or has been, illegitimate love in high places,
the fact can not be very well concealed. Everybody
knows it. The whole court knows that the Queen has
loved Count Louis, and that his marriage, and, above
all, the bringing of his wife to the court is a cruel
insult. One of the Queen's faithful servants, an old
general, determines to avenge her if he can ever get a
chance. And the chance comes. Count Louis soon
afterwards incites a revolution, raises an army and
advances to battle. The old general meets him, cap-
tures him by a cunning trick, and writes the Queen a
letter, saying, "I have him." But the old general does
not quite understand a woman's heart. When a good
woman—and by "good" I mean especially affectionate
—has once loved a man, it is scarcely possible that
anything could make her afterwards really hate him.
There was of course the extraordinary case of Chris-
tina of Sweden, who had her lover stabbed to death
before her eyes, but in such a case as that we do not
believe there was a real affection at any time. Anne
is in a very difficult position; she is very angry with
the prisoner, but she secretly loves him. How is she
to answer the letter of her general? If she says, "Do
not kill him," the general will think that she is very
fond of him. If she says, "Kill him," the general will
think that she is revengeful and the whole world will
think the same thing. If she says, "Let him go free,"
that will only make the general despise her, not to
speak of all the political trouble that would follow.
If she says, "Send him to me that he may be imprisoned at once," that would seem to the world as if she

wished to make love to the prisoner by force, to take
him away from his wife. Whatever she does will seem
in some way wrong. She has placed herself in a false
position to begin with; and now she does not know
what to do. What she really wishes is a reconcilia-
tion with the man who has been so base to her, but
she dares not say that to the leader of her armies.
Therefore she writes a diplomatic letter to him, hoping
that he can understand it. She says that she does not
want to be too severe; she speaks of religion, she
trusts that her general will know what to do. He
determines that the man shall die as quickly as possible.

> Her words he took; her nods and winks
>   Treated as woman's fog,
> The man-dog for his mistress thinks,
>   Not less her faithful dog.
>
> She hugged a cloak old Kraken ripped;
>   Disguise to him he loathed.
> —Your mercy, madam, shows you stripped,
>   While mine will keep your clothed.

That is, the old soldier determined to act exactly
upon the words of the letter; as for suggestions, he
refused to pay any attention to them. "Women," he
thought, "are too weak. She wants to hide her feelings
from me. And she wants to be merciful. By law the
man is a traitor, and ought to be hanged. But I shall
shoot him instead—give him the death of a soldier,
that is mercy enough. My mercy will hide the Queen's
shame; her mercy would proclaim that shame to the
whole world." So Count Louis is shot. Before this,

The Poetry of George Meredith

however, the young wife of Count Louis goes to the Archduchess to beg for her husband's life, and this is a very touching part of the poem. Of course this innocent young wife does not know what has happened in the past, and can not know what pain her presence is giving.

> The Countess Louis from her head
>   Drew veil: "Great Lady, hear!
> My husband deems you Justice dread,
>   I know you Mercy dear.
>
> "His error upon him may fall;
>   He will not breath a nay.
> I am his helpless mate in all,
>   Except for grace to pray.
>
> "Perchance on me his choice inclined,
>   To give his House an heir;
> I had not marriage with his mind,
>   His counsel could not share.
>
> "I brought no portion for his weal
>   But this one instinct true,
> Which bids me in my weakness kneel,
>   Archduchess Anne, to you."

Now you can see that every word here innocently uttered would seem to the Archduchess very cunning or very stupid. Did the young wife know the secret, then every word would be like turning a knife in the heart of the Archduchess. And if she did not know, how horribly stupid she must be to say what seems so wicked. Therefore she is driven away at once. But after she has gone, the Archduchess has to think about what was said, and she feels that after all the young wife really did the very best thing that a woman could have done to save her husband.

Yet it is too late to save him. Presently the news comes that he has been shot. And the result is a civil war; for the party of Count Louis tries to avenge him. There is war also in the heart of the sovereign. How unutterably she hates her faithful old general; yet she must trust to him, for the kingdom is in danger. Pain and sorrow make Anne look already like an old woman. When the war is over she treats her general so ill that he is obliged to leave the country. By one fault, how much unhappiness and destruction comes to pass— revolution, civil war, and the ruin of many lives! And the poem ends with the quatrain often quoted in other connections than the present:

> And she that helped to slay, yet bade
> To spare the fated man,
> Great were her errors, but she had
> Great heart, Archduchess Anne.

Of course, there is just a little bit of cruel irony in the statement, for it obliges us to ask the question whether a great heart can compensate for much foolishness, whether affection can excuse the ruin of a government. I think that the poet here is quietly opposing the moral of the beautiful old Bible story, about the woman forgiven "because she loved much"— *quia multum amavit*. One would say that a person

The Poetry of George Meredith

holding the position of supreme ruler cannot be forgiven simply because she loved much, although we may
pity her with all our hearts.

Pity is not a virtue with Meredith. He reminds us
often of the old Jesuit doctrine, that pity is akin to
concupiscence. For example, Meredith takes a ground
strongly opposed to all romantic precedents when he
treats of the question of adultery. From the time
of the Middle Ages it was the custom of poets to represent unhappy wives secretly in love with strangers,
or to paint the tragedies arising from the consequence
of sexual jealousy. Even in all the versions of the
story of King Arthur, our sympathies are invoked on
behalf of illegitimate love,—even in Tennyson. We
sympathise a good deal with Lancelot and with Guinevere. In Dante, most religious of the old poets, we
have a striking example of this appeal to pity in the
story of Francesca da Rimini. And I need scarcely
speak of various modern schools of poetry who have
imitated the poets of the Middle Ages in this respect.
Meredith takes the opposite view—represents the err-
ing woman always as culpable, and praises the act of
killing her. He gives evolutional reasons for this. For
example, he takes an old Spanish love story, and tells
it over again in a new way. There is a beautiful young
wife alone at home. There is a terrible rascal of a
husband, a fellow who spends all his time in drinking,
gambling, fighting, and making love to other women.
His wife gets tired of his neglect and his brutality
and his viciousness. If he does not love her, somebody
else shall. So she gets a secret lover, while her husband is away. This young man visits her. Suddenly

[329]

her husband returns, and now we leave Meredith to moralise the situation. I think that you will find it both new and interesting.

> Thundered then her lord of thunders;
> Burst the door, and flashing sword,
> Loud disgorged the woman's title:
> Condemnation in one word.
>
> Grand by righteous wrath transfigured,
> Towers the husband who provides
> In his person judge and witness,
> Death's black doorkeeper besides!
>
> .   .   .   .   .   .
>
> How though he hath squandered Honour!
> High of Honour let him scold:
> Gilding of the man's possession,
> 'Tis the woman's coin of gold.
>
> She, inheriting from many
> Bleeding mothers bleeding sense,
> Feels 'twixt her and sharp-fanged nature
> Honour first did plant the fence.
>
> Nature, that so shrieks for justice;
> Honour's thirst, that blood will slake;
> These are women's riddles, roughly
> Mixed to write them saint or snake.
>
> Never nature cherished woman;
> She throughout the sexes' war
> Serves as temptress and betrayer,
> Favouring man, the muscular.

.   .   .   .

[330]

The Poetry of George Meredith

Hard the task: your prison-chamber
Widens not for lifted latch
Till the giant thews and sinews
Meet their Godlike overmatch.

Read that riddle, scorning pity's
Tears, of cockatrices shed;
When the heart is vowed for freedom,
Captaincy it yields to head.

The point upon which the poet here insists is the evolutional signification of female virtue and of all that relates to it. Evidently he does not believe that either men or women were very virtuous in the beginning—not at all; their knowledge of right and wrong had to be developed slowly through great sufferings in the course of thousands of years. In order that the modern woman may be virtuous as she is, millions of her ancestors must have suffered the experience that teaches the social worth of female honour. And a woman who to-day proves unfaithful to her marriage duty is sinning, not simply against modern society, but against the whole experience, the whole modern experience, of the human race. This would make the fault a great one, of course, but would not the fault of the man be as great? By what right, except the right of force, can he punish her, if he himself be guilty of unfaithfulness? I am not sure what answer religion would give to these questions. But Meredith answers immediately and clearly. The fault of the woman is incomparably worse than the fault of the man. It is worse in relation to the injury done to society, to morality, to progress. Society is founded upon the family; the strength of society to defend itself against the enemy, to accumulate wealth, and to find happiness, depends upon the care and the love given to the children. It is in proportion to the love and care given to the young that a nation becomes strong. Now it is especially the mother's duty to look after the interests of the young. This requires no argument. And a sexual weakness upon her part means an injury done to the family in the sense of its very life. The whole interest of society depends upon the chastity and tenderness and moral force of its women. Moral weakness once begun among the women of the people, the decline of that race begins. So indeed perished the finest race that ever existed in this world—the old Greek race.

On the other hand, though unchastity on the part of the man be certainly condemnable—from a purely moral point of view equally condemnable—its consequences are not fraught with the same danger to society, because they are not of a character to destroy the family. Really the part of man in the great struggle of life is the part of the fighter. The all important thing for the man is to be strong. If he can be morally as well as physically strong, so much the better for the race; but the all important thing is that he shall be able to fight, to contend, to conquer. It is not through the man that the moral progress of society is directly effected; it is through the woman and the teaching of the young, it is through the tenderness and love of the home—the only place where a man can rest from his constant battle with the world. It is only in his own home that he can be as good as he may wish to be. Every good home is a little nursing place of

The Poetry of George Meredith

morality, a little garden in which the plants of honour
and truth and courage and gentleness can be cultivated
until they are strong enough to bear the frosts and
the cold winds of the great outside world. In one
generation home life may accomplish very little for
the improvement of a race, but in the course of thousands of years it accomplishes everything. If men are
kinder and wiser and better to-day than they were
thousands of years ago, it is because of the virtues
which have been cultivated in the family. Had the
home of human history been a struggle between men
only, the result would have been very different indeed,
for competition and battle cultivate only the hard
and fierce and cunning side of character. Taking all
these facts together, the poet tells us very plainly
that adultery is something which should never be forgiven in a woman, however it might be forgiven in a
man, because the fault against human society is too
great. And therefore he has written this poem especially to condemn those old romances in which illegitimate affection was the theme—in which, also, every
effort was made to excite the sympathy of the reader
with the sin of the woman. No sympathy has George
Meredith; on the contrary, he praises the man who
kills, in the line where he speaks of the sword—where
he says that the good steel of the sword that killed
was what every man ought to be—hard and penetrat-
ing, hard and terrible to deal with social wrong. It is
very curious to compare this stern view of life with the
tenderness of Michelet, in his books entitled "L'Amour"
and "Les Femmes." Michelet actually says that in
many cases the woman should be forgiven. The two

[333]

opposing kinds of views thus expressed by two great men of different races do really suggest something of the difference of character in the races. Both men are liberal thinkers, both men studied the new philosophy. Yet how very antagonistic their teachings.

I do not wish to give you too much of the moral side of Meredith at one time, for fear that it should become tiresome. So before we take up another philosophical poem, I should like to speak of a poem which is only emotional and descriptive—a tremendous poem, and certainly the greatest thing in verse that Meredith has composed. I mean "The Nuptials of Attila." In some parts it is very hard reading. In other parts it is unmatched in the splendour and strength of its verse.

First we must say a few words about the subject chosen. Doubtless you remember the apparition of Attila in Roman history. You have read how he came from the East with his tempestuous cavalry and threatened to destroy the whole of Western civilization. During his brief career Attila probably wielded the greatest power that has ever been united in the hands of one man. He controlled a larger portion of the earth's surface than that to-day controlled by the Russians, and he might have realized his dream of subduing all the West of Europe, had it not been for one act of folly. That was his marriage to a young girl called Ildico, whom he demanded from her parents against her will. On the night of the wedding there was great drinking and feasting, and when the King retired to the bridal chamber he had probably drunk to excess. At all events he died suddenly in the night, through the bursting of a blood-vessel; and his death

The Poetry of George Meredith

saved Western civilisation. There was not another leader in the vast army capable of keeping it together. The host broke up. The chiefs returned to their several countries, and the great empire of Attila melted away almost as suddenly as frost disappears in the morning sun. What became of Ildico nobody knows. It is the scene of the wedding night, and the scene of the morning following, that the poet describes.

First we have a few lines describing the power of Attila and the hunger of his army for more war:

> Flat as to an eagle's eye,
> Earth hung under Attila,
> Sign for carnage gave he none.
> In the peace of his disdain,
> Sun and rain, and rain and sun,
> Cherished men to wax again,
> Crawl, and in their manner die.
> On his people stood a frost.
> Like the charger cut in stone,
> Rearing stiff, the warrior host,
> Which had life from him alone,
> Craved the trumpet's eager note,
> As the bridled earth the Spring.
> Rusty was the trumpet's throat.
> He let chief and prophet rave;
> Venturous earth around him string
> Threads of grass and slender rye,
> Wave them, and untrampled wave.
> O for the time when God did cry,
> Eye and have, my Attila!

You must remember that Attila was called the Scourge of God. So terrible was the destruction that he wrought, that the Western world of the fifth century thought that he had been sent by God to destroy them as a punishment for sin. He himself accepted this name, and also called himself the Hammer of the World. His own words, translated into Latin, are said to have been "*Stella cadit, tellus fremit, en ego Malleus Orbis*" (the star falls, the earth shudders; lo! I am the hammer of the world). But why this peace? Why does not Attila continue to destroy?

> Scorn of conquest filled like sleep
> Him that drank of havoc deep
> When the Green Cat pawed the globe:
> When his horsemen from his bow
> Shot in sheaves.

This scorn of conquest was only induced by Attila's sudden love for a woman. Perhaps the girl Ildico would rather have died than have been given to Attila; but she had to obey the will and words of the master, and there was no opportunity given her to express her likes or dislikes—no opportunity even to kill herself, for she was well watched. White as death she appeared in her wedding robes upon the night of her awful marriage, and the wedding guests did not like to see her looking so white. Why should she not have been glad? Why should she not have blushed as a bride blushes? Some said that she loved another man; some said that she was frightened; but nobody knew and nobody was pleased, and the wedding ceremony went on. It was a strange banquet that she had to attend, for these terrible men lived upon horse-back, drank

upon horse-back, ate upon horse-back. The wedding
guests entered the hall in all the panoply of war, all
mounted upon their battle steeds—not to sit down, but
to ride furiously round the table.

> Round the banquet-table's load
> Scores of iron horsemen rode;
> Chosen warriors, keen and hard;
> Grain of threshing battle-dints;
> Attila's fierce body-guard,
> Smelling war like fire in flints.
> Grant them peace be fugitive!
> Iron-capped and iron-heeled
> Each against his fellow's shield
> Smote the spear-head, shouting, Live
>   Attila! my Attila!
> Eagle, eagle of our breed,
> Eagle, beak the lamb, and feed!
> Have her, and unleash us! live!
>   Attila! my Attila!

Now to understand how fearful a scene this must
have appeared to the bride, you must understand that
Ildico was a German girl of noble family representing
the highest refinement and delicacy of the old civilisation. To have given her to these savage people was,
of course, a monstrous cruelty. She did not enjoy
the wonderful displays of power and barbaric luxury
about her; she must have felt as one seated alone in
the midst of an earth-quake.

> Fair she seemed surpassingly;
> Soft, yet vivid as the stream

Danube rolls in the moonbeam
Through rock barriers; but she smiled
Never, she sat cold as salt:
Open-mouthed as a young child
Wondering with a mind at fault.
    Make the bed for Attila!

Under the thin hoop of gold
Whence in waves her hair outrolled,
'Twixt her brows the women saw
Shadows of a vulture's claw
Gript in flight; strange knots that sped
Closing and dissolving aye;
Such as wicked dreams betray
When pale dawn creeps o'er the bed.
They might show the common pang
Known to virgins, in whom dread
Hunts their bliss like famished hounds;
While the chiefs with roaring rounds
Tossed her to her lord, and sang
Praise of him whose hand was large,
Cheers for beauty brought to yield,
Chirrups of the trot afield,
Hurrahs of the battle-charge.

Here we suffer with her, so plainly does the figure of
the girl appear before us, silent and white with little
shadows of pain coming and going upon her young
forehead, while all about her shakes the ground under
the hoofs of the battle-horses, under the thunder roar
of the songs and the clashing of steel on steel. These
roaring horsemen are singing of other things than the
past and the present; they are clamouring for the
future, for more war, more slaughter, more destruc-

The Poetry of George Meredith

tion; they are shouting that even their horses are hungry for war.

> Whisper it (the war signal), you sound a horn
> To the grey beast in the stall!
> Yea, he whinnies at a nod.
> O, for sound of the trumpet-notes!
> O, for the time when thunder-shod,
> He that scarce can munch his oats,
> Hung on the peaks, brooded aloof,
> Champed the grain of the wrath of God,
> Pressed a cloud on the cowering roof,
> Snorted out of the blackness fire!
> Scarlet broke the sky, and down,
> Hammering West with print of his hoof,
> He burst out of the bosom of ire,
> Sharp as eyelight under thy frown,
>   Attila! my Attila!
>
> Ravaged cities rolling smoke
> Thick on cornfields dry and black,
> Wave his banners, bear his yoke.
> Track the lightning, and you track
> Attila. They moan: 'tis he!
> Bleed: 'tis he! Beneath his foot
> Leagues are deserts charred and mute;
> Where he passed, there passed a sea.
>   Attila! my Attila!

The splendid and terrible description of the war horse, the Tartar horse, descending over the mountains into Europe, not frightened by things of flesh and bone, but like a thunder-cloud descending upon the cities below—reminds one of the description of Death in the Apocalypse—"I saw a pale horse; and he that sat upon

him was called Death, and all hell followed after him."
In the fifth century this scriptural text was not forgotten; Attila was often compared, with very good reason,
to the rider of the pale horse. Where he conquered,
there was nothing left; the ground became a desert, a
waste of death, dry like the bed of a vanished sea. It
is for another devastation, such another ride, that the
warriors are clamouring at the wedding feast. But
suddenly these men observe that Ildico never smiles, that
she is terribly white like a ghost, and they do not
like this.

> Who breathed on the king cold breath?
> Said a voice amid the host,
> He is Death that weds a ghost,
> Else a ghost that weds with Death?

The barbarian idea of beauty is the red-faced, full-
fleshed woman. They see no beauty in the fair, pale
girl; she seems to them like a phantom. But Attila
only laughs at the ominous exclamation; he knows that
she is beautiful, and he orders her to fulfil her part
of the wedding ceremony by pledging the guests in a
cup of wine.

> Silent Ildico stood up.
> King and chief to pledge her well,
> Shocked sword sword and cup on cup,
> Clamouring like a brazen bell.
> Silent stepped the queenly slave.
> Fair, by heaven! she was to meet
> On a midnight, near a grave,
> Flapping wide the winding sheet.

The Poetry of George Meredith

The last three lines of course are ironical—they represent the criticism of the warriors. Perhaps one may have said, "How beautiful she is! How fair." "Fair!" observes another, "she might seem beautiful in a graveyard at night, wrapped in a white shroud!" To the speaker, such beauty as that is the beauty of the dead; there is something sinister about it. He is not all wrong; for in a little while the mightiest king in the world will die in the woman's arms. It is time for the bride to go to the bridal chamber; see how the women bow down to her as she passes by, not because they love her, but because she has become their queen!

> Death and she walked through the crowd,
> Out beyond the flush of light.
> Ceremonious women bowed
> Following her; 'twas middle night.
>
> .   .   .   .
>
> Attila remained.

He remains, as the master of the feast, to speak a few last words to his faithful chiefs, but even while talking to them he feels impatient to visit his bride, not knowing that she is Death.

> .   .   .   .   as a corse
> Gathers vultures, in his brain
> Images of her eyes and kiss
> Plucked at the limbs that could remain
> Loitering nigh the doors of bliss.
> Make the bed for Attila!

[341]

Pre-Raphaelite and Other Poets

A more terrible comparison could not have been used than this of the dead body attracting vultures. But the warriors want to talk to him a little longer; they want a promise of war; they want to feel sure that, after this wedding, the King will lead them again to battle. They want to capture and sack Rome. And one of them cries out to the King in Latin, "Lead us to Rome!" He answers, he pledges them in wine, he promises that they shall have Rome to sack and burn; and they are happy—they bid him farewell with roars of joy. In the morning he will lead them to Rome, that is enough.

In the morning what a tumult is in the camp, myriads and myriads of squadrons of cavalry, assembling for battle, chanting, cheering, roaring in the gladness of their expectation! But in the pavilion of Attila all is still silent. The chiefs know that their king is seldom late in rising; they are surprised that he does not appear. They make jests about the charm of his new bride, but they do not dare to call him, not for another hour, two hours, three hours, not until midday. At midday the chiefs lose patience, but still all is silent. At last, and only in the evening, after much calling in vain, they break in the door.

> 'Tis the room where thunder sleeps.
> Frenzy, as a wave to shore
> Surging, burst the silent door,
> And drew back to awful deeps,
> Breath beaten out, foam-white.   Anew
> Howled and pressed the ghastly crew,
> Like storm-waters over rocks.
> Attila! my Attila!

The Poetry of George Meredith

One long shaft of sunset red
Laid a finger on the bed.

. . . .

Square along the couch and stark,
Like the sea-rejected thing
Sea-sucked white, behold their King.
Attila! my Attila!

The King is dead! The warriors cannot believe it, do not want to believe. They see, and are struck with horror also because of the incalculable consequence of his death. But certainly he is dead. The red light of the setting sun illuminates his bloodless body lying in a pool of blood, for an artery burst. But what has become of Ildico—the wife?

Name us that
Huddled in the corner dark,
Humped and grinning like a cat,
Teeth for lips!—'tis she! she stares,
Glittering through her bristled hairs.

There is something there, in a dark corner of the room—something crouching like an animal, like a terrified cat, showing its teeth, raising its back, as in the presence of an attacking dog. Is it an animal? It is a woman, with her hair hanging down loose over her face, a woman, laughing horribly, because she is mad. They can see her eyes and her teeth glittering through her long hair. Did she kill him? Some think she did; others know that she did not. Some wish to kill her; cooler heads have resolved to defend her.

[343]

Rend her! Pierce her to the hilt!
She is Murder: have her out!
What! this little fist, as big
As the southern summer fig!
She is Madness, none may doubt.
Death, who dares deny her guilt!
Death, who says his blood she spilt!

.   .   .   .

Each at each, a crouching beast,
Glared, and quivered for the word,
Each at each, and all on that,
Humped and grinning like a cat.
Head bound with its bridal wreath.

.   .   .   .

Death, who dares deny her guilt!
Death, who says his blood she spilt!
Traitor he who stands between!
Swift to hell, who harms the Queen!
She, the wild, contention's cause,
Combed her hair with quiet paws.
        Make the bed for Attila!

Notice the horror of the effect caused by the use
of certain simple words in these verses. The beautiful
Ildico is no longer spoken of as a woman, but as an
insane animal or a thing. First we notice that "it"
and "its" have been substituted for "she" and "hers"
or "her"; then we have the word "paws," making a
very horrible impression. The woman is so mad that
she knows nothing of her danger, knows nothing of
what has happened; through some old habit of wom-

The Poetry of George Meredith

anly instinct, she tries to arrange her poor tossed hair, but with her fingers, as a cat combs itself with its paws.

Then begins the mighty breaking of that tremendous army. First Attila must be buried; and, according to custom, no one must know where the King is buried. A party of slaves are ordered to make the grave; when they have made it, they are killed and buried, in order that none of them may be able to say to strangers where the corpse of Attila reposes. It is not impossible, it is even probable that Ildico was killed and buried with her king, for the barbarians were accustomed to slaughter the attendants of a dead prince, and even his horses, in order that he might have shadowy company and shadowy steeds in the other world. But we do not know. History has nothing to say as to what became of Ildico. The poem closes with a wonderful description of the breaking up of the army, which is likened to the breaking up of the ice in a great river at the approach of spring.

Lo, upon a silent hour,
When the pitch of frost subsides,
Danube with a shout of power
Loosens his imprisoned tides:
Wide around the frighted plains
Shake to hear the riven chains,
Dreadfuller than heaven in wrath,
As he makes himself a path:
High leaps the ice-cracks, towering pile
Floes to bergs, and giant peers
Wrestle on a drifted isle;
Island on ice-island rears;

[345]

Pre-Raphaelite and Other Poets

Dissolution battles fast:
Big the senseless Titans loom,
Through a mist of common doom
Striving which shall die the last:
Till a gentle-breathing morn
Frees the stream from bank to bank.
So the Empire built of scorn
Agonised, dissolved, and sank.
Of the queen no more was told
Than of leaf on Danube rolled.
Make the bed for Attila!

I have said that this poem is emotional rather than didactic; yet there is a moral suggestion in it, the suggestion of what one foolish indulgence in lust may cause. For in the case of Attila, who had already scores and scores of wives, the marriage with Ildico was a mere piece of brutal indulgence and cruelty, and it proved his death. Then again, of course, it was a good thing for the world that Attila died when he did. It would seem as if nature takes very good care that men who are only brutal and cunning shall not be allowed to rule human life for a great length of time. Their own passions or their own follies eventually destroy them.

There is yet another suggestion in the poem, which Meredith is very fond of making, both in his novels and in his verse. He thinks that an old man should never marry a young woman, no matter how great the merit of the old man may be. Here and there will be many to disagree with Meredith, and to quote such cases as that of the great French engineer, De Lesseps, who married only when he was more than sixty

The Poetry of George Meredith

years old, and thereafter raised a very numerous family of remarkably fine children. But in a general way, Meredith is probably right. He expounds his ideas very clearly in a little poem called "The Last Contention." In this "last contention" the poet addresses an old man who wants to marry a young girl. He represents the mind of the man as that of a captain, directing a ship, and the ship is the body, the constitution, the physical part of the individual. With this explanation we may quote a few verses of the poem. It is cruel; but it is very moral and perhaps very just.

> Young captain of a crazy bark!
> O tameless heart in battered frame!
> Thy sailing orders have a mark,
> And hers is not the name.

> For action all thine iron clanks
> In cravings for a splendid prize;
> Again to race or bump thy planks
> With any flag that flies.
>
> .   .   .   .   .

> Admires thee Nature with much pride;
> She clasps thee for a gift of morn,
> Till thou art set against the tide,
> And then beware her scorn.
>
> .   .   .   .   .

> This lady of the luting tongue,
> The flash in darkness, billow's grace,
> For thee the worship; for the young
> In muscle the embrace.

[347]

Pre-Raphaelite and Other Poets

Soar on thy manhood clear for those
Whose toothless Winter claws at May,
And take her as the vein of rose
Athwart an evening grey.

I have left out the most cruel verses; but these are significant enough. The person addressed might be one of those old generals or admirals who figure so often in the novels of Meredith, some brave old man, with a great reputation for courage and skill and the arts of courtesy. Such men may be able to win a young wife, rather by help of their wealth, social position, and reputation than by real love. The poet says that one should not try to do this. And he says that the man who does it, or wishes to do it, is like a skilful captain who trusts too much to his seamanship, forgetting that his vessel is in a state of decay. The heart may be young enough, but that is not sufficient. Nature seems to love and favour grand old men, but not if they do what is not according to Nature's laws. Therefore if marriages between old and young prove to be unfortunate, the fault is in most cases with the old. The old man may admire, may reverence a beautiful young person; but only as we admire a work of art, at a distance, or beautiful colours in the sunset sky. Let me call your attention to the use of the phrases "flash in darkness" and "billow's grace." The Greeks said that life was like a flash between two darknesses—the darkness of the mystery out of which we come, and the darkness of the mystery into which we go. It is a very beautiful and a very profound comparison; the poet here uses it especially in reference to the beautiful pe-

[348]

riod of youth, which is short. He suggests that an old man should have wisdom enough to think of youth and of beauty as passing illusions. "Billow's grace" is a very striking simile. The charm of movement in a graceful person is something which no art can reproduce. It is beauty of motion, and the instant that the motion stops, the charm is not. The beauty of water, flowing water, is of this kind. Even while you admire the motion of a wave, gilded by the sunlight, the wave has passed.

And now we shall turn to a very important division of Meredith's poems—those dealing with the philosophy of life as a whole. On this subject most of the great English poets are apt to be a little didactic in the religious sense. Meredith is also didactic—but not in a religious sense. One peculiarity of his work is the total absence of theological doctrine of any kind. He talks to you about the laws of the universe, the laws of life, the laws of nature—never about the laws of any God or any religion. When he does mention the word God or the word religion, it is always in such a way that you feel he considers such things only as symbols—useful symbols, perhaps, but symbols only. I shall speak only of two remarkable poems of this kind. The first, called "The Woods of Westermain," considers especially the struggle of human life, and the duties of man in that struggle. The other poem, entitled "Earth and Man," treats more largely of the problem of the universe—the great mystery of the questions, Where do we come from? Why do we exist? Whither are we going? Let us first take the "Woods of Westermain."

[349]

Pre-Raphaelite and Other Poets

Why the poem should be called by the name of "The Woods of Westermain," I am not able to tell you; but I think that the name contains a suggestion about occidental life as contrasted with oriental life. However, I am not sure, but, at all events, the subject of the poem is not a real forest, but the forest of human existence, the place in which the struggle of life goes on—therefore, in the true sense, Nature.

The great teaching of this poem is that Nature has given us powers and senses not for pleasure, not for the obtaining of selfish enjoyment, but for battle. All that we know at present about the reason of life is summed up in that fact. The great natural duty of every man is to fight, morally and physically, and though he has a perfect right to enjoy himself, to seek pleasure at proper times and places, he must never allow pleasure to interfere with the supreme duty of struggle in battle; the first requisite, therefore, is courage, the first thing necessary is never to be afraid. In the ancient fairy-tales of Europe, we find many stories about enchanted forests, goblin forests. The knight, the hero of the story, enters a great wood, which seems very green and pleasant to the eye. As he lies down under a tree, however, he sees strange shapes looking at him—shapes of fairies, shapes of demons, shapes of giants. But he rides on, and they do not do him any harm. After a while he arrives safely at his destination. Quite otherwise in the case of the cowardly knight. When he finds himself in the forest he becomes afraid, and terrible shapes rise up about him, come close to him, at last attack him and tear him to pieces. Now the forest of life is just like

the enchanted forest of the old fairy-tales. If you
are afraid, you are destroyed. If you are not afraid,
all is bright and beautiful.

> Enter these enchanted woods,
>   You who dare.
> Nothing harms beneath the leaves
> More than waves a swimmer cleaves.
> Toss your heart up with the lark,
> Float at peace with mouse and worm,
>   Fair you fare.
>
> Only at a dread of dark
> Quaver, and they quit their form:
> Thousand eyeballs under hoods
>   Have you by the hair.
> Enter these enchanted woods,
>   You who dare.
> Here the snake across your path
> Stretches in his golden bath;
> Mossy-footed squirrels leap
> Soft as winnowing plumes of Sleep.
>
> .   .   .   .   .
>
> Each has business of his own;
> But should you distrust a tone,
>   Then beware!
> Shudder all the haunted roods,
> All the eyeballs under hoods
>   Shroud you in their glare.

I am not sure that this imagery can appeal to you
as it was intended to appeal to the Western reader,
because it partly depends for effect upon the knowl-

edge of the old fairy-tale pictures. In Western ghost stories and fairy stories, goblins and other phantoms are usually represented in long robes with hoods over their faces, and very big, wicked eyes. That is why the poet speaks so often of the hoods and the eyeballs. The meaning is that, in this world, just so soon as you begin to suspect and to be afraid, everything really becomes to you terrible—even as in the old fairy-tales a tree was only a tree to the sight of a brave man, but to the cowardly man its roots became feet and its branches horrible arms and claws, and its crest a goblin face.

Then follows a wonderful description of wood life— the life of insect, reptile, bird and little animals—the poet taking care to show how each and all of these represent something of human life and moral truth. But it is one of the most difficult poems in English literature to read; and I shall not try to quote much from it. Enough to say that the same lesson is taught all the way through the poem, the lesson of what Nature means. She must not be thought of as a cruel Sphinx: she is cruel only if you imagine her to be cruel. Nature will always be what you think her to be. Think of her as beautiful and good; then she will be good and beautiful for you. Think of her as cruel; then she will be cruel to you. Do not think of her as pleasure; if you do, she will give you pleasure, but she will destroy you at the same time. She is the spirit and law of Eternal Struggle; and it is thus only that you should think of her, as a divinity desiring you to be brave, active, generous, ambitious. Above all things, you must not hate. Hate Nature, and you are instantly de-

stroyed. You must not allow even a thought of hate
to enter your mind.

> Hate, the shadow of a grain;
> You are lost in Westermain:
> Earthward swoops a vulture sun
> Nighted upon carrion:
> Straightway venom winecups shout
> As to One whose eyes are out:
> Flowers along the reeling floor
> Drip henbane and hellebore;
> Beauty, of her tresses shorn,
> Shrieks as nature's maniac:
> Hideousness on hoof and horn
> Tumbles, yapping in her track:
> Haggard Wisdom, stately once,
> Leers fantastical and trips.
>
> .   .   .   .   .   .
>
> Imp that dances, imp that flies
> Imp o' the demon-growing girl,
> Maddest! whirl with imp o' the pits
> Round you, and with them you whirl
> Fast where pours the fountain—rout
> Out of Him whose eyes are out.

The foregoing must seem to you very difficult verse;
and it is really very difficult for the best English
readers. But at the same time it is very powerful; and
I think that you ought to have at least one example
of the difficult side of Meredith. This is a picture—a
horrible picture, such as old artists used to make in
the fifteenth or sixteenth century to illustrate the temptations of a saint by devils, or the terrors of a sinner
about to die, and surrounded by ghastly visions. Really

[353]

if you hate Nature, the universe will at once for you become what it seemed to the superstitious of the past ages and to the disordered fancies of insane fanatic. The very sun itself will no longer appear as a glorious star, but as a creature of prey, devouring the dead. Perhaps the poet here wishes also to teach us that we must not think too much about the ugly side of death as an appearance—the corruption, the worms, the darkness of the grave. To think about those things, as the monks of the Middle Ages did, is to hate Nature. Everything seems foul to the man whose imagination is foul. Everything which should be nourishing becomes poison, everything which should seem beautiful becomes hideous. The reference to "One whose eyes are out," is, you know, a reference to the old fashioned pictures of death, as a goblin skeleton, seeing without eyes. In some frightful pictures death was represented also as an eyeless corpse, out of which all kinds of goblins, demons, and bad dreams were swarming, like maggots. Of course such are the pictures referred to here by the poet. Believe in goblins and devils, and you will see them; believe that all men are wicked, and you will find them wicked; believe that Nature is evil, and Nature will certainly destroy you, just as the demons in the mediæval story tore to pieces the magician who had not learned the secret of making them obey.

Very much more easy to understand are the stanzas upon "Earth and Man." These attempt to explain the real problem of man's existence. The poet represents the earth as a person, a mother, a nurse. But this mother, this nurse, this divine person is not able to do

The Poetry of George Meredith

everything for man. She can give him life; she can feed him; but she cannot help him otherwise, except upon the strange condition that he helps himself. She makes him and embraces him, but that is all. Otherwise he must make his own future, his own happiness or misery.

> For he is in the lists
> Contentious with the elements, whose dower
> First sprang him; for swift vultures to devour
> If he desists.
>
> His breath of instant thirst
> Is warning of a creature matched with strife,
> To meet it as a bride, or let fall life
> On life's accursed.

That is, man in this world is like an athlete, or a warrior in the lists—in the place of contests. With what must he contend? First of all, he must contend with the very elements of nature, with the very same forces which brought him into being, or as the poet says "sprang him." And if he hesitates to fight with those forces, then quickly the vultures of death seize upon him. The condition of his existence is struggle. Even the first cry of the child, the cry of thirst for the mother's milk, signifies that man is born to desire and to toil and to contend. He must either meet the duty of struggle as gladly as he would meet a bride, or he must acknowledge himself unfit to live, and cursed by his own mother, Nature. Nature is not to be thought of as a mother that pets her child and weeps over its small sorrows; no, she is a good mother, but very rough, and she loves only the child that fights and conquers.

She has no pity upon him except as he fights and wins. She cannot do certain things for him; she cannot develop his mind—he must do that for himself. She makes him do it by pain, by terror, by punishing him fearfully for his mistakes. By the consequence of mistakes only does she teach him. She urges him forward by hunger and by fear, but there is no mercy for him if he blunders. I want you to remember that the poet is not speaking of the separate individual man, but of mankind and of the history of the human race. According to modern science, man was at the beginning nothing more than an animal; he has become what he is through knowledge of suffering, and the poet describes his sufferings in the beginning:

> By hunger sharply sped
> To grasp at weapons ere he learns their use,
> In each new ring he bears a giant's thews,
>   An infant's head.

> And ever that old task
> Of reading what he is and whence he came,
> Whither to go, finds wilder letters flame
>   Across her mask.

That is to say, man first is impelled by hunger to use weapons, in order to kill animals, and these weapons he at first must use very clumsily. You must understand the word "ring" to mean an age or cycle. The poet wishes to say that through many past ages in succession, man had the strength of a giant, but his brain,

The Poetry of George Meredith

his mind, was feeble and foolish like that of a little child—not even a child in the common meaning of the word, for the poet uses the term "infant," signifying a child before it has yet learned how to speak. It is supposed that primitive man had no developed languages. But, as time goes on, man learns how to express thought by speech, and presently he begins to think about himself—to wonder what he is, where he came from, and where he is going. Then he invents religious theories to account for his origin. But the mystery always remains. There are ancient stories about a magical writing. When you looked at this writing, at first it seemed to be in one language, and to have one meaning, but when you looked at it a second time, the letters and the meaning had changed, and every succeeding time that you looked at it, again it changed. Like this magical writing is the mystery of Nature, of the Universe; so that poet represents Nature as wearing a mask upon which such ever-changing characters appear in letters of fire. No matter how much we learn or theorise, the infinite riddle cannot be read. And one factor of this terrible riddle is Death. Death of all things most puzzles and terrifies man. He sometimes suspects that Nature herself is Death, and purely evil. He began by worshipping her through fear, but his worship did not change his destiny in the least.

> The thing that shudders most
> Within him is the burden of his cry.
> Seen of his dread, she is to his blank eye
> The eyeless Ghost.

[357]

Pre-Raphaelite and Other Poets

Once worshipped Prime of Powers,
She still was the Implacable; as a beast,
She struck him down and dragged him from the feast
    She crowned with flowers.

.   .   .   .

He may entreat, aspire,
He may despair, and she has never heed.
She drinking his warm sweat will soothe his need,
    Not his desire.

She prompts him to rejoice,
Yet scares him on the threshold with the shroud.
He deems her cherishing of her best-endowed
    A wanton's choice.

If man thought of the spirit of Nature as the cruel
spirit of death and destruction, surely he had reason to
do so in the time of his primitive ignorance. Pleasure
seemed to him of Nature—offered to him by Nature,
and yet to indulge it often brought upon him destruction. Joy seemed to him natural, yet whenever he
most rejoiced, the shadow of death would appear
somewhere near him. Always this Nature seemed to be
putting out temptations to joy and pleasure, only as
a bird hunter scatters food on the ground to attract
birds into his snare. And again this Nature would
never listen to man's prayer. He found out that by
working hard he could obtain food enough to live
upon; thus Nature seemed to allow him the right
of life, or as the poet says, "to soothe his needs"; but
never would she grant him his "desire," his prayer
for supernatural help. When it came to the matter

The Poetry of George Meredith

of help, he found out that he must help himself. But why was it, again, that the wicked and the cruel were permitted to succeed and to become prosperous, while the good and the gentle perished from the face of the earth? To ancient mankind this was indeed a most terrible problem, a problem which has not been perfectly solved even at this day. Was Nature a wanton—that is, a wicked woman, preferring the evil characters, the murderer, the thief, the robber, to the upright and just? Such was the question which millions of men must have asked themselves in the past. Evidently the poet does not think so; he calls the successful, "the best endowed." What does this mean? It means that the choice of Nature in her favours, however immoral that choice may seem to us, is really a choice of the best, according to her judgment. You may say, if you like, that these or those successful men are bad, that they have broken all moral rules, that they have sinned against all the ethics of society, that they are scoundrels who ought to be in prison. But Nature says, "No, those are my best children. You may not like them, and doubtless they are not good to your thinking, but they are very much more clever and much stronger than you. I want my children to be cunning and to be strong." Are we to suppose, therefore, that Nature wishes to cultivate only wicked cunning and brutal strength? No, but cunning and strength are the foundations upon which intellect and moral power are eventually built. It is like the statement of Herbert Spencer, that the first thing necessary for success in life is "to be a good animal." If you can be both a good animal and a

moral and kind person, so much the better. But while
the development is going on, the chances always are
that Nature will favour the animal man at the expense
of the moral man who has no strength and no cleverness. For those who have neither strength nor cunning must disappear from the face of the earth. Nature does not want to help weakness; she prefers strong
wickedness to helpless goodness. And if we reflect
upon this, we shall find that the whole tendency is not
to evil but to good. It is by considering the past history of man that we can learn how much he has gained
through this cruel policy of Nature.

> . . . Thereof he has found
> Firm roadway between lustfulness and pain;
> Has half transferred the battle to his brain,
>   From bloody ground;
>
> He will not read her good,
> Or wise, but with the passion Self obscures;
> Through that old devil of the thousand lures,
>   Through that dense hood:
>
> Through terror, through distrust;
> The greed to touch, to view, to have, to live;
> Through all that makes of him a sensitive
>   Abhorring dust.

Which means that, if we will really think about the
matter from an evolutional standpoint, we shall find
that it has been through the destruction of the weak
that mankind has become strong. At first he knew
only desire, like an animal; his wants were only like

those of an animal. But gradually nobler desires came to him, because they were forced upon him by his constant struggle against death. He learns that one must be able to control one's desire as well as to fight against other enemies. From the day man discovered that the greatest enemy was Self, he became a higher being, he was no longer a mere animal. When the poet speaks of him as "transferring the battle to his brain from bloody ground," he means that the struggle of existence to-day has become a battle of minds, instead of being, as it used to be, a trial of mere physical strength. We must every one of us fight, but the fight is now intellectual. Notwithstanding this progress, we are still very stupid, for we try to explain the laws of the Universe according to our little feeble conceptions of moral law. Or, as the poet says, we insist on thinking about Nature "with the passion Self obscures" —with that selfishness in our hearts which judges everything to be bad that gives us pain. Until we can get rid of that selfishness, we shall never understand Nature.

Now the question is, shall we ever be able to understand Nature? I shall let the poet answer that question in his own way. It is an optimistic way, and it has the great merit of being quite different from anything else written upon the subject by any English poet.

> But that the senses still
> Usurp the station of their issue mind,
> He would have burst the chrysalis of the blind:
>   As yet he will;

As yet he will, she prays,
Yet will when his distempered devil of Self;—
The glutton for her fruits, the wily elf
  In shifting rays;—

That captain of the scorned;
The coveter of life in soul and shell,
The fratricide, the thief, the infidel,
  The hoofed and horned;—

He singularly doomed
To what he execrates and writhes to shun;—
WHEN FIRE HAS PASSED HIM VAPOUR TO THE SUN,
AND SUN RELUMED.

Here we might well imagine that we were listening to a Buddhist, not to an English poet, for the thought is altogether the thought of an Oriental philosopher, though it happens also to be in accord with the philosophy of Western science. The lines which I put in capital letters seem to me the most remarkable and the most profound that any Western poet has yet written about the future of mankind. Let us loosely paraphrase the verses quoted:

The end to which the senses of man have been created is the making of Mind. If man were not blinded and deceived by his senses, he would know what Nature is, because the divine sight, perhaps the infinite vision, would be opened to him. But the time will come when he shall be able to know and to see.

What time?

The time when the selfishness of man shall have ceased, when he shall no longer think of life as given

[362]

The Poetry of George Meredith

to him only for the pursuit of pleasure; when he shall have learned that he must not desire to live too much, and that the body is only the shell of the mind; when crime and cruelty shall have become impossible—when this world shall have come to an end.

But when the world shall have come to an end, will there still be man? Yes, in the poet's faith; for man is part of the eternal, and the destruction of the universe cannot affect his destiny. It is not, however, when this world shall have come to an end that man will know. The earth will go back to the sun, out of which it came, and the sun itself will burn out into ashes, and the universe will disappear, and there will thereafter be another universe, with other suns and worlds, and only then, after passing through the fires of the sun, perhaps of many suns, will man obtain the supreme knowledge. Never in this world can he become wise enough and good enough to be perfectly happy. But in some future universe, under the light of some sun not yet existing, he may become an almost perfect being.

It may seem strange to you to hear such a prediction from an English poet, though the thought of the poem is very ancient in Indian philosophy. Yet Meredith did not reach this thought through the study of any Oriental teaching. He obtained it from the evolutional philosophy of the present century, adding, indeed, a little fancy of his own, but nothing at all in antagonism to the opinions of science, so far as fact is concerned.

What is the teaching of science in regard to the future and the past of the present universe? It is that

[363]

in the course of enormous periods of time this universe passes away into a nebulous condition, and out of that condition is reformed again. Mathematically it has been calculated that the forces regulating the universe must have in the past formed the same kind of universes millions of times, and will do the same thing in the future, millions of times. Every modern astronomer recognizes the studies upon which these calculations are based. It is certainly curious that when science tells us how the universe with its hundreds of millions of suns, and its trillions of worlds, regularly evolves and devolves alternately—it is curious, I repeat, that this science is telling us the very same thing that Indian philosophers were teaching thousands of years ago, before there was any science. They taught that all worlds appear and disappear by turns in the infinite void, and they compared these worlds to the shadows of the dream of a god. When the Supreme awakens from his sleep, then all the worlds disappear, because they were only the shapes of his dream.

Herbert Spencer would not go quite so far as that. But he would confirm Indian philosophy as to the apparition and disparition of the universes. There is another point upon which any Western man of science would also confirm the Oriental teaching—that the essence of life does not cease and cannot cease with the destruction of our world. Only the form dies. The forces that make life cannot die; they are the same forces that spin the suns. Remember that I am not talking about a soul or a ghost or anything of that kind; I am saying only that it is quite scientific to believe that all the life which has been in this world will

The Poetry of George Meredith

be again in some future world, lighted by another sun.
Meredith suggests perhaps more than this—only suggests. Take his poem, however, as it stands, and you
will find it a very noble utterance of optimism, inspir-
ing ideas astonishingly like the ideas of Eastern meta-
physicians.

I am going to conclude this lecture upon Meredith
with one more example of his philosophy of social life.
It is a poem treating especially of the questions of
love and marriage, and it shows us how he looks at matters which are much closer to us than problems about
suns and souls and universes.

The name of the poem is "The Three Singers to
Young Blood"—that is to say, the three voices of the
world that speak to youth. In order to understand this
composition rightly, you must first know that in Western countries generally and in England particularly,
the most important action of a man's early life is marriage. A man's marriage is likely to decide, not only
his future happiness or misery, but his social position,
his success in his profession, his ultimate place even
in politics, if he happens to enter the service of the
state. I am speaking of marriage among the upper
classes, the educated classes, the professional classes.
Among the working people, the tradesmen and me-
chanics, most of whom marry quite young, marriage
has not very much social significance. But among the
moneyed classes it is all important, and a mistake in
choosing a wife may ruin the whole career of the most
gifted and clever man. This is what Meredith has in
mind, when he speaks of the three voices that address
youth. The first voice, simply the voice of healthy na-

ture, urges the young man to seek happiness by making a home for himself. The second voice is that of society, of worldly wisdom and calculating selfishness. The third voice is the voice of reckless passion, caring nothing about consequences. Which of the three shall the young man listen to? Let us hear the first voice.

> As the birds do, so do we,
> Bill our mate, and choose our tree.
> Swift to building work addressed,
> Any straw will help a nest.
> Mates are warm, and this is truth,
> Glad the young that come of youth.
> They have bloom i' the blood and sap
> Chilling at no thunder-clap.
> Man and woman on the thorn,
> Trust not Earth, and have her scorn.
> They who in her lead confide,
> Wither me if they spread not wide!
> Look for aid to little things,
> You will get them quick as wings,
> Thick as feathers; would you feed,
> Take the leap that springs the need.

In other words, the advice of this first voice is, Do not be afraid. Choose your companion as the bird does; make a home for yourself; do not be afraid to try, simply because you have no money. Do not wait to become rich. If you know how to be contented with little, you will find that you can make a small home very easily. A wife makes life more comfortable, and the children of young parents are the strongest and the happiest. Such children are healthy, and they

The Poetry of George Meredith

grow up brave and energetic. You must confide in Nature. Men and women who are afraid to trust to Nature, because they happen to be poor, lose all chance of ever finding real happiness. Nature turns from them in scorn. But those who trust to Nature—how they increase and multiply and prosper! Do not wait for somebody to help you. Watch for opportunities; and you will find them, quickly, and in multitude. If you want anything in this world, do not wait for it to come to you; spring for it, as the bird springs from the tree to seize its food.

There is nothing very bad about this advice, though it is opposed to the rules of social success. The majority of young people act pretty much in the way indicated, and it is interesting to observe in this connection that both Mr. Galton and Mr. Spencer have declared that if it were required to act otherwise, the consequences would be very unfortunate for the nation. It is not from cautious and long delayed marriages that a nation multiplies; on the contrary, it is from improvident marriages by young people. Yet there is something to be said on the other side of the question. No doubt a great deal of unhappiness might be avoided if young men and women were somewhat less rash than they now are about entering into marriage.

But let us listen to the second voice. Each of the three speaks in exactly the same number of lines— sixteen.

> Contemplate the rutted road;
> Life is both a lure and goad.
> Each to hold in measure just,
> Trample appetite to dust.

Pre-Raphaelite and Other Poets

Mark the fool and wanton spin:
Keep to harness as a skin.
Ere you follow nature's lead,
Of her powers in you have heed;
Else a shiverer you will find
You have challenged humankind.
Mates are chosen marketwise:
Coolest bargainer best buys.
Leap not, nor let leap the heart:
Trot your track, and drag your cart.
So your end may be in wool,
Honoured, and with manger full.

This is the voice of worldly wisdom, of hard selfishness, and, I am sorry to say, of cunning hypocrisy; but it sounds very sensible indeed, and thousands of very successful men act upon the principles here laid down. Let us paraphrase:

Take a good look at the road of life—see how rough it is! Understand that there are two opposite principles of life; there are things that attract to danger, and there are powers that compel a man to make the greatest effort of which his strength is capable. Consider all pleasure as dangerous; if you want to be safe and sure, kill your passions, and master all your desires. Observe how hard foolish people and sensual people find life. Wrap yourself up in self-control, keep always on your guard against pleasure, keep on distrust as a suit of armour—no, rather as a skin, never to be taken off. Before you allow yourself to follow any natural impulse, remember how dangerous natural impulses are. Beware of Nature! Otherwise you will

[368]

The Poetry of George Meredith

soon find out, with trembling, that the whole world is against you, that human experience is against you, that you have become an enemy of society. And as for a wife, remember that you should choose a wife exactly as you would buy a horse, or as you would make any business purchase. In business bargaining, it is the man who keeps his temper the longest and conceals his feelings the most cunningly, that gets the best article. Never allow an impulse to guide you. Never follow the guidance of your heart. Life is hard, make up your mind to go steadily forward and bear your burden, and if you will do this while you are young, you will become comfortably rich when you get old, and will have the respect of society and the enjoyment of everything good in this world. I have said that this advice is very immoral, although it is in one way very sensible. I say that it is immoral only for this reason, that it tells people to act sensibly, not for the love of what is good and true, but merely for the sake of personal advantages. I cannot believe that a man is good who lives virtuously only because he finds virtue a profitable business. All this is pure selfishness, but there is no doubt that a great many successful men live and act exactly according to these principles. Now let us consider the third voice, the voice of mere passion, esthetic passion, which is especially strong with generous minds. It is not usually the dullard nor the hypocrite nor the egotist who goes to his ruin by following the impulses of such a passion as that here described. It is rather the man of the type of Byron, or still more of the type of Shelley. It is against danger of this voice that the artist and the poet must especially be on guard.

[369]

Pre-Raphaelite and Other Poets

O the rosy light! it fleets,
Dearer dying than all sweets.
That is life: it waves and goes;
Solely in that cherished Rose
Palpitates, or else 'tis death.
Call it love with all thy breath.
Love! it lingers: Love! it nears:
Love! O Love! the Rose appears,
Blushful, magic, reddening air.
Now the choice is on thee: dare!
Mortal seems the touch, but makes
Immortal the hand that takes.
Feel what sea within thee shames
Of its force all other claims,
Drowns them. Clasp! the world will be
Heavenly Rose to swelling sea.

This will need a good deal of explanation, though I am sure that you can feel the general meaning without any explanation. The poet is making a reference to the rose of the alchemist's dream—the strange old fairy-tale of the Rosicrucians. It was believed in the Middle Ages and even later, that an Elixir of Life might be formed by chemistry—that is to say, a magical drink that would make old men young again, or prolong life through hundreds of years. It was said that whenever this wonderful drink was made in a laboratory, there would appear in the liquid the ghostly image of a luminous Rose. It would take much too long to go into the history of this curious and very poetical fancy. Suffice to say that the poet here uses the symbol of the rose of the alchemist to signify life itself—the essence of youth, and the essence of passion and the worship of beauty. Now we can attempt to paraphrase:

How wondrous beauty is! How wondrous life and love! Yet quickly these must pass away. Of what worth is life without love? Better to love and die quickly. The desire of the lover is, in its way, a desire for sacrifice; he is willing to give his life a thousand times over for the being he adores. He thinks that love is life, that there is nothing else worth existing for. His passion gives new and strange colour to all his thoughts, new intensity to all his senses; the world becomes more beautiful for him. Even as if the colour of the sunlight were changed, so do all things appear changed to the vision of the man who is then bewitched. But, even during the bewitchment, he is faintly conscious of duty, of right and wrong, of a voice within him warning against dangers. He knows, he fears, but he will not heed. He reasons against his conscience. Is not this attraction really divine? She is only a woman, yet merely to touch her hand gives a shock, as of something supernatural. Then the very strength of passion itself makes it seem more natural. The poet compares it to a sea—the tide of impulse could not be better described, because of its depth and force. And always the urging of this passion is "Take her! Do not care! That will be heaven for you!"

The last stanza has a strange splendour, as well as a strange power; reckless passion has never been more wonderfully described in sixteen lines. And to which of the three voices does the poet give preference? Not to any of them. He says that all of them are deficient in true wisdom. The first he calls "liquid"—meaning sweet, like the cry of a dove. But that does not mean that it is altogether commendable. The second voice he calls a "caw"—meaning that it is dismal and harsh, like the cry of a black crow. As for the last, he says only that it is "the cry that knows not law!" By this he means that which suffers no restraint, and which therefore is incomparably dangerous. Yet I suppose that it is better than the caw. What the poet thinks is that the three different voices united together, so that each makes harmony with the others, so that the good which is in each could make accord—would be "music of the sun!"

> Hark to the three. Chimed they in one,
> Life were music of the sun.
> Liquid first, and then the caw,
> Then the cry that knows not law.

This utterance is not nearly so commonplace as we might think at first reading. There is a great deal of deep philosophy in it. Meredith means that all our impulses, all our passions, all our selfishness, and even our revolts against law, have their value in the eternal order of things. In a perfect man all these emotions and sentiments would still exist, but they would exist only in such form that they would beautifully counterbalance each other. But there is no such thing as human perfection, and the individual is therefore very likely to be dominated by selfishness if he acts cautiously, and dominated by passion when he acts without judgment.

I think I have quoted enough of Meredith to give

The Poetry of George Meredith

you some notion of his particular quality. At all
events I hope that you may become interested in him.
He is especially the poet of scholars; the poet of men
of culture. Only a man of culture can really like him
—just as only a man long accustomed to good living
can appreciate the best kinds of wine. Give fine wine
to a poor man accustomed only to drink coarse spirits,
and he will not care about it. So the common reader
cannot care about Meredith. He is what we call a
"test-poet"—your culture, your capacity to think and
feel, is tested by your ability to like such a poet. The
question, "Do you like Meredith?" is now in English
and even in French literary circles, a test. But remember that Meredith has great faults. If he did not
have, he would rank at the very top of the Victorian
poets. But he has the fault of obscurity, like Browning,
he often tortures language into the most amazing forms,
and he is about the most difficult of all English poets
to read. His early work is much better than his later
in this respect. But the difficulty of Meredith is not
only a difficulty of language. No one can understand
him who does not also understand the philosophical
thought of the second half of the nineteenth century.
He is especially the poet of a particular time, and for
that reason it is very much to be regretted that he is
less clear than almost any literary artist of his period.

CHAPTER VII

"THE SHAVING OF SHAGPAT"

I HAVE spoken to you a great deal about the poetry of George Meredith, but I have not yet found an opportunity to tell you about his having written what I believe to be one of the greatest fables—certainly the greatest fable imagined during the nineteenth century. I imagine also that this fable will live, will even become a great classic,—after all his novels have been forgotten. For his novels, great as they are, deal almost entirely with contemporary pictures of highly complicated English and Italian aristocratic society. They picture the mental and moral fashions of a generation, and all such fashions quickly change. But the great fable pictures something which is, which has been, and which always will be in human nature; it touches the key of eternal things, just as his poetry does—perhaps even better; for some of his poetry is terribly obscure. Mr. Gosse has written a charming essay upon the fable of which I am going to speak to you; but neither Mr. Gosse nor anybody else has ever attempted to explain it. If the book is less well known, less widely appreciated than it deserves, the fact is partly owing to the want of critical interpretation. Even to Mr. Gosse the book makes its appeal chiefly as a unique piece of literary art. But how many people in conservative England either care for literary art in itself, or are

[374]

"The Shaving of Shagpat"

capable of estimating it? So long as people think that
such or such a book is only a fairy tale, they do not
trouble themselves much to read it. But prove to them
that the fairy tale is the emblem of a great moral fact,
then it is different. The wonderful stories of Andersen
owe their popularity as much to the fact that they teach
moral fact, as to the fact that they please children.

Meredith's book was not written to please children;
there is perhaps too much love-making in it for that.
I do not even know whether it was written for a particular purpose; I am inclined to think that there was
no particular purpose. Books written with a purpose
generally fail. Great moral stories are stories that have
been written for art's sake. Meredith took for model
the manner of the Arabian story tellers. The language,
the comparisons, the poetry, the whole structure of his
story is in the style of the Arabian Nights. But as
Mr. Gosse observes, the Arabian Nights seem to us
cold and pale beside it. You can not find in the Arabian
Nights a single page to compare with certain pages
of "The Shaving of Shagpat"; and this is all the more
extraordinary because the English book is written in
a tone of extravagant humour. You feel that the author is playing with the subject, as a juggler plays with
half a dozen balls at the same time, never letting one of
them fall. And yet he has done much better than the
Orientals who took their subject seriously. Even the
title, the names of places or of persons, are jokes,
—though they look very much like Arabian or Persian
names. "Shagpat" is only the abbreviation of "shaggy
pate," "pate" being an old English word for head—
so that the name means a very hairy and rough look-

ing head. When you begin to see jokes of this kind even in the names, you may be inclined to think that the book is trifling. I thought so myself before reading it; but now that I have read it at least half a dozen times, and hope to read it many times more, I can assure you that it is one of the most delightful books ever written, and that it can not fail to please you. With this introduction, I shall now begin to say something about the story itself, the fantastic plot of it.

Who is Shagpat? Shagpat is a clothing merchant and the favourite of a king. Shagpat wears his hair very long, contrary to the custom of Mohammedan countries, where all men shave their heads, with the exception of one tuft on the top of the head, by which tuft, after death, the true believer is to be lifted up by angels, and carried into Paradise. Mohammedans are as careful about this tuft as the Chinese are careful about their queues. How comes it that in a Mohammedan city a true believer should thus wear his hair long? It is because in his head there has been planted one magical hair taken out of the head of a Djinn or Genie; and this hair, called the Identical, has the power to make all men worship the person on whose head it grows. Therefore it is that the king reverences this clothing merchant, and that all the people bow down before him. Also an order is given that all men in that country must wear their hair long in the same manner, and that no barbers are to be allowed to exercise their trade in any of the cities.

A barber, not knowing these regulations,—a barber of the name of Shibli Bagarag—comes to the principal city and actually proposes to shave Shagpat. He

[376]

"The Shaving of Shagpat"

is at once seized by slaves, severely beaten, and banished from the city. But outside the city he meets a horrible old woman, so ugly that it pains him to look at her; and she tells him that she can make his fortune for him if he will promise to marry her. Although he is in a very unhappy condition, the idea of marrying so hideous a woman terrifies him; nevertheless he plucks up courage and promises. She asks him then to kiss her. He has to shut his eyes before he can do that, but after he has done it she suddenly becomes young and handsome. She is the daughter of the chief minister of the king, and she is ugly only because of an enchantment cast upon her. This enchantment has been caused by the power of Shagpat, who desired to marry her. For her own sake and for the sake of the country and for the sake of all the people, she says that it is necessary that the head of Shagpat should be shaved. But to shave Shagpat requires extraordinary powers— magical powers. For the magical hair in that man's head cannot be cut by any ordinary instrument. If approached with a knife or a razor, this hair suddenly develops tremendous power as of an electric shock, hurling far away all who approach it. It is only a hair to all appearances at ordinary times, but at extraordinary times it becomes luminous, and stands up like a pillar of fire reaching to the stars. And the daughter of the minister tells Bagarag that if he has courage she can teach him the magic that shall help him to cut that hair,—to shave the shaggy pate of Shagpat.

I have gone into details this far only to give you a general idea of the plan of the story. The greater part of the book deals with the obstacles and dangers of

[377]

Shagpat, and recounts, in the most wonderful way, the struggle between the powers of magic used on both sides. For Shagpat is defended against barbers by evil spirits who use black magic; while Bagarag is assisted by his wife, and her knowledge of white magic. In his embraces she has become the most beautiful woman in the world, and the more he loves her the more beautiful she becomes. But he is given to understand that he must lose her if his courage fails in the fight against Shagpat. To tell you here how his courage is tested, and how he triumphs over all tests, would only spoil your pleasure in the story when you come to read it. Here I shall only say that the grandest chapter in the part of the book recounting Bagarag's adventures is the chapter on the Sword of Aklis, the magical sword with which the head of Shagpat at last is shaved. The imagining of this sword is one of the most wonderful things in any literature; for all the ancient descriptions of magical swords are dull and uninteresting compared with the description of the sword of Aklis. It can only be looked at by very strong eyes, so bright it is; it can be used as a bridge from earth to sky; it can be made so long that in order to use it one must look through a telescope; it can be made lighter than a moon beam, or so heavy that no strength could lift it. I want to quote to you a few sentences of the description of the sword, because this description is very beautiful, and it will give you a good idea of Meredith's coloured prose style. The passages which I am going to read describe the first appearance of the sword to Bagarag, after he has washed his eyes with magical water:

[378]

"The Shaving of Shagpat"

His sight was strengthened to mark the glory of the
Sword, where it hangs in slings, a little way from the wall.
. . . Lo! the length of it was as the length of crimson
across the sea when the sun is sideways on the wave, and
it seemed full a mile long, the whole blade sheening like an
arrested lightning from the end to the hilt; the hilt two
large live serpents twined together, with eyes like sombre
jewels, and sparkling spotted skins, points of fire in their
folds, and reflections of the emerald and topaz and ruby
stones, studded in the blood-stained haft. Then the seven
young men, sons of Aklis, said to Shibli Bagarag, . . .
"Grasp the handle of the sword!"

Now, he beheld the sword and the ripples of violet heat
that were breathing down it, and those two venomous serpents twining together, and the size of it, its ponderousness;
and to essay lifting it appeared to him a madness, but he
concealed his thought, and . . . went forward to it boldly,
and piercing his right arm between the twists of the serpents, grasped the jewelled haft. Surely, the sword moved
from the slings as if a giant had swayed it! But what
amazed him was the marvel of the blade, for its sharpness
was such that nothing stood in its way, and it slipped
through everything, as we pass through still water,—the
stone columns, blocks of granite by the walls, the walls of
earth, and the thick solidity of the ground beneath his
feet. They bade him say to the Sword, "Sleep!" and it
was no longer than a knife in the girdle. Likewise, they
bade him hiss on the heads of the serpents, and say,
"Wake!" and while he held it lengthwise it shot lengthen-
ing out.

In fact, it lengthens across the world, if the owner
so desires, to kill an enemy thousands of miles away.
With this wonderful sword at last Shagpat is shaved.

[379]

But notwithstanding the power of thousands of good spirits who help the work, and the white magic of the beautiful Noorna, the shaving is an awfully difficult thing to do. The chapter describing it reads as magnificently as the description of the Judgment Day, and you will wonder at the splendour of it.

What does all this mean, you may well ask. What is the magical hair? What is the sword? What is every impossible thing recounted in this romance? Really the author himself gives us the clue, and therefore his meaning ought to have been long ago clearly perceived. At the end of the story is this clue, furnished by the words—

The Sons of Aklis were now released from the toil of sharpening of the sword a half-cycle of years, to wander in delight on the fair surface of the flowery earth, breathing its roses, wooing its brides; for the mastery of an event lasteth among men the space of one cycle of years, and after that a fresh illusion springeth to befool mankind, and the Seven must expend the concluding half-cycle in preparing the edge of the Sword for a new mastery.

From this it is quite evident to anybody who has read the book that the sword of Aklis is the sword of science, —the power of exact scientific knowledge, wielded against error, superstition, humbug, and convention of every injurious kind.

Do not, however, imagine that this bit of interpretation interprets all the story; you must read it more than once, and think about it a great deal, in order to perceive the application of its thousand incidents to real human nature.

When Bagarag first, in his ignorance, offers to shave Shagpat, he has no idea whatever of the powers arrayed against him. What he wants is not at all in itself wrong; on the contrary it is in itself quite right. But what is quite right in one set of social conditions may seem to be quite wrong in another. Therefore the poor fellow is astonished to discover that the whole nation is against him, that the king is particularly offended with him, that all public opinion condemns him, would refuse him even the right to live in its midst. Is not Bagarag really the discoverer, the scientific man, the philosopher with a great desire to benefit other men, discovering that his kind wish arouses against him the laws of the government, the anger of religions, and all the prejudice of public opinion? Bagarag is the reformer who is not allowed to reform anything,—threatened with death if he persists. Reformers must be men of courage, and Bagarag has courage. But courage is not enough to sustain the purpose of the philosopher, the reformer, the man with new ethical or other truth to tell mankind. Much more than courage is wanted— power. How is power to come? You remember about the horrible old woman who asks Bagarag to kiss her, and when he kisses her she becomes young and divinely beautiful. We may suppose that Noorna really represents Science. Scientific study seems very ugly, very difficult, very repellent at first sight, but if you have the courage and the capacity to master it, if you can bravely kiss it, as Bagarag kissed the old woman, it becomes the most delightful mistress; nor is that all—it finds strange powers and forces for you. It can find for you even a sword of Aklis.

Now certain subjects are supposed to be beneath the dignity of literary art; and some of the subjects in this extraordinary book might appear to you too trivial for genius to busy itself with. The use of a barber as hero is not at all inartistic; it is in strict accordance with the methods of the Arabian story-tellers to make barbers, fishermen, water-carriers, and other men of humble occupations, the leading characters in a tale. But that the whole plot of the narrative should turn upon the difficulty of cutting one hair; and that this single hair should be given so great an importance in the history—this might very well seem to you beneath the dignity of art—that is, until you read the book. Yet the manner in which the fancy is worked out thoroughly excuses such triviality. The symbol of the hair is excellent. What is of less seeming importance than a hair? What is so frail and light and worthless as a hair? Now to many reformers and teachers the errors, social, moral, or religious, which they wish to destroy really appear to have less value, less resistance than a hair. But, as a great scientific teacher observed a few years ago, no man is able to conceive the strength in error, the force of error, the power of prejudice, until he has tried to attack it. Then all at once the illusion, the lie, that seems frail as a hair, and even of less worth, suddenly reveals itself as a terrible thing, reaching from Earth to Sky, radiating electricity and lightning in every direction. Observe in the course of modern European history what an enormous effort has been required

"The Shaving of Shagpat"

to destroy even very evident errors, injustices, or illusions. Think of the hundreds of years of sturdy endeavour which we needed before even a partial degree of religious freedom could be obtained. Think of the astonishing fact that one hundred years ago the man risked his life who found the courage to say that witchcraft was an illusion. One might mention thousands of illustrations of the same truth. No intellectual progress can be effected within conservative countries by mere discovery, mere revelation of facts, nor by logic, nor by eloquence, nor even by individual courage. The discovery is ridiculed; the facts are denied; the logic is attacked; the eloquence is met by greater eloquence on the side of untruth; the individual courage is astounded, if not defeated, by the armies of the enemies summoned against it. Progress, educational or otherwise, means hard fighting, not for one lifetime only but for generations. You are well aware how many generations have elapsed since the educational system of the Middle Ages was acknowledged by all men of real intelligence as inadequate to produce great results. One would have thought that the mediæval fetish would have been thrown away in the nineteenth century, at least. But it is positively true that in most English speaking universities, even at the present time, a great deal of the machinery of mediæval education remains, and there is scarcely any hope of having it removed even within another hundred years. If you asked the wise men of those universities what is the use of preserving certain forms of study and certain formalities of practice that can only serve to increase the obstacles to educational progress, they would answer you truthfully that it is of no use at all, but they would also tell you something about the difficulty that would attend any attempted change; and you would be astonished to learn the extent and the immensity of those difficulties.

Now you will perceive that the single hair in our study actually represents, perhaps, better than any more important object could do, the real story of any social illusion, any great popular error. The error seems so utterly absurd that you cannot understand how any man in his senses can believe it, and yet men quite as intelligent as yourselves, perhaps even more so, speak of it with respect. They speak of it with respect simply because they perceive better than you do what enormous power would be needed to destroy it. It appears to you something so light that even a breath would blow it away forever, or the touch of pain break it so easily that the breaking could not even be felt. You think of wisdom crushing it as an elephant might crush a fly, without knowing that the fly was there. But when you come to put forth your strength against this error, this gossamer of illusion, you will find that you might as well try to move a mountain with your hand. You must have help: you must have friends to furnish you with the sword of Aklis. Even with that mighty sword the cutting of the hair will prove no easy job.

Afterwards what happens? Why, exactly the same thing that happens before. Men think that because the world has made one step forward in their time, all illusions are presently going to fade away. This is the greatest of social mistakes that a human being can possibly make. The great sea of error immediately closes

again behind the forms that find strength to break out
of it. It is just the same as before. One illusion may
indeed be eventually destroyed, but another illusion
quickly forms behind it. The real truth is that wisdom
will be reached when human individuals as well as human society shall have become infinitely more perfect
than they now are; and such perfection can scarcely be
brought about before another million of years at least.

These are the main truths symbolised in this wonderful story. But while you are reading the "Shaving of
Shagpat," you need not consider the moral meanings
at all. You will think of them better after the reading.
Indeed, I imagine that the story will so interest you
that you will not be able to think of anything else until
you have reached the end of it. Then you find yourself
sorry that it is not just a little bit longer.

CHAPTER VIII

A NOTE ON ROBERT BUCHANAN

AMONG the minor poets of the Victorian period, Robert Buchanan cannot be passed over unnoticed. A contemporary of all the great singers, he seems to have been always a little isolated; I mean that he formed no strong literary friendships within the great circle. Most great poets must live to a certain extent in solitude; the man who can at once mix freely in society and find time for the production of masterpieces is a rare phenomenon. George Meredith is said to be such a person. But Tennyson, Rossetti, Swinburne, Browning, Fitzgerald, were all very reserved and retired men, though they had little circles of their own, and a certain common sympathy. The case of Buchanan is different. His aloofness from the rest has been, not the result of any literary desire for quiet, but the result, on the contrary, of a strong spirit of opposition. Not only did he have no real sympathy with the great poets, but he represented in himself the very prejudices against which they had to contend. Hard headed Scotchman as he was, he manifested in his attitude to his brother poets a good deal of the peculiar, harsh conservatism of which Scotchmen seemed to be particularly capable. And he did himself immense injury in his younger days by an anonymous attack upon the morals, or rather upon the moral tone, of such poets as Rossetti and Swinburne.

A Note on Robert Buchanan

Swinburne's reply to this attack was terrible and withering. That of Rossetti was very mild and gentle, but so effective that English literary circles almost unanimously condemned Buchanan, and attributed his attack to mere jealousy. I think the attack was less due to jealousy than to character, to prejudice, to the harshness of a mind insensible to particular forms of beauty. And for more than twenty years Buchanan has suffered extremely from the results of his own action. Thousands of people have ignored him and his books simply because it was remembered that he gave wanton pain to Rossetti, a poet much too sensitive to endure unjust criticism. I suppose that for many years to come Buchanan will still be remembered in this light, notwithstanding that he tried at a later day to make honourable amends to the memory of Rossetti, by dedicating to him, with a beautiful sonnet of apology, the definitive edition of his own works.

But the time has now passed when Buchanan can be treated as an indifferent figure in English literature. In spite of all disadvantages he has been a successful poet, a successful novelist, and a very considerable influence in the literature of criticism. Besides, he has written at least one poem that will probably live as long as the English language, and he has an originality quite apart and quite extraordinary, though weaker than the originality of the greater singers of his time. As to his personal history, little need to be said. He was educated at Glasgow University, and his literary efforts have always been somewhat coloured by Scotch sentiment, in spite of his long life in literary London.

Three volumes represent his poetical production. In

[387]

these are contained a remarkable variety of poems—
narrative, mystical, fantastic, classical, romantic, rang-
ing from the simplest form of ballad to the complex
form of the sonnet and the ode. The narrative poems
would, I think, interest you least; they are gloomy
studies of human suffering, physical and moral, among
the poor, and are not so good as the work of Crabbe in
the same direction. The mystical poems, on the contrary, are of a very curious kind; for Buchanan actually made a religious philosophy of his own, and put
it into the form of verse. It is a Christian mysticism,
an extremely liberal Unitarianism forming the basis of
it; but the author's notions about the perpetual order
of things are all his own. He has, moreover, put these
queer fancies into a form of verse imitating the ancient
Celtic poetry. We shall afterward briefly consider the
mystical poetry. But the great production of Buchanan
is a simple ballad, which you find very properly placed
at the beginning of his collected poems. This is a beautiful and extraordinary thing, quite in accordance with
the poet's peculiar views of Christianity. It is called
"The Ballad of Judas Iscariot." If you know only this
composition, you will know all that it is absolutely
necessary to know of Robert Buchanan. It is by this
poem that his place is marked in nineteenth century
literature.

Before we turn to the poem itself, I must explain to
you something of the legend of Judas Iscariot. You
know, of course, that Judas was the disciple of Christ
who betrayed his master. He betrayed him for thirty
pieces of silver, according to the tradition; and he betrayed him with a kiss, for he said to the soldiers whom

A Note on Robert Buchanan

he was guiding, "The man whom I shall kiss is the man you want." So Judas went up to Christ, and kissed his face; and then the soldiers seized Christ. From this has come the proverbial phrase common to so many Western languages, a "Judas-kiss." Afterwards Judas, being seized with remorse, is said to have hanged himself; and there the Scriptural story ends. But in Church legends the fate of Judas continued to be discussed in the Middle Ages. As he was the betrayer of a person whom the Church considered to be God, it was deemed that he was necessarily the greatest of all traitors; and as he had indirectly helped to bring about the death of God, he was condemned as the greatest of all murderers. It was said that in hell the very lowest place was given to Judas, and that his tortures exceeded all other tortures. But once every year, it was said, Judas could leave hell, and go out to cool himself upon the ice of the Northern seas. That is the legend of the Middle Ages.

Now Robert Buchanan perceived that the Church legends of the punishment of Judas might be strongly questioned from a moral point of view. Revenge is indeed in the spirit of the Old Testament; but revenge is not exactly in the spirit of the teaching of Christ. The true question as to the fate of Judas ought to be answered by supposing what Christ himself would have wished in the matter. Would Christ have wished to see his betrayer burning for ever in the fires of hell? Or would he have shown to him some of that spirit manifested in his teachings, "Do good unto them that hate you; forgive your enemies"? As a result of thinking about the matter, Buchanan produced his ballad. All

[389]

that could be said against it from a religious point of view is that the spirit of it is even more Christian than Christianity itself. From the poetical point of view we must acknowledge it to be one of the grandest ballads produced in the whole period of Victorian literature. You will not find so exquisite a finish here as in some of the ballads of Rossetti; but you will find a weirdness and a beauty and an emotional power that make up for slenderness in workmanship.

In order to understand the beginning of the ballad clearly, you should know the particulars about another superstition concerning Judas. It is said that all the elements refused to suffer the body to be committed to them; fire would not burn it; water would not let it sink to rest; every time it was buried, the earth would spew it out again. Man could not bury that body, so the ghosts endeavoured to get rid of it. The Field of Blood referred to in the ballad is the Aceldama of Scriptural legend, the place where Judas hanged himself.

> 'Twas the body of Judas Iscariot
>   Lay in the Field of Blood;
> 'Twas the soul of Judas Iscariot
>   Beside the body stood.
>
> Black was the earth by night,
>   And black was the sky;
> Black, black were the broken clouds,
>   Though the red Moon went by.
>
> .   .   .   .
>
> Then the soul of Judas Iscariot
>   Did make a gentle moan—

[390]

A Note on Robert Buchanan

"I will bury underneath the ground
  My flesh and blood and bone.

. . . . . .

"The stones of the field are sharp as steel,
  And hard and bold, God wot;
And I must bear my body hence
  Until I find a spot!"

'Twas the soul of Judas Iscariot
  So grim, and gaunt, and grey,
Raised the body of Judas Iscariot
  And carried it away.

And as he bare it from the field
  Its touch was cold as ice,
And the ivory teeth within the jaw
  Rattled aloud, like dice.

The use of the word "ivory" here has a double function; dice are usually made of ivory; and the suggestion of whiteness heightens the weird effect.

As the soul of Judas Iscariot
  Carried its load with pain,
The Eye of Heaven, like a lanthorn's eye,
  Opened and shut again.

Half he walk'd, and half he seemed
  Lifted on the cold wind;
He did not turn, for chilly hands
  Were pushing from behind.

The first place that he came unto
  It was the open wold,

And underneath were pricky whins,
  And a wind that blew so cold.

The next place that he came unto
  It was a stagnant pool,
And when he threw the body in
  It floated light as wool.

He drew the body on his back,
  And it was dripping chill,
And the next place he came unto
  Was a Cross upon a hill.

A Cross upon the windy hill,
  And a Cross on either side,
Three skeletons that swing thereon,
  Who had been crucified.

And on the middle cross-bar sat
  A white Dove slumbering;
Dim it sat in the dim light,
  With its head beneath its wing.

And underneath the middle Cross
  A grave yawned wide and vast,
But the soul of Judas Iscariot
  Shiver'd, and glided past.

We are not told what this hill was, but every reader
knows that Calvary is meant, and the skeletons upon
the crosses are those of Christ and the two thieves
crucified with him. The ghostly hand had pushed Judas
to the place of all places where he would have wished
not to go. We need not mind the traditional discrep-

A Note on Robert Buchanan

ancy suggested by the three skeletons; as a matter of fact, the bodies of malefactors were not commonly left upon the crosses long enough to become skeletons, and of course the legend is that Christ's body was on the cross only for a short time. But we may suppose that the whole description is of a phantasm, purposely shaped to stir the remorse of Judas. The white dove sleeping upon the middle cross suggests the soul of Christ, and the great grave made below might have been prepared out of mercy for the body of Judas. If the dove had awoke and spoken to him, would it not have said, "You can put your body here, in my grave; nobody will torment you"? But the soul of Judas cannot even think of daring to approach the place of the crucifixion.

> The fourth place that he came unto,
>   It was the Brig of Dread,
> And the great torrents rushing down
>   Were deep, and swift, and red.
>
> He dared not fling the body in
>   For fear of faces dim,
> And arms were waved in the wild water
>   To thrust it back to him.

There is here a poetical effect borrowed from sources having nothing to do with the Judas tradition. In old Northern folklore there is the legend of a River of Blood, in which all the blood ever shed in this world continues to flow; and there is a reference to this river in the old Scotch ballad of "Thomas the Rhymer."

[393]

Pre-Raphaelite and Other Poets

It was mirk, mirk night, and there was nae light,
And they waded in red blude up to the knee,
For a' the blude that's shed on earth,
Rins through the springs o' that countrie.

Judas leaves the dreadful bridge and continues his wanderings over the mountain, through woods and through great desolate plains:

For months and years, in grief and tears,
  He walked the silent night;
Then the soul of Judas Iscariot
  Perceived a far-off light.

A far-off light across the waste,
  As dim as dim might be,
That came and went like a lighthouse gleam
  On a black night at sea.

'Twas the soul of Judas Iscariot
  Crawled to the distant gleam;
And the rain came down, and the rain was blown
  Against him with a scream.

.   .   .   .

'Twas the soul of Judas Iscariot,
  Strange, and sad, and tall,
Stood all alone at dead of night
  Before a lighted hall.

And the wold was white with snow,
  And his foot-marks black and damp,
And the ghost of the silver Moon arose,
  Holding her yellow lamp.

A Note on Robert Buchanan

And the icicles were on the eaves,
  And the walls were deep with white,
And the shadows of the guests within
  Passed on the window light.

The shadows of the wedding guests
  Did strangely come and go,
And the body of Judas Iscariot
  Lay stretch'd along the snow.

But only the body. The soul which has carried it
does not lie down, but runs round and round the lighted
hall, where the wedding guests are assembled. What
wedding? What guests? This is the mystical banquet
told of in the parable of the New Testament; the bridegroom is Christ himself; the guests are the twelve disciples, or rather, the eleven, Judas himself having been
once the twelfth. And the guests see the soul of Judas
looking in at the window.

'Twas the Bridegroom sat at the table-head,
  And the lights burned bright and clear—
"Oh, who is that," the Bridegroom said,
  "Whose weary feet I hear?"

'Twas one look'd from the lighted hall,
  And answered soft and slow,
"It is a wolf runs up and down
  With a black track in the snow."

The Bridegroom in his robe of white
  Sat at the table-head—
"Oh, who is that who moans without?"
  The blessed Bridegroom said.

[395]

'Twas one looked from the lighted hall,
　And answered fierce and low,
" 'Tis the soul of Judas Iscariot·
　Gliding to and fro."

'Twas the soul of Judas Iscariot
　Did hush itself and stand,
And saw the Bridegroom at the door
　With a light in his hand.

The Bridegroom stood in the open door,
　And he was clad in white,
And far within the Lord's Supper
　Was spread so long and bright.

The Bridegroom shaded his eyes and looked,
　And his face was bright to see—
"What dost thou here at the Lord's Supper
　With thy body's sins?" said he.

'Twas the soul of Judas Iscariot,
　Stood black, and sad, and bare—
"I have wandered many nights and days;
　There is no light elsewhere."

'Twas the wedding guests cried out within,
　And their eyes were fierce and bright—
"Scourge the soul of Judas Iscariot
　Away into the night!"

The Bridegroom stood in the open door
　And he waved hands still and slow,
And the third time that he waved his hands
　The air was thick with snow.

A Note on Robert Buchanan

And of every flake of falling snow,
   Before it touched the ground,
There came a dove, and a thousand doves
   Made sweet sound.

'Twas the body of Judas Iscariot
   Floated away full fleet,
And the wings of the doves that bare it off
   Were like its winding-sheet.

'Twas the Bridegroom stood at the open door,
   And beckon'd, smiling sweet;
'Twas the soul of Judas Iscariot
   Stole in, and fell at his feet.

"The Holy Supper is spread within,
   And the many candles shine,
And I have waited long for thee
   Before I poured the wine!"

It would have been better, I think, to finish the ballad at this stanza; there is one more, but it does not
add at all to the effect of what goes before. When the
doves, emblems of divine love, have carried away the
sinful body, and the Master comes to the soul, smiling
and saying: "I have been waiting for you a long time,
waiting for your coming before I poured the wine"—
there is nothing more to be said. We do not want to
hear any more; we know that the Eleven had again become Twelve; we do not require to be told that the wine
is poured out, or that Judas repents his fault. The
startling and beautiful thing is the loving call and the

welcome to the Divine Supper. You will find the whole of this poem in the "Victorian Anthology," but I should advise any person who might think of making a Japanese translation to drop the final stanza and to leave out a few of the others, if his judgment agrees with mine.

Read this again to yourselves, and see how beautiful it is. The beauty is chiefly in the central idea of forgiveness; but the workmanship of this composition has also a very remarkable beauty, a Celtic beauty of weirdness, such as we seldom find in a modern composition touching religious tradition. It were interesting to know how the poet was able to imagine such a piece of work. I think I can tell a little of the secret. Only a man with a great knowledge and love of old ballads could have written it. Having once decided upon the skeleton of the story, he must have gone to his old Celtic literature and to old Northern ballads for further inspiration. I have already suggested that the ballad of "Thomas the Rhymer" was one source of his inspiration, with its strange story of the River of Blood. Thomas was sitting under a tree, the legend goes, when he saw a woman approaching so beautiful that he thought she was an angel or the Virgin Mary, and he addressed her on his knees. But she sat down beside him, and said, "I am no angel nor saint; I am only a fairy. But if you think that I am so beautiful, take care that you do not kiss me, for if you do, then I shall have power over you." Thomas immediately did much more than kiss her, and he therefore became her slave. She took him at once to fairy land, and on their

[398]

A Note on Robert Buchanan

way they passed through strange wild countries, much
like those described in Robert Buchanan's ballad; they
passed the River of Blood; they passed dark trees
laden with magical food; and they saw the road that
reaches Heaven and the road that reaches Hell. But
Buchanan could take only a few ideas from this poem.
Other ideas I think were inspired by a ballad of Goethe's,
or at least by Sir Walter Scott's version of it, "Frederick and Alice." Frederick is a handsome young soldier
who seduces a girl called Alice under promise of marriage, and then leaves her. He rides to join the army in
France. The girl becomes insane with grief and shame;
and the second day later she dies at four o'clock in the
morning. Meantime Frederick unexpectedly loses his
way; the rest I may best tell in the original weird form.
The horse has been frightened by the sound of a church
bell striking the hour of four.

> Heard ye not the boding sound,
>   As the tongue of yonder tower,
> Slowly, to the hills around,
>   Told the fourth, the fated hour?
>
> Starts the steed, and snuffs the air,
>   Yet no cause of dread appears;
> Bristles high the rider's hair,
>   Struck with strange mysterious fears.
>
> Desperate, as his terrors rise,
>   In the steed the spur he hides;
> From himself in vain he flies;
>   Anxious, restless, on he rides.

[399]

Seven long days, and seven long nights,
  Wild he wandered, woe the while!
Ceaseless care, and causeless fright,
  Urge his footsteps many a mile.

Dark the seventh sad night descends;
  Rivers swell, and rain-streams pour;
While the deafening thunder lends
  All the terrors of its roar.

At the worst part of his dreary wandering over an
unknown and gloomy country, Frederick suddenly sees
a light far away. This seems to him, as it seemed in
Buchanan's ballad to the soul of Judas, a light of hope.
He goes to the light, and finds himself in front of a vast
and ruinous looking church. Inside there is a light;
he leaps down from his horse, descends some steps, and
enters the building. Suddenly all is darkness again;
he has to feel his way.

Long drear vaults before him lie!
  Glimmering lights are seen to glide!—
"Blessed Mary, hear my cry!
  Deign a sinner's steps to guide!"

Often lost their quivering beam,
  Still the lights move slow before,
Till they rest their ghastly gleam
  Right against an iron door.

He is really in the underground burial place of a
church, in the vaults of the dead, but he does not know
it. He hears voices.

A Note on Robert Buchanan

Thundering voices from within,
　　Mixed with peals of laughter, rose;
As they fell, a solemn strain
　　Lent its wild and wondrous close!

'Midst the din, he seem'd to hear
　　Voice of friends, by death removed;—
Well he knew that solemn air,
　　'Twas the lay that Alice loved.

Suddenly a great bell booms four times, and the iron
door opens. He sees within a strange banquet; the
seats are coffins, the tables are draped with black, and
the dead are the guests.

Alice, in her grave-clothes bound,
　　Ghastly smiling, points a seat;
All arose, with thundering sound;
　　All the expected stranger greet.

High their meagre arms they wave,
　　Wild their notes of welcome swell;
"Welcome, traitor, to the grave!
　　Perjured, bid the light farewell!"

I have given the greater part of this strange ballad
because of its intrinsic value and the celebrity of its
German author. But the part that may have inspired
Buchanan is only the part concerning the wandering
over the black moor, the light seen in the distance, the
ghostly banquet of the dead, and the ruined vaults. A
great poet would have easily found in these details the
suggestion which Buchanan found for the wandering of

[401]

Judas to the light and the unexpected vision of the dead assembling to a banquet with him—but only this. The complete transformation of the fancy, the transmutation of the purely horrible into a ghostly beauty and tenderness, is the wonderful thing. After all, this is the chief duty of the poet in this world, to discover beauty even in the ugly, suggestions of beauty even in the cruel and terrible. This Buchanan did once so very well that his work will never be forgotten, but he received thereafter no equal inspiration, and the "Ballad of Judas" remains, alone of its kind, his only real claim to high distinction.

The poetry of Robert Buchanan is not great enough as poetry to justify many quotations, but as thinking it demands some attention. His third volume is especially of interest in this respect, because it contains a curious exposition of his religious idealism. Buchanan is a mystic; there is no doubt that he has been very much influenced by the mysticism of Blake. The whole of the poems collectively entitled "The Devil's Mystics," must have been suggested by Blake's nomenclature. This collection belongs to "The Book of Orm," which might have been well called "The Book of Robert Buchanan." Orm ought to be a familiar name to students of English literature, one of the old English books also being called "The Ormulum," because it was written by a man named Orm. Buchanan's Orm is represented to be an ancient Celt, who has visions and dreams about the mystery of the universe, and who puts these visions and dreams, which are Buchanan's, into old-fashioned verse.

The great Ernest Renan said in his "Dialogues Phi-

A Note on Robert Buchanan

losophiques" that if everybody in the world who had
thought much about the mystery of things were to
write down his ideas regarding the Infinite, some great
truth might be discovered or deduced from the result.
Buchanan has tried to follow this suggestion; for he
has very boldly put down all his thoughts about the
world and man and God. As to results, however, I can
find nothing particularly original except two or three
queer fancies, none of which relates to the deeper rid-
dles of being. In a preface in verse, the author further
tells us that when he speaks of God he does not mean
the Christian God or the God of India nor any particular God, but only the all-including Spirit of Life. Be
that as it may, we find his imagery to be certainly borrowed from old Hebrew and old Christian thinkers;
here he has not fulfilled expectations. But the imagery
is used to express some ideas which I think you will find
rather new—not exactly philosophical ideas, but moral
parables.

One of these is a parable about the possible consequences of seeing or knowing the divine power which is
behind the shadows of things. Suppose that there were
an omnipotent God whom we could see; what would be
the consequences of seeing him? Orm discovered that
the blue of the sky was a blue veil drawn across Immensity to hide the face of God. One day, in answer
to prayer, God drew aside the blue veil. Then all
mankind were terrified because they saw, by day and by
night, an awful face looking down upon them out of the
sky, the sleepless eyes of the face seeming to watch
each person constantly wherever he was. Did this make
men happy? Not at all. They became tired of life,

finding themselves perpetually watched; they covered their cities with roofs, and lived by lamp light only, in order to avoid being looked at by the face, God. This queer parable, recounted in the form of a dream, has a meaning worth thinking about. The ultimate suggestion, of course, is that we do not know and see many things because it would make us very unhappy to know them.

An equally curious parable, also related in the form of a dream, treats of the consolations of death. What would become of mankind if there were no death? I think you will remember that I told you how the young poet William Watson took up the same subject a few years ago, in his remarkable poem, "A Dream of Man." Watson's supposition is that men became so wise, so scientific, that they were able to make themselves immortal and to conquer death. But at last they became frightfully unhappy, unutterably tired of life, and were obliged to beg God to give them back death again. And God said to them, "You are happier than I am. You can die; I cannot. The only happiness of existence is effort. Now you can have your friend death back again." Buchanan's idea was quite different from this. His poem is called "The Dream of the World without Death." Men prayed to God that there might be no more death or decay of the body; and the prayer was granted. People continued to disappear from the world, but they did not die. They simply vanished, when their time came, as ghosts. A child goes out to play in the field, for example, and never comes back again; the mother finds only the empty clothes of her darling. Or a peasant goes to the fields to work, and

[404]

his body is never seen again. People found that this
was a much worse condition of things than had been
before. For the consolation of knowledge, of certainty, was not given them. The dead body is a
certificate of death; nature uses corruption as a seal,
an official exhibit and proof of the certainty of death.
But when there is no body, no corpse, no possible sign,
how horrible is the disappearance of the persons we
love. The mystery of it is a much worse pain than
the certain knowledge of death. Doubt is the worst
form of torture. Well, when mankind had this experience, they began to think, that, after all, death was
a beautiful and good thing, and they prayed most fer-
vently that they might again have the privilege of dying
in the old way, of putting the bodies of their dead into
beautiful tombs, of being able to visit the graves of
their beloved from time to time. So God took pity on
them and gave them back death, and the poet sings his
gratitude thus:

> And I cried, "O unseen Sender of Corruption,
> I bless thee for the wonder of Thy mercy,
> Which softeneth the mystery and the parting.
>
> "I bless Thee for the change and for the comfort,
> The bloomless face, shut eyes, and waxen fingers,—
> For Sleeping, and for Silence, and Corruption."

This idea is worth something, if only as a vivid
teaching of the necessity of things as they are. The
two fantasies thus commented upon are the most original things in the range of this mystical book. I could

not recommend any further reading or study of the poet, except perhaps of his "Vision of the Man Accurst." But even this has not the true stamp of originality; and only the "Ballad of Judas Iscariot" is certain not to be soon forgotten.

CHAPTER IX

THIS poet, one of the greatest of the English minor poets of our time, and represented in literature by a very considerable bulk of work, happens to be one of the least known. He was never popular; and even to-day, when recognition is coming to him slowly, almost as slowly as it came to George Meredith, he is chiefly read by the cultivated classes. There are several reasons for this. One is that he is altogether an old-fashioned poet, writing with the feeling of the eighteenth rather than of the nineteenth century, so that persons in search of novelty are not likely to look at him. Then again he is not a thinker, except at the rarest moments, not touched at all by the scientific ideas of the nineteenth century. For that reason a great many people, accustomed to look for philosophy in poetry, do not care about his verse. I must confess that I myself should not have read him, had it not been for a beauti-. ful criticism of his work published some five years ago. That tempted me to study him, with pleasant results. But I then found a third reason for his unpopularity— want of passion. When everything else is missing that attracts intellectual attention to a poet, everything strange, novel, and philosophical, he may still become popular if he has strong emotion, deep feeling. But Robert Bridges has neither. He is somewhat cool, even

[407]

when he is not cold; his colours are never strong,
though they are always natural; and there is something
faint about his music that makes you think of the music
of insects, of night crickets or locusts. You may therefore begin to wonder that I should speak about him at
all. If a poet has no philosophy, no originality, and
no passion, what can there be in him? Well, a great
deal. It is not necessary to be original in order to be a
poet; it is only necessary to say old things somewhat
better than they have been said before. Such a non-
original poet of excellence may be a great lover of nature; for nature has been described in a million ways,
and we are not tired of the descriptions. Again, the
feeling need not be very strong; it is not strong in
Wordsworth, except at moments. I think that the
charm of Robert Bridges, who is especially a nature-
poet, lies in his love of quiet effects, pale colours, small
soft sounds, all the dreaminess and all the gentleness
of still and beautiful days. Some of us like strong
sounds, blazing colours, heavy scents of flowers and
fruits; but some of us do not—we prefer rest
and coolness and quiet tones. And I think that to
Japanese feeling Robert Bridges ought to make an
appeal. Much of his work makes me think of the
old Japanese colour prints of spring, summer,
autumn, and winter landscapes. He is particularly
fond of painting these; perhaps half of his poetry,
certainly a third of it, deals with descriptions of the
seasons. There is nothing tropical in these descriptions, because they are true to English landscape, the
only landscape that he knows well. Now there is a
good deal in English landscape, in the colours of the

Robert Bridges

English seasons, that resembles what is familiar to us in the aspects of Japanese nature.

I cannot tell you very much about the poet himself; he has left his personality out of the reach of public curiosity. I can only tell you that he was born in 1844 and that he is a country doctor, which is very interesting, for it is not often that a man can follow the busy duties of a country physician and find time to make poetry. But Dr. Bridges has been able to make two volumes of poetry which take very high rank; and a whole school of minor poets has been classed under the head of "Robert Bridges and his followers" in the new Encyclopedia of English poets.

I do not intend at once to tire you by quoting this poet's descriptions of the seasons; I only want to interest you in him, and if I can do that, you will be apt to read these descriptions for yourselves. I am going to pick out bits, here and there, which seem to me beautiful in themselves, independently of their subjects. Indeed, I think this is the way that Robert Bridges wants us to read him. At the beginning of Book IV, of the shorter poems (you will be interested to know that most of his poems have no titles), he himself tells us what his whole purpose is, in these pretty stanzas:

> I love all beauteous things,
>   I seek and adore them;
> God hath no better praise,
> And man in his hasty days
>   Is honored for them.

[409]

Pre-Raphaelite and Other Poets

I too will something make,
   And joy in the making;
Although to-morrow it seem
Like the empty words of a dream
   Remembered on waking.

With this hint I have no hesitation in beginning
this lecture on Robert Bridges by picking out what
seems to me almost the only philosophical poem in the
whole of his work. The philosophy is not very deep,
but the poem is haunting.

EROS

Why hast thou nothing in thy face?
Thou idol of the human race,
Thou tyrant of the human heart,
The flower of lovely youth that art;
Yea, and that standest in thy youth
An image of eternal Truth,
With thy exuberant flesh so fair,
That only Pheidias might compare,
Ere from his chaste marmoreal form
Time had decayed the colours warm;
Like to his gods in thy proud dress,
Thy starry sheen of nakedness.

Surely thy body is thy mind,
For in thy face is nought to find,
Only thy soft unchristen'd smile
That shadows neither love nor guile,
But shameless will and power immense,
In secret sensuous innocence.

Robert Bridges

O king of joy, what is thy thought?
I dream thou knowest it is nought,
And wouldst in darkness come, but thou
Makest the light where'er thou go.
Ah yet no victim of thy grace,
None who e'er longed for thy embrace,
Hath cared to look upon thy face.

The divinity here described is not the infant but
the more mature form of the god of Love, Eros (from
whose name is derived the adjective "erotic," used in
such terms as "erotic poetry"). This Eros was represented as a beautiful naked boy about twelve or thirteen years old. Several statues of him are among the
most beautiful works of Greek art. It is one of these
statues that the poet refers to. And you must understand his poem, first of all, as treating of physical
love, physical passion, as distinguished from love which
belongs rather to the mind and heart and which is
alone real and enduring. There is always a certain
amount of delusion in physical attraction, in mere bodily beauty; but about the deeper love, which is perfect
friendship between the sexes, there is no delusion, and
it only grows with time. Now the god Eros represented only the power of physical passion, the charm
of youth. Looking at the face of the beautiful statue,
the poet is startled by something which has been from
ancient times noticed by all critics of Greek art, but
which appears to him strange in another way—there
is no expression in that face. It is beautiful, but it
is also impersonal. So the faces of all the Greek gods
were impersonal; they represented ideals, not realities.

[411]

Pre-Raphaelite and Other Poets

They were moved neither by deep love nor by deep hate—not at least in the conception of the artist and sculptor. They were above humanity, above affection, therefore above pity. Here it is worth while to remark the contrast between the highest Eastern ideals in sculpture and the highest Western ideals. In the art of the Far East the Buddha is also impersonal; he smiles, but the smile is of infinite pity, compassion, tenderness. He represents a supreme ideal of virtue. Nevertheless he is, though impersonal, warmly human for this very reason. The more beautiful Greek divinity smiles deliciously, but there is no tenderness, no compassion, no affection in that smile. It is not human; it is superhuman. Looking at the features of a Greek Aphrodite, an Eros, a Dionysius, you feel that they could smile with the same beautiful smile at the destruction of the world. What does the smile mean? You are charmed by it, yet it is mysterious, almost awful. It represents nothing but supreme content, supreme happiness—not happiness in the spiritual sense of rest, but happiness of perfect youth and innocence of pain. That is why there is something terrible about it to the modern thinker. It is without sympathy; it is only joy.

Now you will see the poem in its inner meaning. Let us paraphrase it:

"Why is there no expression in that divinely beautiful face of thine, O fair god, who art forever worshipped by the race of men, forever ruling the hearts of its youth without pity, without compassion! Thou who art the perfect image of the loveliness of youth, and the symbol of some eternal and universal law, so fair, so lovely that only the great Greek sculptor Pheidias could represent thee in pure marble, thou white as that marble itself, before time had faded the fresh colour with which thy statue had been painted! Truly thou art as one of his gods in the pride of thy nakedness—which becomes thee more than any robe, being itself luminous, a light of stars. But why is there no expression in thy face?

"It must be that thy body represents thy mind. Yet thy mind is not reflected in thy face like the mind of man. There I see only the beautiful old pagan smile, the smile of the years before the Religion of Sorrow came into this world. And that smile of thine shows neither love nor hate nor shame, but power incalculable and the innocence of sensuous pleasure.

"Thou king of Joy, of what dost thou think? For thy face no-wise betrays thy thought. Truly I believe thou dost not think of anything which troubles the minds of sorrowing men; thou thinkest of nothing. Thou art Joy, not thought. And I imagine that thou wouldst prefer not to be seen by men, to come to them in darkness only, or invisibly, as thou didst to Psyche in other years. But thou canst not remain invisible, since thy body is made of light, and forever makes a great shining about thee. For uncounted time thou hast moved the hearts of millions of men and of women; all have known thy presence, felt thy power. But none, even of those who most longed for thee, has ever desired to look into thy beautiful face, because it is not the face of humanity but of divinity, and because there is in it nothing of human love."

There is a good deal to think about in this poem, but

[413]

to feel the beauty of it you ought to have before your eyes, when studying it, a good engraving of the statue. However, even without any illustration you will easily perceive the moral of the thought in it, that beauty and youth alone do not signify affection, nor even anything dear to the inner nature of man.

Now I shall turn to another part of the poet's work. Here is a little verse about a grown man looking at the picture of himself when he was a little child. I think that it is a very charming sonnet, and it will give you something to think about.

> A man that sees by chance his picture, made
> As once a child he was, handling some toy,
> Will gaze to find his spirit within the boy,
> Yet hath no secret with the soul portray'd:
> He cannot think the simple thought which play'd
> Upon those features then so frank and coy;
> 'Tis his, yet oh! not his: and o'er the joy
> His fatherly pity bends in tears dismay'd.

There is indeed no topic which Robert Bridges has treated more exquisitely and touchingly than certain phases of childhood, the poetry of childhood, the purity of childhood, the pathos of childhood. I do not think that any one except Patmore, and Patmore only in one poem, "The Toys," has even approached him. Take this little poem for example, on the death of a little boy. It is the father who is speaking.

Robert Bridges

ON A DEAD CHILD

Perfect little body, without fault or stain on thee,
  With promise of strength and manhood full and fair!
    Though cold and stark and bare,
The bloom and the charm of life doth awhile remain on thee.

Thy mother's treasure wert thou;—alas! no longer
  To visit her heart with wondrous joy; to be
    Thy father's pride;—ah, he
Must gather his faith together, and his strength make
      stronger.

To me, as I move thee now in the last duty,
  Dost thou with a turn or gesture anon respond;
    Startling my fancy fond
With a chance attitude of the head, a freak of beauty.

Thy hand clasps, as 'twas wont, my finger, and holds it:
  But the grasp is the clasp of Death, heartbreaking and
        stiff;
    Yet feels my hand as if
'Twas still thy will, thy pleasure and trust that enfolds it.

So I lay thee there, thy sunken eyelids closing,—
  Go lie thou there in thy coffin, thy last little bed;—
    Propping thy wise, sad head,
Thy firm, pale hands across thy chest disposing.

So quiet!—doth the change content thee?—Death, whither
      hath he taken thee?
  To a world, do I think, that rights the disaster of this?
    The vision of which I miss,
Who weep for the body, and wish but to warm thee and
      awaken thee?

[415]

Ah! little at best can all our hopes avail us
  To lift this sorrow, or cheer us, when in the dark
    Unwilling, alone we embark,
And the things we have seen and have known and have
    heard of, fail us!

You will see the exquisiteness of this more fully after a little explanation. The father is performing the last duty to his little dead son: washing the body with his own hands, closing the eyes, and placing the little corpse in the coffin, rather than trust this work to any less loving hands. The Western coffin, you must know, is long, and the body is placed in it lying at full length as upon a bed, with a little pillow to support the head. Then the hands are closed upon the heart in the attitude of prayer. The poem describes more than the feelings of a father, during these tender offices. As he turns the little body to wash it, the small head changes its position now and then, and the motion is so much like the pretty motions made by that little head during life, that it is very difficult to believe there is now no life there. In all modern English poetry there is nothing more touching than the lines:

    Startling my fancy fond
With a chance attitude of the head, a freak of beauty.

The word "freak" is incomparably beautiful in this line, for it has a sense of playfulness; it means often a childish fancy or whim or pretty mischievous action. The turning of the dead head seems so like the motion of the living head in play. Then as the hands were washed by the father, the relaxed muscles caused the opened fingers to close upon the father's finger, just as in other days when the two walked about together, the little boy's hands were too small to hold the great hands of the father, and therefore clasped one finger only. Then observe the very effective use of two most simple adjectives to picture the face of the dead child—"wise" and "sad." Have you ever seen the face of a dead child? If you have, you will remember how its calmness gives one the suggestion of strange knowledge; the wise smile little, and fond fancy for thousands of years has looked into the faces of the unsmiling dead in search of some expression of supreme knowledge. Also there is an expression of sadness in the face of death, even in the faces of children asleep, although relaxation of muscles is the real explanation of the fact. All these fancies are very powerfully presented in the first five verses.

In the last two verses the sincerity of grief uniquely shows itself. "Where do you think the little life has gone?" the father asks. "Do you want me to say that I think it has gone to a happier world than this, to what you call Heaven? Ah, I must tell you the truth. I do not know; I doubt, I fear. When a grief like this comes to us, all our religious imaginations and hopes can serve us little."

You must read that over and over again to know the beauty of it. Here is another piece of very touching poetry about a boy, perhaps about the same boy who afterward died. It will require some explanation, for it is much deeper in a way than the previous piece. It is called "Pater Filio," meaning "the father to the son."

[417]

Sense with keenest edge unusèd,
　　Yet unsteel'd by scathing fire;
Lovely feet as yet unbruisèd
　　On the ways of dark desire;
Sweetest hope that lookest smiling
O'er the wilderness defiling!

Why such beauty, to be blighted
　　By the swarm of foul destruction?
Why such innocence delighted,
　　When sin stalks to thy seduction?
All the litanies e'er chaunted
Shall not keep thy faith undaunted.

　　　·ㆍ　　·ㆍ　　·ㆍ　　·　　·

Me too once unthinking Nature,
　　—Whence Love's timeless mockery took me,—
Fashion'd so divine a creature,
　　Yea, and like a beast forsook me.
I forgave, but tell the measure
Of her crime in thee, my treasure.

The father is suffering the great pain of fathers
when he speaks thus, the pain of fearing for the future
of his child; and the mystery of things oppresses him,
as it oppresses everybody who knows what it is to be
afraid for the sake of another. He wonders at the
beautiful fresh senses of the boy, "yet unsteeled by
scathing fire"—that is, not yet hardened by experience
of pain. He admires the beauty of the little feet tot-
tering happily about; but in the same moment dark
thoughts come to him, for he remembers how blood-
stained those little feet must yet become on the ways
of the world, in the streets of cities, in the struggle
of life. And he delights in the smile of the child, full

[418]

of hope that knows nothing of the great foul wilderness of the world, in which envy and malice and passions of many kinds make it difficult to remain either good or hopeful. And he asks, "Why should a child be made so beautiful, only to lose that beauty at a later day, through sickness and grief and pain of a thousand kinds? Why should a child come into the world so charmingly innocent and joyful, only to lose that innocence and happiness later on through the encountering of passion and temptation? Why should a child believe so deeply in the gods and in human nature? Later on, no matter how much he grieves, the time will come when that faith in the powers unseen must be sadly warped."

And lastly the father remembers his own childhood, thinking, "I too was once a divine little creature like that. Love, the eternal illusion, brought me into the world, and Nature made me as innocent and trustful as this little boy. Later on, however, the same Nature abandoned me, like the animal that forsakes her young as soon as they grow a little strong. I forgave Nature for that abandonment," the father says, turning to the child, "but it is only when I look at you, my treasure, that I understand how much I lost with the vanishing of my own childhood."

Nobody in the whole range of English literature has written anything more tender than that. It is out of the poet's heart.

One would expect, on reading delicacies of this kind, that the poet would express himself not less beautifully than tenderly in regard to woman. As a matter of fact, he certainly ranks next to Rossetti as a love poet,

even in point of workmanship. I am also inclined to
think, and I believe that critics will later recognise
this, that his feeling in regard to the deeper and nobler
qualities of love can only be compared to the work
of Browning in the same direction. It has not Browning's force, nor the occasional sturdiness that approaches roughness. It is altogether softer and
finer, and it has none of Browning's eccentricities. A
collection of sonnets, fifty-nine in number, entitled "The
Growth of Love" may very well be compared with Rossetti's sonnet-sequence, "The House of Life." But it
is altogether unlike Rossetti's work; it deals with
thought more than sensation, and with joy more than
sorrow. But before we give an example of these, let
me quote a little fancy of a very simple kind, that gives
the character of Robert Bridges as a love poet quite
as well as any long or elaborate poem could do.

> Long are the hours the sun is above,
> But when evening comes I go home to my love.
>
> I'm away the daylight hours and more,
> Yet she comes not down to open the door.
>
> She does not meet me upon the stair,—
> She sits in my chamber and waits for me there.
>
> As I enter the room she does not move;
> I always walk straight up to my love;
>
> And she lets me take my wonted place
> At her side, and gaze in her dear dear face.

[420]

Robert Bridges

There as I sit, from her head thrown back
Her hair falls straight in a shadow black.

Aching and hot as my tired eyes be,
She is all that I wish to see.

And in my wearied and toil-dinned ear,
She says all things that I wish to hear.

Dusky and duskier grows the room,
Yet I see her best in the darker gloom.

When the winter eves are early and cold,
The firelight hours are a dream of gold.

And so I sit here night by night,
In rest and enjoyment of love's delight.

But a knock at the door, a step on the stair
Will startle, alas, my love from her chair.

If a stranger comes she will not stay:
At the first alarm she is off and away.

And he wonders, my guest, usurping her throne,
That I sit so much by myself alone.

You feel the mystery of the thing beginning at the second stanza, but not until you get to the sixth stanza do you begin to perceive it. This is not a living woman, but a ghost. The whole poetry of the composition is here. What does the poet mean? He has not told us anywhere, and it is better that he should not have told us, because we can imagine so many things, so

[421]

many different circumstances, which the poem would
equally well illustrate. Were this the fancy of a young
man, we might say that the phantom love means the
ideal wife, the unknown bride of the future, the beautiful
dream that every young man makes for himself about
a perfectly happy home. Again, we might suppose that
the spirit bride is not really related at all to love in
the common sense, but figures or symbolises only the
devotion of the poet to poetry, in which case the spirit
bride is art. But the poet is not a young man; he is
an old country doctor, coming home late every night
from visiting his patients, tired, weary, but with plenty
of work to do in his private study. Who, then, may
be the shadowy woman with the long black hair always
waiting for him alone? Perhaps art, perhaps a memory, most likely the memory of a dead wife, and we may
even imagine, the mother of the little boy about whose
death the poet has so beautifully written elsewhere.
I do not pretend to explain; I do not want to explain;
I am only anxious to show you that this composition
fulfils one of the finest conditions of poetry, by its sug-
gestiveness. It leaves many questions to be answered
in fancy, and all of them are beautiful.

Let me now take a little piece about the singing of
the nightingale. I think you remember that I read to
you, and commented upon Keats's poem about the nightingale. That is the greatest English poem, the most
perfect, the most unapproachable of poems upon the
nightingale. And after that, only a very, very skilful
poet dare write seriously about the nightingale, for his
work, if at all imperfect, must suffer terribly by com-
parsion with the verses of Keats. But Robert Bridges

Robert Bridges

has actually come very near to the height of Keats in a three stanza poem upon the same subject. The treatment of the theme is curiously different. The poem of Keats represents supreme delight, the delight which is so great that it becomes sad. The poem of Bridges is slightly dark. The mystery of the bird song is the fact that he chiefly considers; and he considers it in a way that leaves you thinking a long time after the reading of the verses. The suggestions of the composition, however, can best be considered after we have read the verses.

NIGHTINGALES

Beautiful must be the mountains whence ye come,
And bright in the fruitful valleys the streams, wherefrom
   Ye learn your song:
Where are those starry woods? O might I wander there,
Among the flowers, which in that heavenly air
   Bloom the year long!

Nay, barren are those mountains and spent the streams:
Our song is the voice of desire, that haunts our dreams,
   A throe of the heart,
Whose pining visions dim, forbidden hopes profound,
No dying cadence nor long sigh can sound,
   For all our art.

Alone, aloud in the raptured ear of men
We pour our dark nocturnal secret; and then,
   As night is withdrawn
From these sweet-springing meads and bursting boughs of
   May,
Dream, while the innumerable choir of day
   Welcome the dawn.

[423]

Pre-Raphaelite and Other Poets

Other poets, following the popular notion that birds are happy when they sing, often speak of the nightingale as an especially happy bird because of the extraordinary sweetness of its song. The Greek poets thought otherwise; to them it seemed that the song of the birds was the cry of infinite sorrow and regret, and one of the most horrible of all the Greek myths is the story of Philomela, transformed into a nightingale. Matthew Arnold, you may remember, takes the Greek view. So in a way does Robert Bridges, but there are other suggestions in his verse, purely human. Paraphrased, the meaning is this (a man speaks first):

"When I listen to your song, I feel sure that the country from which you come must be very beautiful; and very sweet the warbling music of the stream, whose sound may have taught you how to sing. O how much I wish that I could go to your wonderful world, your tropical world, where summer never dies, and where flowers are all the year in bloom." But the birds answer: "You are in error. Desolate is the country from which we come; and in that country the mountains are naked and barren, and the rivers are dried up. If we sing, it is because of the pain that we feel in our hearts, the pain of great desire for happier things. But that which we desire without knowing it by sight, that which we hope for in vain, these are more beautiful than any song of ours can express. Skilful we are, but not skilful enough to utter all that we feel. At night we sing, trying to speak our secret of pain to men; but when all the other birds awake and salute the sun with happy song, while all the flowers open their leaves to the light, then we do not sing, but dream on in silence and shadow."

Is there not in this beautiful verse the suggestion of the condition of the soul in the artist and the poet, in those whose works are beautiful or seem beautiful, not because of joy, but because of pain—the pain of larger knowledge and deeper perception? I think it is particularly this that makes the superior beauty of the stanzas. You soon find yourself thinking, not about the nightingale, but about the human heart and the human soul.

Here and there on almost every page of Bridges are to be found queer little beauties, little things that reveal the personality of the writer. Can you describe an April sky, and clouds in the sky, and the light and the colour of the day, all in two lines? It is not an easy thing to do; but there are two lines that seem to do it in a poem, which is the sixth of the fourth book:

On high the hot sun smiles, and banks of cloud uptower
In bulging heads that crowd for miles the dazzling South.

Notice the phrase "bulging heads." Nothing is so difficult to describe in words, as to form, than ordinary clouds, because the form is indefinite. Yet the great rounding masses do dimly suggest giant heads, not necessarily the heads of persons, much oftener heads of trees. The word "bulging" means not only a swelling outwards but a soft baggy kind of swelling. No other adjective in the English language could better express the roundish form here alluded to. And we know that they are white, simply by the poet's use of the word dazzling that completes the picture. But there is more to notice; the poet has called these clouds banks of cloud, and has spoken of them as crowding the sky for miles. Remember that a bank of clouds always implies masses of cloud joined together below. Now on a beautiful clear day you must have often noticed in the sky that a clear space, straight as any line upon a map, marks off the lower part of the cloud. Between the horizon and this line there is only clear blue; then the clouds, all lined and joined together at the bottom, are all rounded, bulgy at the top. This is what the two lines which I have quoted picture to us.

In the simplest fancies, however, the same truth to Nature is observable, and comes to us in like surprises. Here is a little bit about a new moon shining on the sea at night—the fourth poem in the fourth book:

> She lightens on the comb
>   Of leaden waves, that roar
> And thrust their hurried foam
>   Up on the dusky shore.
>
> Behind the Western bars
>   The shrouded day retreats,
> And unperceived the stars
>   Steal to their sovran seats.
>
> And whiter grows the foam,
>   The small moon lightens more;
> And as I turn me home,
>   My shadow walks before.

You feel that this has been seen and felt, that it is not merely the imagination of a man sitting down to

Robert Bridges

manufacture poetry at his desk. I imagine that you have not seen the word "comb" used of wave motion very often, though it is now coming more and more into poetical use. The comb of the wave is its crest, and the term is used just as we use the word comb in speaking of the crest of a cock. But there is also the verb "to comb"; and this refers especially to the curling over of the crest of the wave, just before it breaks, when the appearance of the crest-edge resembles that of wool being pulled through a comb (*kushi*). Thus the word gives us two distinct and picturesque ideas, whether used as noun or as adjective. Notice too the use of "leaden" in relation to the colour of waves where not touched by moonlight; the dull grey could not be better described by any other word. Also observe that as night advances, though the sea becomes dark, the form appears to become whiter and whiter. In a phosphorescent sea the foam lines appear very beautiful in darkness.

I shall quote but one more poem by Robert Bridges, choosing it merely to illustrate how modern things appear to this charming dreamer of old-fashioned dreams. One would think that he could not care much about such matters as machinery, telegraphs, railroads, steamships. But he has written a very fine sonnet about a steamship; and the curious thing is that this poem appears in the middle of a collection of love poems:

> The fabled sea-snake, old Leviathan,
> Or else what grisly beast of scaly chine
> That champ'd the ocean-wrack and swash'd the brine,
> Before the new and milder days of man,

Had never rib nor bray nor swingeing fan
Like his iron swimmer of the Clyde or Tyne,
Late-born of golden seed to breed a line
Of offspring swifter and more huge of plan.

Straight is her going, for upon the sun
When once she hath look'd, her path and place are
    plain;
With tireless speed she smiteth one by one
The shuddering seas and foams along the main;
And her eased breath, when her wild race is run,
Roars through her nostrils like a hurricane.

While this is true to fact, it is also fine fancy; the
only true way in which the practical and mechanical
can appeal to the poet is in the sensation of life and
power that it produces.

I think we have read together enough of Robert
Bridges to excite some interest in such of his poetry
as we have not read. But you will have perceived that
this poet is in his own way quite different from other
poets of the time, and that he cannot appeal to com-
mon-place minds. His poetry is like fine old wine, mild,
mellowed wine, that only the delicate palate will be able
to appreciate properly.

THE END

INDEX

Index

[430]

Index

Index